CROSSBILL GUIDES

Lesbos

Greece

Crossbill Guides: Lesbos – Greece
First print: 2016

Initiative, text and research: Alex Tabak
Additional research, text and information: Dirk Hilbers
Editing: John Cantelo, Dirk Hilbers, Brian Clews, Cees Hilbers,
Riet Hilbers, Kim Lotterman
Illustrations: Alex Tabak
Maps: Alex Tabak
Design: Oscar Lourens
Print: Drukkerij Tienkamp, Groningen

ISBN 978-94-91648-08-3
© 2016 Crossbill Guides Foundation, Arnhem, The Netherlands

This book is produced with best practice methods ensuring lowest possible environmental impact, using waterless offset, vegetable based inks and FSC-certified paper.

All rights reserved. No part of this book may be reproduced in any form by print, photocopy, microfilm or any other means without the written permission of the Crossbill Guides Foundation.

The Crossbill Guides Foundation and its authors have done their utmost to provide accurate and current information and describe only routes, trails and tracks that are safe to explore. However, things do change and readers are strongly urged to check locally for current conditions and for any changes in circumstances. Neither the Crossbill Guides Foundation nor its authors or publishers can accept responsibility for any loss, injury or inconveniences sustained by readers as a result of the information provided in this guide.

Published by Crossbill Guides in association with KNNV Publishing.

KNNV Publishing

www.crossbillguides.org
www.knnvpublishing.nl

CROSSBILL GUIDES FOUNDATION

This guidebook is a product of the non-profit foundation Crossbill Guides. By publishing these books we want to introduce more people to the joys of Europe's beautiful natural heritage and to increase the understanding of the ecological values that underlie conservation efforts. Most of this heritage is protected for ecological reasons and we want to provide insight into these reasons to the public at large. By doing so we hope that more people support the ideas behind nature conservation.
For more information about us and our guides you can visit our website at:

WWW.CROSSBILLGUIDES.ORG

Highlights of Lesbos

Birdwatching in the Kalloni saltpans

1. Join the ranks of birdwatchers in the Gulf of Kalloni and western Lesbos, where several outstanding wetlands and scrublands offer a magnificent show of birds. (route 7, 8 and 16).

2. Get off the beaten track – Lesbos abounds in little visited areas, where, on forgotten trails, you find wildflowers, birds, reptiles and dragonflies that everyone else overlooks (routes 5, 9, 13, 14, 16 and sites E, I, L, T and U).

Walking on Mount Olymbos

3. Follow one of Lesbos's rivers upstream from coastal wetland up to the source. The oriental plane forest on the river banks are among the most impressive woodlands of Europe (route 2).

Oriental Plane

4. Stroll through Lesbos's fantastic olive groves. Age-old olive trees and drifts of orchids and anemones await you (routes 1, 3 and sites C, G, H, I).

Olive grove around the Gulf of Gera

HIGHLIGHTS OF LESBOS

5 Go hiking through the Olymbos range, where Komper's Orchid and Krüper's Nuthatch are just two of the many attractive species (routes 2, 4 and sites K).

Krüper's Nuthatch

6 Head to west Lesbos where, amidst the rocky scrub, lies a geological gem: a 'forest' of petrified, prehistoric trees – the largest of its kind in the world (route 16).

Petrified tree

7 Sit down on a village square on a balmy evening and enjoy local food in the relaxed Greek atmosphere. Much of the food is home grown, picked in the countryside or freshly harvested from the sea (see page 195).

Stifádo (Στιφάδο)

8 Discover Lesbos's archeological and cultural heritage, including ancient monuments, old watermills and monasteries (see page 198).

Church of Petra

About this guide

This guide is meant for all those who enjoy being in and learning about nature, whether you already know all about it or not. It is set up a little differently from most guides. We focus on explaining the natural and ecological features of an area rather than merely describing the site. We choose this approach because the nature of an area is more interesting, enjoyable and valuable when seen in the context of its complex relationships. The interplay of different species with each other and with their environment is astonishing. The clever tricks and gimmicks that are put to use to beat life's challenges are as fascinating as they are countless.

Take our namesake the Crossbill: at first glance it is just a big finch with an awkward bill. But there is more to the Crossbill than meets the eye. This bill is beautifully adapted for life in coniferous forests. It is used like scissors to cut open pinecones and eat the seeds that are unobtainable for other birds. In the Scandinavian countries where Pine and Spruce take up the greater part of the forests, several Crossbill species have each managed to answer two of life's most pressing questions: how to get food and avoid direct competition. By evolving crossed bills, each differing subtly, they have secured a monopoly of the seeds produced by cones of varying sizes. So complex is this relationship that scientists are still debating exactly how many different species of Crossbill actually exist. Now this should heighten the appreciation of what at first glance was merely a plumb red bird with a beak that doesn't close properly. Once its interrelationships are seen, nature comes alive, wherever you are.

To some, impressed by the 'virtual' familiarity that television has granted to the wilderness of the Amazon, the vastness of the Serengeti or the sublimity of Yellowstone, European nature may seem a puny surrogate, good merely for the casual stroll. In short, the argument seems to be that if you haven't seen a Jaguar, Lion or Grizzly Bear, then you haven't seen the 'real thing'. Nonsense, of course.

But where to go? And how? What is there to see? That is where this guide comes in. We describe the how, the why, the when, the where and the how come of Europe's most beautiful areas. In clear and accessible language, we explain the nature of Lesbos and refer extensively to routes where the area's features can be observed best. We try to make Lesbos come alive. We hope that we succeed.

How to use this guide

This guidebook contains a descriptive and a practical section. The descriptive part comes first and gives you insight into the most striking and interesting natural features of the area. It provides an understanding of what you will see when you go out exploring. The descriptive part consists of a landscape section (marked with a red bar), describing the habitats, the history and the landscape in general, and a flora and fauna section (marked with a green bar), which discusses the plants and animals that occur in the region.
The second part offers the practical information (marked with a purple bar). A series of routes (walks and car drives) are carefully selected to give you a good flavour of all the habitats, flora and fauna that Lesbos has to offer. At the start of each route description, a number of icons give a quick overview of the characteristics of each route. These icons are explained in the margin of this page. The final part of the book (marked with blue squares) provides some basic tourist information and some tips on finding plants, birds and other animals.
There is no need to read the book from cover to cover. Instead, each small chapter stands on its own and refers to the routes most suitable for viewing the particular features described in it. Conversely, descriptions of each route refer to the chapters that explain more in depth the most typical features that can be seen along the way.
In the back of the guide we have included a list of all the mentioned plant and animal species, with their scientific names and translations into German and Dutch. Some species names have an asterix (*) following them. This indicates that there is no official English name for this species and that we have taken the liberty of coining one. We realise this will meet with some reservations by those who are familiar with scientific names. For the sake of readability however, we have decided to translate the scientific name, or, when this made no sense, we gave a name that best describes the species' appearance or distribution. Please note that we do not want to claim these as the official names. We merely want to make the text easier to follow for those not familiar with scientific names. An overview of the area described in this book is given on the map on page 13. For your convenience we have also turned the inner side of the back flap into a map of the area indicating all the described routes. Descriptions in the explanatory text refer to these routes.

 car route

 walking route

 beautiful scenery

 interesting history

 interesting geology

 interesting flora

 interesting invertebrate life

 interesting reptile and amphibian life

 interesting wildlife

 interesting birdlife

 site for snorkelling

 visualising the ecological contexts described in this guide

TABLE OF CONTENTS

Table of contents

Landscape	11
Geographical overview	12
Geology	14
Habitats	20
Coastal wetlands, inland lakes and temporary pools	22
Rivers and streams	26
Scrubland	29
Forests	33
Olive groves, arable land and fields	38
Cliffs, rocky outcrops and screes	41
History	43
Nature conservation	50
Flora and fauna	55
Flora	58
Mammals	76
Birds	78
Reptiles and amphibians	90
Insects and other invertebrates	98
Practical Part	107
Route 1: Amali Peninsula	108
Route 2: Along Evergetoulas river to Mount Olymbos	112
Route 3: Hiking the olive grove trails	117
Route 4: Through the heart of the Olymbos massif	122
Route 5: From Ambeliko to Vatera	127
Route 6: Gulf of Kalloni – along the eastern shore	131
Route 7: Kalloni Saltpans	135
Route 8: Potamia Valley	138
Route 9: Palios	141
Route 10: The north slopes of Mount Lepetimnos	145
Route 11: Skala Sikaminia to Eftalou	149
Route 12: Lafionas	152
Route 13: Voulgaris river valley and northwest coast	154
Route 14: Liota	158
Route 15: Faneromeni	161
Route 16: Between Eresos and Sigri – the volcanic west	163

TABLE OF CONTENTS

Route 17: Ipsilou Monastery	169
Additional sites	172

Tourist information & observation tips	**187**
Travel and accommodation	187
Convenient travel and safety issues	189
Additional information	192
Observation tips	200
Birdlist Lesbos	**202**
Acknowledgements & Picture credits	**208**
Species list & translation	**210**

List of text boxes

Volcanic structures	18
Tectonic windows	19
Degradation of Mediterranean forest	32
The noble Oriental Plane	37
Philosophers, poets and painters of Lesbos	44
Some of the key wildflowers of Lesbos	59
Facing the elements in scrubland	63
Splitters and lumpers	74
Main groups of *Ophrys*	75
Migration routes	88
Human impact on the reptiles and amphibians of Lesbos	96
White butterfly of white rocks	100
Browns and Graylings	101

LANDSCAPE

In the course of time, the Greek island of Lesbos has gone by many names. It has been called *Lassia* (the densely forested one) as well as *Aithiope* (the sun-drenched island) and even *Imerti* (the island one longs for). All these names apply today. Lesbos offers its visitors even more: it is not only a tranquil island with beautiful shady woods and sun-drenched mountainscapes, it is also *Thaleri* (the one with the bountiful nature).

Lesbos has a deserved reputation of being an excellent destination for birdwatchers and naturalists. Its main attraction has always been the rich birdlife and diverse hiking, but the island offers much more. It boasts a wide range of Mediterranean habitats in a relatively small area, which results in a high diversity of species, many of which occur in abundance. Apart from the bird-filled marshes and hedgerows dripping with migrant birds, there are huge drifts of orchids, olive groves speckled with wild anemones. The forest floors are bustling with lizards, snakes and other reptiles, while agamas and Persian Squirrels run back and forth over the ancient stone walls. The island even offers a tangible insight into the fascinating world of geology, with the amazing Petrified Forest being the highlight.

On Lesbos, there is never a dull moment, not even when you have visited it several times. Nature differs greatly depending on season and location. Since many visitors don't stray from the well-known hotspots, there are always new places waiting to be discovered: secluded valleys, remote peaks or rural tracks leading into the middle of nowhere. Although you never know what you'll find, Lesbos does offer you one certainty: at the end of the day, there is always a little village where a taverna awaits, serving you the finest of foods. What is in western Europe the latest trend – eating local, organic food, picked in the wild – never went out of fashion on Lesbos. Most tavernas serve great local food, fresh from the sea, forest and vegetable garden and with a menu changing with the seasons.

This book guides you on your visit to this island full of natural delights. We've balanced well-known sites with new ones that we've discovered ourselves or local residents have recommended. Whether your interest lies in birdwatching, rambling through the countryside, searching for wildflowers, reptiles and amphibians, insects or discovering the geological or ancient history, this book will help you to make the most out of your visit!

Impressive coastal cliffs on the south coast (site J)

GEOGRAPHICAL OVERVIEW

Geographical overview

The beautiful island of Lesbos – often also written *Lesvos* – lies in the eastern part of the Aegean Sea, about 10 km off the coast of Turkey. It is Greece's third largest island, only surpassed by Crete and Evia. Lesbos at its greatest extent measures 90 km by 50 km amounting to an area of about 1630 km2, which makes it about the size of Greater London or the province of Utrecht in the Netherlands. The varied coastline is about 370 km long ranging from flat coastal plains to steep cliffs rising from the sea. Two large saltwater bodies, the Gulf of Kalloni and the Gulf of Gera, cut deep into the island's southern flank resulting in the island's distinctive shape.

The total population of Lesbos is about 100,000 people. The capital Mytilini (Greeks often call the whole island Mytilini) is the commercial centre of Lesbos. With approximately 38,000 inhabitants, it is by far the most densely populated area. The rest of the inhabitants live scattered across the island in small towns and villages. Other population centres of any size are the Kalloni area in the centre of Lesbos and the conglomerate of villages on the western shore of the Gulf of Gera, each

Overview of Lesbos

GEOGRAPHICAL OVERVIEW

housing about 7,000 people. Plomari and Polichnitos are considerable towns in the south (3,500 and 3,000 inhabitants respectively). Molyvos in the north (2,500 people) is the island's modest tourism centre, while Eresos, Andissa, Agra and Mesotopos (each housing about 1,000 people) are the only sizable settlements in the western part of the island.

Being thinly populated, Lesbos is a rural island with small-scale farmland consisting of a mixture of olive groves, fields and arable land, cut by rivers and streams. In addition, large areas of land, often unsuitable for cultivation, are covered with scrub, pine forest and deciduous woodland. The scrublands are used as grazing land for the numerous sheep and goats, which are a familiar sight all over the island.

Travelling from east to west through the interior you cross three different regions, each with a distinct topography and land use.

The southeast is the greenest part of the island. It receives the greatest amount of rain and is covered in extensive olive groves, pine forests and chestnut woodlands. Geologically, this is the oldest part of the island, consisting of carbonate-rich rocks that support a lush vegetation and a proliferation of wildflowers. The hills are intersected by deep valleys. The area is dominated by the 967 m high Mount Olympos. The tranquil Gulf of Gera, fringed by olive groves and brackish marshes is enclosed to the east by the Amali peninsula where Mytilini is situated.

The central part, a wide strip along the line Molyvos, Kalloni and Polichnitos, consists of volcanic rocks and is mainly covered with a patchwork of maquis, oak woodland, pine forests, arable land and olive groves. The highest peak is Mount Lepetimnos (968 m) in the north. The central chain of hills on the western side of the Gulf of Kalloni hosts the main volcanic centres, dominated by Profitis Ilias of Parakila Forest (799 m). South of here, the Gulf of Kalloni is an important area for its nature. The coastal marshes and saltpans are famous for their rich birdlife.

In the far west, the area around the towns of Andissa, Sigri, Eresos and Agra, is where Lesbos's most dramatic volcanic landscapes are found. The empty and barren grazing land is covered with a typical low and thorny scrubland known as *phrygana* (see page 30). At places it is even completely devoid of vegetation. This part offers superb birding areas in both the uplands and at the mouths of the rivers near the coast. Amazing geological features, like the Petrified Forest, are found here as well. In a small area in the north, around the village of Gavathas, there's something different: calcareous rocks covered with well-developed oak woodland with a rich flora.

GEOLOGY

Geology

Geological map of Lesbos

Geological units

 Oldest rocks

 Ophiolite

 Relocated rocks

 Volcanic rocks

 Freshwater limestones

 Alluvial sediments

 Main volcanic centres

The geology of Lesbos is highly varied and complex, but can be summarized as consisting of alpine and pre-alpine bedrock (300-150 million years old) that is overlain in part by a much younger layer of volcanic rock of the Lower Miocene (roughly between 21.5 and 16.5 million years ago). The latter covers the western and central part of the island while the former dominates the east, making the west and east of the island strikingly different. This distinction is so visibly reflected in the landscape, flora and fauna that it is even noticed by the most casual of visitors.

But there is more to the geology of Lesbos – much more. In fact, thanks to the geological complexity, together with the unscathed geological phenomena, the whole island was given the status of Global Geopark of UNESCO in 2012.

As you delve deeper into the geological history of Lesbos, you'll discern five different geological units, each stemming from a different era, each with its own typical rock formations, structure, vegetation cover, geomorphology and land use – but all still present on the surface on the island.

The geological built-up of Lesbos is best understood by looking at its genesis chronologically.

Oldest rocks

First, there are the oldest rocks still in place of its original formation. They surface in the south-eastern part of the island around the Gulf of Gera (routes 1, 2, 3, 4 and sites A, B, C, E) and small isolated areas near Sigri and Gavathas (see route 14). These rocks consists of a basic carbonate-rich type of schist (calc-schists in jargon), sandstones and marbles, alternated with small areas of limestone – which are of great interest for botanists. The rocks date back to the Permian and Triassic eras (300-200 million years old) and represent a fragment of an old microcontinent called *Cimmeria*. In this period there were two great landmasses: *Gondwana* (which are today part of Africa, South America, India, Australia, Arabia, Antarctica and the Balkans) and *Laurasia* (the current continents Europe, Asia and North America except what we now call the Balkans and India). The Cimmerian microcontinent started as a ribbon-shaped renegade part of Gondwana, that gradually drifted towards Laurasia, leaving a gap in which the great Tethys ocean formed (of which the Mediterranean Sea is a small remainder; see map). Today, only slivers of the Cimmerian microcontinent are found along a long, narrow strip from Bulgaria up to Malaysia.

Ophiolite and relocated rocks

The second geological component was formed later, during the Jurassic and Cretaceous periods (roughly between 175 and 90 million years ago), when the Cimmerian microcontinent partly subducted under the continent Laurasia. During this process, fragments of oceanic crust and deep sea sediments of the Tethys ocean were reshaped, pushed up and overthrusted the continental landmass. Geological formation of this origin are called ophiolites and consist of marine sediments and basic and ultrabasic rocks (for example serpentine). They are mainly distributed in the central part of Lesbos between Polichnitos and Agia Paraskevi, while a much smaller area is found on the Amali peninsula (routes 1, 2 and 5). Ophiolitic rocks contain often high concentrations of metals (for example nickel), which create a stressful environment for plants. Only a limited number of species are able to cope in such an environment. Freed from competition with other plants, some grow in abundance. One of these species is the Turkish Pine, which forms dense and monotonous stands here. Another example is the endemic metal tolerant plant Lesbos Alison* (*Alyssum lesbiacum*).

Northward drift of the Cimmerian microcontinent over time, closed the Paleo-Tethys ocean and opened the Neo-Tethys ocean. The red dot roughly marks the position of Lesbos.

Ophiolites were not the only formations that emerged when the Cimmerian continent pushed itself underneath the Laurasian plate. A complex mixture of ancient volcanic rocks and their sediments were pushed up too, often severely reshaped and relocated by immense pressure and temperature. This complex potpourri of shales and marbles dominates a wide strip along the southeast coast of Lesbos. The incredible force associated with the subduction of the Cimmerian microcontinent also reshaped the land, leaving impressive rock outcrops and cliffs, some of which still feature prominently in Lesbos's landscape (see sites G, H, I, and J).

GEOLOGY

Volcanic rocks

Much later, in the Tertiary Period – roughly between 21.5 and 16.2 million years ago – Lesbos experienced a period with intense volcanic eruptions, which added thick layers of volcanic rocks. These almost completely cover the central, northern and western parts of Lesbos (best found on routes 9, 16, 17 and sites T, U, V). The island was situated in a volcanic arc that extended from South Bulgaria (see Crossbill Guide Eastern Rhodopes), southwards over the Central Aegean Sea before arching across to Northern Turkey.

Rather than a single event, a number of volcanic eruptions occurred over time, resulting in several formations with different types of rocks. This is the reason Lesbos has so many different volcanic landforms, like volcanic craters (see textbox on page 18) and lava domes (e.g. that of Ipsilou – route 17). The main attraction however, is the superb geological oddity created by the Sigri Pyroclastic Formation: the eruption that produced the Petrified Forest of Lesbos (see page 17).

Petrified tree on the islet Nisiopi (opposite Sigri), uncovered by erosion by the sea. Clearly visible are the volcanic layers with pyroclastic material.

Freshwater limestones and alluvial sediments

The geologically youngest parts of Lesbos are deposits of freshwater sediments. In several locations, pockets of marls, marly limestones and sandstones occur, formed between 20 and 2 million years ago. These layers are again a treasure trove of prehistoric nature. In the area of Gavathas and Liota for example (route 14), marlstones originating from long gone lakes have revealed the fossil of an ancestral elephant species – at 18 million years, the earliest known occurrence of elephants in Europe.

The most recent material are river sediments consisting of sand and pebbles deposited in the last 2 million years. These sedimentary layers often formed wide coastal plains, such as the Kalloni and Polichnitos saltpans, Faneromeni, Kambos and Gera (see routes 7, 13, 15 and sites D, O, and V). The river sediments in the area of Vatera have proven to be important sites for the excavation of two million year old mammal fossils (see route 5).

GEOLOGY

Petrified Forest of Lesbos

From a network of trails in the Petrified Forest Park, you are witness to a unique and impressive phenomenon: huge trunks of trees lie haphazardly in the open landscape. Some are snags whilst others are forest giants up to 20 m long. And they are all made of solid rock! The trees retain exceptional details of bark, wood structure and capillary systems in a great variety of colours. Massive tree stumps show wide and thick root systems, frozen in time as if recently cut. It is an alienating sight: the stark contrast of the green, grassy slope, with its ghostly tree trunks, lying there as if life was wiped out overnight. And so it was.

You are looking at the remains of a 17 million year-old subtropical forest, still *in situ* where they grew – underlining the uniqueness of this geological masterpiece.

This was a period of intense volcanic activity. One particularly explosive eruption created enormous amounts of ash and rock which were ejected violently into the atmosphere and covered large areas around the volcano. A powerful blast of hot gasses felled the trees (which is why today most of the trunks are lying horizontally). Subsequent heavy rainfall caused huge debris flows so that masses of volcanic ash engulfed the vegetation.

The abrupt event swallowed the trees so fast that they were completely sealed off from the atmosphere, creating the ideal conditions for their fossilisation. The hot silica-rich debris penetrated the organic matter. Over time it transformed every cell into a perfect stone copy on a microscopic level.

The Petrified Forest of Lesbos represents one of the most splendid geological monuments known worldwide. Whilst Arizona's petrified forest is the most famous, that on Lesbos is the world's largest. Although the Petrified Forest Park itself is quite small, the actual forest is all around you. You just can't see it because the trees are hidden in the volcanic rock. Petrified remains are present within the entire triangle between Eresos, Andissa and Sigri, even extending onto the sea floor along the western coast. There must be many thousands of petrified trees.

Two impressive petrified trunks with vibrant colours and well preserved wood structure (route 16).

LANDSCAPE

GEOLOGY

Volcanic structures

The immense Tertiary volcanic eruptions that battered Lesbos for millions of years, produced striking structures throughout the central and western part of the island. Ancient volcanic craters are located in the area of Pterounda, Agra and Lepetimnos (see sites T and U). The first is most visible. It has a diameter of about 6 km, with a crater edge rising from the surrounding land (see map on page 14).

Other conspicuous volcanic structures are lava domes, of which there are several. A good example is the hill of Ipsilou (route 17). Lava domes are the result of slow volcanic eruptions where lava piles up instead of flowing away. Imagine the way whipped cream expands when it comes out of a spray can. In similar fashion lava accumulates when it comes to the surface.

The rock on which the church of Petra is built, was in fact created within an active volcano vent. It consists of hardened magma. Over time, erosion caused the softer surrounding rocks to vanish, leaving only the hard rock of the lava plug (see page 5).

Small dome-shaped volcanic rock along the main road Eresos – Andissa (route 16). In the background a volcanic dike is visible, a linear rock structure formed by a pathway of magma inside rocks which is now exposed.

The forest is a time capsule revealing the prehistoric flora of this part of the world. It gives a unique insight into the natural world and climatic conditions of the late Oligocene – middle Miocene. Studies show that the mixed forest was composed of ancestors of both conifers (pines and redwood) and angiosperms (laurel, beech, maple and oak) within different vegetation zones. Not only tree trunks were fossilised, but also many branches, fruits and leaves.

We recommend combining a visit to the park with a visit to the Natural History Museum in Sigri. This fine museum offers insightful exhibitions about the geological evolution of the Aegean Sea and a variety of geological processes, together with a display of fossils. Around the museum is another 2 ha area, Plaka Park, with petrified trees.

Recent tectonic activity

Present-day Lesbos still lies in a minor active tectonic zone and is subjected to forces which are visible in the landscape by the numerous geological faults on the island. The displacements of rocks created huge cracks, of which the imposing scarp near the Dipi Larisos marsh is the best example (see route 2). Since classical times, the tectonic activity also caused powerful earthquakes, for example the one that destroyed the ancient

GEOLOGY

city of Pyrra around 230 BC (see page 134). Recently, bigger earthquakes occurred in 1867 and 1968. The latter destroyed the village of Chalikas on the flanks of Mount Lepetimnos (see route 10).

A more relaxing aspect of recent tectonic activity is the occurrence of thermal baths on the island, situated around natural hot springs produced by heated groundwater emerging from the earth's crust. Some renowned thermal baths are found in Kendro, Eftalou and Polichnitos. The latter is fed by one of the hottest springs in Europe (68°C to 92°C), and is housed in historic domed buildings (see page 200). Small natural hot springs are numerous on Lesbos. They are found along route 11 and site J.

Natural hot springs of Polychnitos, feeding the thermal baths close by. They create an amazing scene of steaming ponds with beautiful colours created by heat-loving micro organisms.

Tectonic windows

Tectonic windows are discontinuities in the upper rock layer that expose the underlying, older formations. They are formed by erosion or when rocks are displaced along a geological fracture. Sometimes a window is simply a depression with the older layer surfacing at the bottom. However, the displacement or erosion may also cause the older stratum to stick out of the surrounding, younger layers. On Lesbos, a very good example of a tectonic window that is also an outcrop, is Mount Olymbos (see route 2). The summit is the edge of a geological unit consisting of bright white marble rocks, still in the place of its original formation. It was uplifted and finally broke through the younger layers that now surround the mountain. Other rather curious examples of tectonic windows are seen along the east side of the main road Eresos – Andissa (route 16). The white outcrops are in fact very old marble escarpments in a 'sea' of young volcanic rocks.

Mount Olymbos is an impressive tectonic window.

LANDSCAPE

HABITATS

Habitats

Even though Lesbos is modest in size and altitude, it sports a good variety of Mediterranean habitats. A thorough exploration of the island will take you to treeless, dry and rocky habitats, shady deciduous woodlands, extensive pine forests, lush river valleys, picturesque olive groves, steep cliffs and damp coastal wetlands.

None of these habitats is unique of Lesbos. Still, there are two aspects that give them a unique quality here and which are a hallmark of the island. The first is the intactness of these habitats. The woodlands, the groves of Sweet Chestnut and Olive are of exceptional high quality. They may not be a fully natural landscape untouched by human hands, but represent a very traditional form of land use. They were created by centuries of farming, pruning, burning and herding. The landscape, ecology and species adapted to this traditional human use. This is the case everywhere in the Mediterranean, but on Lesbos the traditional way of tending the land has largely remained unchanged, resulting in the same flowery and bird-rich landscapes that are fast disappearing elsewhere.

The second feature of the landscape of Lesbos is its geological complexity, which creates a patchwork of sometimes subtly different habitats, which, adding them all up, offer a place for a far larger number of species than you'd expect from an island, as already noted, of such a modest size and altitude.

Irrespective of the patchwork of small scale habitats, when you look at Lesbos as a whole, one salient feature demands attention: the island is divided into a dry rocky western part and a much more vegetated and damp eastern part. Thorny *phrygana* scrub reigns the west, while the olive groves, woodlands and forests are in command in the east. This sharp contrast is largely determined by the geology and further intensified by a

CROSSBILL GUIDES • LESBOS

HABITATS

difference in rainfall: the eastern part receives far more precipitation and has deeper soils to retain water, resulting in greater vegetation cover.

Unlike many areas in northern Europe, the habitats on Lesbos are not neatly outlined. There are many subtle transitions, making you sometimes wonder how to categorise the habitat before you. For example, scrubland comes in different forms and varieties, depending on environmental conditions and human impact. To make this even more complex, in many places scrubland habitat is mixed with small fields, olive groves or woodland. As a result, animals and wildflowers that elsewhere are considered typical of a specific habitat, may occur in a wider range of landscape types here. It is this unpredictability that makes Lesbos such an exciting place for the naturalist.

In the following section the habitats are described in further detail, spiced up by mentioning some of their most attractive species.

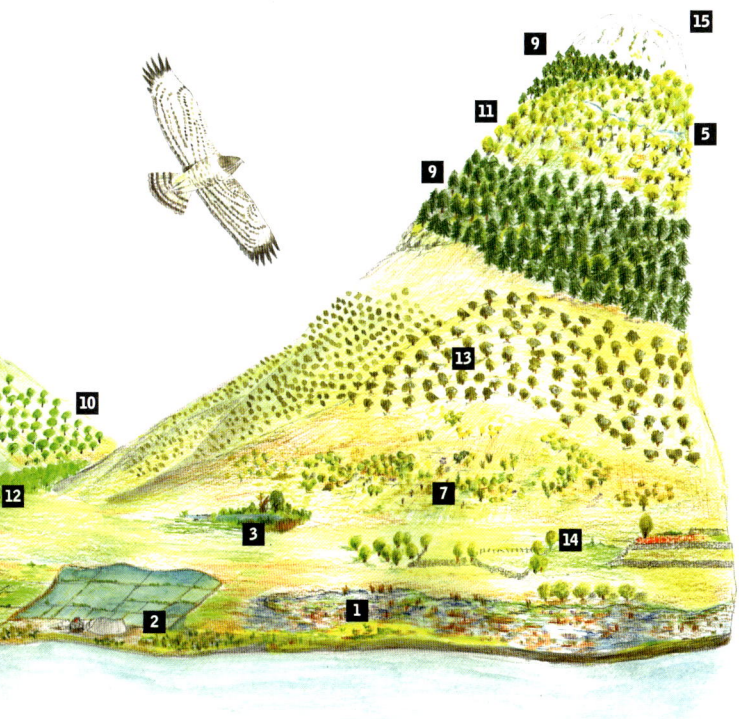

Overview of the habitats of Lesbos.

1 - Saline wetland
2 - Saltpans
3 - Inland lake
4 - River mouth
5 - Mountain stream
6 - River
7 - Maquis
8 - Phrygana
9 - Pine forest
10 - Oak woodland
11 - Chestnut forest
12 - Riverine forest
13 - Olive grove
14 - Arable field
15 - Cliffs and rocky outcrops

LANDSCAPE

COASTAL WETLANDS, INLAND LAKES AND TEMPORARY POOLS

Coastal wetlands, inland lakes and temporary pools

> Saline wetlands feature on routes 6 and 7 while coastal freshwater marshes are present on routes 1, 2 and site D. Saltpans are explored on route 7 and site O. Inland lakes are found on route 12, 16 and site M. Many routes feature small standing waters, but some stick out, such as routes 9, 16 and site L. The most interesting river mouths along the coast are explored on routes 2, 5, 6, 15, 16 and sites P and V.

Along its 370 km long coastline, Lesbos offers a great variety of flat coastal wetlands which are in great contrast to the inaccessible steep cliffs also found here. The coastal lowland habitats range from freshwater temporary pools and river mouths to wet meadows and large saline muddy areas. All are great places to explore.

Coastal wetlands form naturally in flat terrain where sediments carried down by rivers are deposited at the seashore. Where there are strong currents, the sea has deposited a bar of sand and pebbles parallel to the coastline. This acts as a natural barrier, preventing the outflow of water to the sea, and eventually aids the forming of marshes, lagoons and pools. These wetlands are fed with fresh water from the mountains while saline water seeps in from the sea, creating a diverse wetland with both fresh and saline areas and a wide range of intermediates.

In this chapter we describe all these coastal habitats plus some freshwater sites further inland as they often share a similar nature and wildlife.

Saline wetlands

Most saline wetlands are situated in the Gulf of Kalloni, which drives a wedge between the western and eastern parts of the island. This calm bay, protected from eroding currents, provides ideal conditions for the formation of extensive coastal plains with saline wetlands. Typically, this habitat experiences extreme seasonal swings in salinity and water levels. In winter, freshwater input from rivers and direct rainfall dilute the salt concentration, while in spring and summer – when drought kicks in – salinity levels rise through evaporation.

The challenges that come with highly saline soils are daunting for plants. Only few, highly adapted species have mastered the art of surviving here.

Roughly three different vegetation zones can be distinguished along the Gulf of Kalloni, which occur in a line of decreasing salinity from the sea

COASTAL WETLANDS, INLAND LAKES AND TEMPORARY POOLS

to the interior. First there are pioneer plant communities growing on flooded mudflats soaked in salt water. This zone is characterised by the dominance of annual plants that complete their biological cycle in the short winter and spring period, during which conditions are a little better. They are able to survive simply by avoiding the worst season. This is the domain of Common Glasswort and Sea Pearlwort. The Common Glasswort gives the plains a distinctive purplish-brown colour.

The second zone has less dynamic water levels and is not often flooded. It is covered with perennial plants like Button Glasswort, Glaucous Glasswort and Sea Purslane. Finally, the third zone is found on the higher banks where soil salinity is much lower, allowing a wider variety of plants to grow. Here you find meadows of rushes, in which some attractive flowers can be found, most notably Oriental Iris, Narbonne Sea-lavender* (*Limonium narbonense*), Hairy Sea-heath and Sea Aster.

Away from the influence of salt water, other ecosystems emerge. Depending on slope and soil, there are damp meadows, steppe-like grasslands and dune scrublands, which, together with the saline zone, form a complex and rich ecosystem. Two areas where this is particularly well developed is at Mesa and Skala Kalloni. It is no wonder that these sites are top-notch places for naturalists (see routes 6 and 7).

Above all, the coastal wetlands are excellent for birds. Close to the coast, the direct influence of the sea brings large amounts of nutrients into the ecosystem, which make a rich fare for all kinds of invertebrates like molluscs, worms and Brine Shrimp. In turn they form a huge resource for the thousands of migrating shorebirds visiting the wetlands in spring. The shallow waters are feeding grounds for a variety of waders, terns, ducks, flamingos and herons, while the exposed mud flats attract plovers, stints and sandpipers.

The damp grasslands and sandy terrain surrounding the saline marshes not only provide an excellent resource for hungry migrants such as yellow wagtails, various species of wheatear and the rare Collared Pratincole and Spur-winged Plover, but

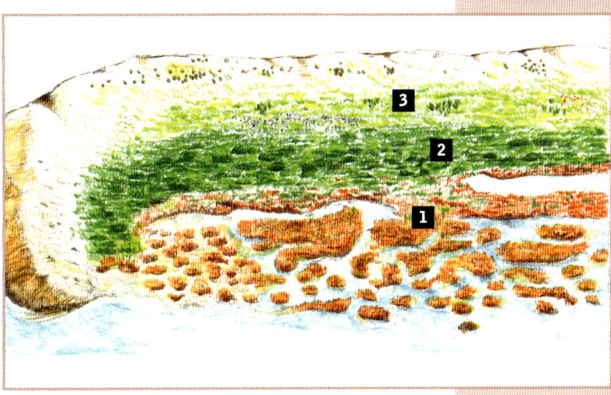

A representation of three vegetation zones that can be distinguished along the Gulf of Kalloni around Mesa and Skala Kalloni, creating a complex of habitats.

1 - pioneer plant communities
2 - perennial plants
3 - meadows of rushes

LANDSCAPE

COASTAL WETLANDS, INLAND LAKES AND TEMPORARY POOLS

The saltpans of Kalloni (route 7). The banks and surrounding grasslands offer breeding grounds for Stone Curlew (top).

also fine hunting grounds for raptors like Red-footed Falcon, Long-legged Buzzard and Montagu's and Pallid Harriers. The grasslands are breeding grounds for Stone Curlew and Short-toed Lark. The area supports a wide variety of wildlife in the proximity of salt marshes, with butterflies attracted to flowery parts, dragonflies and reptiles like Grass Snake and Snake-eyed Lizard.

Saltpans

The saltpans of Kalloni (260 ha) and Polichnitos (60 ha) are a special kind of saline coastal wetland. Although they are man-made, they are similar to the salt marsh ecosystem. The flocks of bright pink Greater Flamingos and the multitude of waterbirds makes you almost forget that they are basically working industrial sites primarily used for salt production. Both complexes are surrounded by a ditch and contain shallow evaporation basins with varying water levels. As with the saltmarshes, the mud is full of marine invertebrate life, which attracts scores of shorebirds. Needless to say, all offer exquisite birdwatching.

Freshwater marshes, inland lakes and small standing waters

The freshwater marshes along the Gulf of Gera form a radically different kind of coastal wetland. Here are no saline soils to limit the vegetation, which, in its pursuit of sunlight, grows much taller. Only close to the sea is there a narrow brackish zone with saltworts and tamarisks. Dipi Larisos is the largest freshwater marsh on Lesbos, fed by the Evergetoulas river (see route 2). The river brings down large amounts of calcium and nutrient-rich water in winter. The seasonal pools in the delta are the haunt of rare dragonflies (see page 113), while in other parts, dense reedbeds and wet meadows harbour terrapins and the usual birds of this habitat like Sedge, Reed and Great Reed Warbler. The diversity of plant species is

COASTAL WETLANDS, INLAND LAKES AND TEMPORARY POOLS

quite low in these wetlands, but typical plants here are Southern Cattail, Sea Club-rush and Sharp Rush, plus, in the meadows, a fine display of three species of marsh orchids around early May (see route 2).
These meadows are not restricted to Dipi Larisos, but occur in a fringe along the western shore of the Gulf of Gera (see site D). Unfortunately, some are under threat of being drained.
Metochi Lake (route 12) and Mikri Limni (site M) are the few natural inland lakes found on Lesbos. Since these have a similar ecology to the coastal freshwater marshes, they are included in this chapter. Fed by water from the surrounding hills, the water level of these lakes depends heavily on rainfall, so they are largely dry in summer. The lakes are fringed by dense reedbeds and rushes, providing excellent habitat for terrapins, dragonflies and – especially in the case of Metochi Lake – wetland birds. Megali Limni, a third natural lake, was drained in the 19th century, both to eradicate malaria from the island and to use its water for irrigation. The former lake is now a large slab of arable land along the main road from Agiasos to Vasilika. In addition to these few sizable freshwater lakes, there are a large number of temporary pools and small standing waters on the island. They form on impenetrable bedrocks like granite, schist and hard compact volcanic rocks, or near rivers and springs. These microhabitats are often in sharp contrast with the surrounding dry landscapes, and are the haunt of dragonflies and amphibians such as Eastern Spadefoot and Levant Water Frog.

Great part of the natural lake Mikri Limni (site M) is covered by rushes.

LANDSCAPE

RIVERS AND STREAMS

River mouths

Most rivers on Lesbos don't have a permanent outlet to the sea but are blocked, for most of the year, by a sand bar. Continuously fed by small amounts of water from the mountains, even during the hot period, the lower reaches of rivers do not dry out. They create elongated freshwater coastal wetlands, fringed by a dense vegetation of reeds, oleanders and tamarisks. By the beach, they typically form a U-shaped marsh enclosing the water. Only larger rivers (e.g. Evergetoulas, Tsiknias and Vouvaris) carry enough water to overcome the barrier of sand and pebbles. They form river mouths with muddy margins with a nearly year-round outlet to the sea.

The river mouth of the Vergias river west of Skala Eresou is fringed by dense vegetation, supporting herons, egrets and warblers. It may hold water the whole year. On the beach a sand-bar prevents outflow of water to the sea.

The river mouths are ecological gems, especially where they form complexes with other habitats such as fields, dunes and scrubland. Good examples are found at Ancient Andissa, Faneromeni and Chrousos (routes 13, 15 and site V). The secluded lakes act as a magnet for migrating birds, like Little Ringed Plover and herons and egrets. The riparian vegetation along the banks provide hiding places for aquatic invertebrates and amphibians. The sandy shores and rocks in the water and are places where Balkan Terrapin bask in the sun, they also provide a retreat for water snakes.

Rivers and streams

> Beautiful streams feature on routes 2, 3, 4, 10, 16 and sites C, I, K, N and T. The best routes for rivers are 2, 5, 13, 16 and site P.

Lesbos has a large number of rivers and streams. Most of them are seasonal, flowing strongly during the wet winters and the occasional heavy rain in early spring, but reduced to just a trickle in summer. The deltas of these rivers have been described in the previous chapter. Here we deal with the river valleys, starting at the source in the mountains and ending in the lowlands.

RIVERS AND STREAMS

Mountain streams

Most streams start in the uplands of Mount Olymbos, Mount Lepetimnos and Parakila Forest. Although several of them are fed by small springs and don't dry up completely during summer, the volume of water depends greatly on the season – what is a powerful stream in early spring is nothing more than a damp gully a few months later.

Still, a damp gully is a radically different habitat than the surrounding hillsides. The cool, moist and shady habitat forms a stark contrast with the hot, dry and often exposed surrounding. Hence, the mountain stream ecosystem hosts a special kind of wildlife, which varies somewhat according to the topography and bedrock of a given area. In the marble and base rich rocks of eastern Lesbos, there are streams lined with Oriental Planes and their banks form a floral bed of peonies and several rare arum species. The small streams in the Parakila Forest with its acid volcanic soil are the only places where the striking Pontic Azalea is found (see page 59). It occurs together with Royal Fern, which is rather common in northern Europe but very rare in Greece.

The streams harbour attractive dragonflies and damselflies like Odalisque, Eastern Spectre and Turkish Goldenring, while those that run through the upper regions of the chestnut forests of Agiasos are home to the rare Blue-eyed Goldenring (see page 126).

Between Eresos and Andissa, in the western part, there is a stream fed by an underground water reservoir which has a steady flow throughout the year. An old lava duct connects with an opening in the bedrock (see route 16).

As this is also the driest part of the island, this permanent stream forms a crucial refuge for wildlife and a vital water source for birds, mammals and reptiles. It is also home to freshwater crabs, dragonflies and amphibians like Eastern Spadefoot.

Even though the other streams dry up completely in spring, the streambed retains enough moisture to allow leafy trees and shrubs to grow alongside them, acting as migrant traps for birds and a retreat for reptiles and mammals.

The specialized and rare Blue-eyed Goldenring (bottom) is restricted to mountain streams east of Mount Olymbos (top).

LANDSCAPE

RIVERS AND STREAMS

Middle section of the river Evergetoulas near Asomatos, where the valley widens. At this spot the thick riverine forest with Oriental Plane is alternated by orchards and meadows, thus creating a diverse environment.

Middle and lower sections

Further downstream, the middle section of river runs through a wider valley where the streambed is often fringed by thick belts of riverine forest with Oriental Plane. These are luxuriant jungles, with climbing plants that create a deep shade, from which the exotic songs of Golden Oriole, Nightingale and Cetti's Warbler are heard. In places where smaller rivers cut through olive groves, the banks are often cloaked in dense vegetation, in which Laurel, Pendulous Sedge and, locally, the peculiar False Hemp grow (see page 59).

The middle section of most rivers fall dry in summer. Along the larger rivers, pools of standing water remain, which vary considerably in depth and temperature, and in the amount of shade available. During the hot season, they are vital for amphibians, water snakes and dragonflies.

Another feature of rivers with widely fluctuating water levels is the large quantity of sediments in the streambed brought here during peak flows, but left exposed as flows diminish during the dry period. You'll find them, dotted with tamarisks, in the lower sections of the Evergetoulas and Tsiknias rivers.

The river habitat is linear. Whilst there are plants and animals that are exclusive to this habitat, one of the main attractions of rivers is that they add three vital elements to the surrounding habitats: food, water and breeding sites. Woodpeckers, Bee-eaters, snakes, lizards and tortoises – none of which can be called riverine species – all profit from a river running through their territory. The river can't be considered separately from the surrounding cliffs, scrubland, fields and olive groves and its birds, mammals and reptiles. Combined with the variation in environmental conditions on north and south facing slopes, river valleys host a rich flora and fauna, which makes them such great places to explore.

Scrubland

> Almost all routes described in this guidebook will lead through some scrubland. The most interesting *maquis* is found along routes 1, 5, 9, 11, 14 and site B. Extensive areas of superb *phrygana* are found on routes 16 and site U and V.

A major element of Lesbos's landscape is scrubland. It appears to be, at first glance, a rather uniform cloak that covers one hillside after the other. At closer inspection, the scrubland is a fascinating world, full of colour, scent and the buzzing of countless insects.
The Mediterranean scrubland is unlike any habitat found in temperate Europe. The species that live here have adapted to cope with the strong seasonality of the Mediterranean climate with its very hot and dry summers and relatively cool and wet winters.
Springtime is by far the best time to enjoy the scrubland. The countryside is bursting with life. Wildflowers, reptiles and birds are everywhere. When summer arrives and the temperature rises, the hillsides quickly turn into hot, dry and inhospitable places. The summer is clearly the challenging period for life in the scrublands. The vegetation responds to this with a number of survival strategies – each species has its own way to cope with drought. A large number of plants are equipped with thick, leathery or hairy leaves – all to retain as much of the precious water as possible.
Extensive grazing by goats is another big problem that plants have to cope with. Spiny or thorny leaves and branches are effective tools to prevent being chewed by hungry mouths, as well as aromatic oils, which makes the plants unpalatable. Oddly, these oils are what make many scrubland plants smell so wonderful.
In places, the scrublands of Lesbos form vast thickets of almost impenetrable thorny shrubs, but there is also a more inviting version where the bushes form a mosaic with open patches of grassland and rocks. This form of the Mediterranean scrub is found in places with a lot of local variation in soil thickness, slope, bedrock type and human activities.
The scrubland often reflects centuries of degradation and soil erosion, through burning and cutting wood, which prevented the further development to woodland (see text box page 32). But in some areas, the growth of trees is limited by environmental factors, like steep slopes, very thin soils or perpetual desiccating winds. Then the scrubland is the natural climax habitat.

SCRUBLAND

In 'Mediterranean' regions over the world, scrublands show a wide range of growth forms depending on the environmental conditions in the area. For this reason, Mediterranean scrublands go by many different names, many of which originate from local language or early colonists: *maquis* and *garrigue* (French), *matorral* (Spanish), *chapparal* (Spanish-American) and *fynbosch* (Dutch-South-African). Lesbos has two different and very distinctive types of scrubland: *phrygana* and *maquis*. Each grows in different places, formed under different circumstances and has a distinct flora and fauna.

Maquis

Maquis is a type of scrubland, made up of evergreen shrubs and small trees 1 to 4 metres tall. The individual bushes often stand a little apart, allowing room for grassy patches with all kinds of wildflowers, especially in places with a more developed soil. The most dominant shrub is Kermes Oak. This is the only oak species to grow commonly in the maquis (the Holm Oak, which is widespread in the Mediterranean, and often a typical element in scrublands, does not occur on Lesbos). The Kermes Oak shares its habitat with a large number of shrubs and small trees, including Eastern Strawberry Tree, Carob Tree, Mastic Tree and Prickly Juniper. Maquis develops in damper (or less dry) conditions, mostly found on the eastern and northern part of the island. Maquis is found on both volcanic and calcareous substrates, while phrygana is found in very dry areas.

Typical of maquis on Lesbos is that flowering occurs in two periods: an exuberant spring bloom and a more modest flowering period in autumn. Maquis consist predominantly of evergreens shrubs. Rather than shedding their leaves all at once, they replace their leaves, dropping the old ones as the new ones appear which they do before the challenging dry summer.

Subalpine Warbler is a typical bird of maquis.

In the landscape, areas with maquis are often interspersed with fields and olive groves. Together, they form a lovely blend, both as a backdrop for hiking and as a habitat for finding wildlife. Many species of birds and reptiles occur in maquis, dry fields and olive groves, but have their highest density and variety where these three habitats meet.

Phrygana

Phrygana refers to the dwarf shrub vegetation that covers the driest areas of the island. It is much lower and scantier than maquis. Cushion-forming, thorny shrubs and herbs no taller than 60 cm

SCRUBLAND

dominate – just high enough to be a serious nuisance to anyone who decides to cross a phrygana.

In extreme, dry environments, leathery leaves or a layer of fine hairs don't cut it. More serious protection against drought is called for which is why typical shrubs of the phrygana – most noteably Thorny Burnet, a member of the rose family, and the greenweed *Genista acanthoclada* – change their wardrobe depending on the season. The winter coat consists of bigger and greener leaves which are replaced by tiny leaves in summer. Other species, like Spiny Broom, have no leaves at all in that period.

Maquis (left) is found on various soil types in the eastern and northern part of Lesbos, while phrygana (right) dominates the dry western part of the island.

On Lesbos, phrygana is found predominantly in the volcanic western part and along the northern and southern coastal strip, where rainfall is the lowest, exposure to the sun highest and soils are mostly thin and rocky. Like the maquis, the phrygana has a spring peak of wildflowers, but this show takes place earlier in the season (roughly in early April) and is short-lived. Unlike the maquis, there is no autumnal encore – by late spring most plants have died down, giving the landscape a brown appearance that lasts until next winter.

Next to the natural phrygana of the poor dry soils, a similar vegetation develops under pressure of human activities like fire and overgrazing. This is the dominant form. Hence, phrygana is often regarded as a step further down the ladder of degradation – placing it between maquis and semi-desert (see text box on the next page). In its most degraded form, phrygana is composed of few shrubs, scattered over large areas of rocky terrain with hardly any soil and, during most of the year, nearly devoid of plants. This kind of phrygana is a result of desertification (see page 50). As phrygana is often framed in this negative way, it is important to realise that not all phrygana is the result of degradation.

LANDSCAPE

SCRUBLAND

Degradation of Mediterranean forest
The development of the Mediterranean scrubland is a very ancient and complex process, which began in prehistoric times and which reflects the growing impact of human activities on the environment. It is generally thought that, after the last ice age, the dominant vegetation in the Mediterranean basin, including Lesbos, was evergreen and deciduous oak forest. Scrubland was the natural vegetation only where environmental conditions prevented the development of true forest (for example near the coast, on exposed slopes and peaks or in areas with very thin soils).

Roughly 5.000 years ago, man's impact on the environment – activities like felling trees, grazing domesticated livestock, burning woodland and increasing agricultural exploitation – resulted in the degradation of large areas of forests into maquis. Where maquis was further overexploited (through, for example, overgrazing or through cutting for making charcoal) the vegetation was further degraded into phrygana (a good example of human-induced, 'degradation phrygana' can be seen on route 16). If human activities cease, evergreen forest may recover to some degree, but this is usually a slow process. On poor soils, like in the west of Lesbos, the soil is often extremely degraded and eroded. Due to the thin soil the forest will not return in the foreseeable future.

Wildlife of scrubland

In the eyes of many people, scrubland, both in its appearance as maquis and as phrygana, is an uninviting trouser-shredding wasteland of spiny shrubs under, in summer at least, a burning sun. This reputation makes it rather underwatched, which is a pity as it is a superb place to find wildlife of all sorts. Whether your interest lies in birds, reptiles or insects, the scrublands are a prime habitat to visit. The combination of available hiding places and an abundance of food makes it a perfect habitat for wildlife. Nearly all of the reptiles occurring on Lesbos can be found in scrubland. Remarkable species like Snake-eyed Lizard, Sand Boa, Cat and Dwarf Snakes feel perfectly at home here. The scrubland is equally good for its birdlife. Apart from being a favoured hunting ground for the Short-toed Eagle (in search for the above-mentioned snakes), the scrub harbours an array of songbirds. Many species of warblers are common in or even

The secretive Cat Snake has eyes with vertical pupils, like a cat, hence its name. During the day it hides underneath flat stones and only becomes active at dusk and dawn. It hunts lizards and small snakes.

restricted to scrublands. On Lesbos the common maquis-dwellers are Subalpine and Olivaceous Warblers, but look out too for Orphean (where scrub is mixed with some tall trees), Sardinian (near the coast) and the sought-after Rüppell's Warblers. In phrygana, especially where mixed with barren rocks, you will encounter Isabelline and Black-eared Wheatears, Rufous Bush Robin, Cretzschmar's and Cinereous Bunting (routes 16, 17 and site U).

The open patches between the shrubs harbour a dazzling number of wildflowers, above all rockroses, orchids, clovers and umbellifers (members of the carrot family; see page 60 for more details). The abundance of nectar bearing plants hosts a rich and diverse insect life, with many species of bumblebees and hoverflies buzzing about.

The most rewarding scrublands in terms of finding wildlife are those that border other habitats – spots where scrubland merges with (dry) stream beds, alternates with bare rocky patches or cliffs, or borders fields and patches of oak woodland. In the route section of this guidebook we describe some of the most interesting sites, which are easy to explore from trails and tracks.

Forests

> Turkish pine forests feature on routes 1, 2, 4, 6 and sites E, L, M, N and T. Black pine forest is found on site T. Oak woodland is encountered on routes 10, 14 and 17. Chestnut woodland can be explored on routes 2, 3, 4, and site K. Riverine forests feature along routes 2, 3, 5, 10, 13, 16 and site S.

Pine forest

The Turkish pine forest is the most common forest type on Lesbos, covering about one fifth of the total land surface. Vast areas in the central, western and southern part of the island are clad in endless pine forests. This forest is special in the sense that the dominant (and often only) tree in this forest, the Turkish Pine, only just reaches north-eastern Greece and the eastern Aegean islands. It is very much an oriental forest type.

Much of this forest breathes an air of peace and silence, perhaps even dullness. You can walk here for hours without seeing a human soul and not much wildlife either.

In spite of the general uniform character of the pine forests, there is some variation between stands that grow on different types of bedrock. In areas with ophiolite (mainly in the central part of Lesbos) the understory is

FORESTS

usually sparse with few shrubs and wildflowers. Their growth is inhibited by both drought and the chemical composition of ophiolite rocks (see page 15). This is not the type of pine forest in which you'd want to spend much time. On all other types of bedrock the undergrowth is much denser, with shrubs such as Kermes Oak and Prickly Juniper and – locally – attractive wildflowers such as the rare Komper's Orchid and Spurred Helleborine.

Birds are indifferent to the bedrock – it is the age of the trees that count. Although the pine forest is not the best habitat for birdwatching, the stands with old trees are home to one 'high profile' bird: the Krüper's Nuthatch (see route 4 and 6). Other breeding species to expect in its company are Spotted Flycatcher, Serin, Short-toed Treecreeper and, occasionally, Black Stork.

In places, Turkish Pine forms stable and mature forests with even-aged stands, which remain unchanged for many years. The trees can grow to become old, impressive trees – with 200 year old trees being no exception. In such old, dense stands, regeneration does not take place regularly. Only where forests are disturbed by fire, storm damage or human impacts, young trees appear in large numbers. Where this happens the result is a young, uniform forest. Rejuvenation of Turkish Pine is actually prompted by fire. Its cones remain dormant and closed until a fire opens them to release the seeds. This is in sharp contrast to another, quite rare kind of pine forest that consists of Austrian or Black Pine. To these trees, which regenerate only very slowly, fires are a threat because it destroys their cones.

Black Pine forest is typically found in the Balkans and the higher mountains of the Mediterranean region, but it is quite scarce in its range. On Lesbos it only occurs on the higher summits of Parakila Forest (site T). Unfortunately, a few decades ago another patch, south of Agiasos, burnt after a fire and was replaced by the fast-growing Turkish Pines.

The Turkish pine forests with their sparse understory on ophiolitic rocks in the central part of Lesbos, form a great contrast with the spectacular display of wildflowers in the nearby olive groves and chestnut woodlands (route 2). The Violet Bird's-nest Orchid in the foreground is one of the few orchids to find here.

Oak woodland

On the rolling hills in the north-western part of Lesbos, a pleasant landscape with oak woodlands prevails. It represents a hybrid of an ancient man-made and natural forest, maintained for extracting tanning agents for leather (derived from the acorn cups of Valonia Oak), food for livestock

FORESTS

and firewood. Typical is the occurrence of Valonia Oak – a species of south-eastern Europe. It has a beautiful broad domed crown and the acorn is almost completely enclosed by an exceptionally large, hairy cup. It is a resilient tree, capable of surviving fires and resisting hot and dry conditions. It grows alongside three other oaks, all of which are quite common: Downy, Turkey and Gall Oaks. Downy Oak has typical silvery hairs on its young leaves whilst Turkey Oak can be recognized by its saw-toothed leaves. Both are rather widespread in southern Europe. The Gall Oak is again a south-eastern species and has leathery leaves which are full with shiny galls caused by the insect *Cynips tinctoria*.

Woodland with Valonia Oak is a typical landscape in the north-western part of Lesbos (top). The characteristic large scales of the acorn cup contain about 45% tannin, traditionally used for treating animal hides to produce leather and for making ink (bottom).

In the open patches between the trees, plants of the maquis occur, such as Cretan Cistus, Silver Sage and the thyme *Coridothymus capitatus*. In oak woods on calcareous soil, plenty of orchids occur, including Narrow-leaved Helleborine and Monkey and Horned Orchids. Some beautiful sites like these are found in the old woodlands of Liota (route 14). On steep and inaccessible slopes, these woods may even be largely or entirely natural. Younger woodland established itself on now abandoned terraced fields.

Valonia Oak woodlands have a fragmented distribution throughout the East Mediterranean, and are under threat due to extensive cutting and the gradual shift from small-scale farming toward intensive agricultural practices.

Chestnut woodland

The forests and groves with Sweet Chestnut around Agiasos are an outstanding feature of Lesbos. On a fine spring day, the extensive groves with their massive old trees are a lovely and peaceful place. If it weren't for the spiny chestnut shells and for the risk of crushing the local flora, it would be the perfect place to just lie down and close your eyes.

FORESTS

Damp and shady forests of Oriental Plane found along rivers and streams are unique to the eastern Mediterranean region. They constitute one of the most natural forest types on Lesbos.

The main expanse of chestnut woodland is found east of the bold marble summit of Mount Olymbos at an altitude between roughly 500 and 800 m, where the conditions are cooler and damper than elsewhere on Lesbos. The woodland is testimony of an ancient chestnut cultivation which may easily go back more than 2000 years. Shaped by centuries of management for chestnut production and pruning for timber, the groves form an open woodland, mixed here and there with small fruit orchards and patches of arable land.

Its allure is underlined by the impressive wealth of wildflower species, above all orchids, tulips, anemones, Grape-hyacinths and arums. On your stroll through the open woodland, Three-lined and Snake-eyed Lizards will frequently cross your path. Leopard and Dwarf Snakes are widespread snake species here, although they are secretive and hard to find. Good places to encounter them are in cultivations in woodland clearings.

The highly nutritional chestnuts are a food resource for Persian Squirrel and Wild Boar. The latter reveals its presence by digging and trotterprints, but the shy animal itself is rarely seen. As for birdlife, Bonelli's Warbler is found in the chestnut groves, together with birds of temperate Europe, like Middle-spotted Woodpecker, Song Thrush, Short-toed Treecreeper, Nuthatch and Robin.

On steep slopes in damp stream valleys, a dense and mossy variety of chestnut forest has developed. There is not much of a herb layer as a consequence

FORESTS

of the deep shade. Tall leafy plants and a number of temperate species (e.g. Common Twayblade) growing near the stream banks complements the distinct northern feel of the forest.

The bright green chestnut woodlands are a joy to explore, especially as there is an extensive web of paths and ancient *kalderimi* (cobbled paths). Although some of the kalderimi have been concreted over the years, the whole area still breathes an atmosphere of the old countryside of the Mediterranean mountains.

The chestnut woodland is clearly a forest type of the relatively cool and moist higher parts of Lesbos. However, it is not only the altitude and accompanying climate that determines where the chestnuts grow. The strict limit of this woodland south east of Agiassos illustrates the effect the bedrock can have on the vegetation. Sweet Chestnut is *calcifuge* or limestone-fleeing – it grows only on schist and sandstone that contain almost no carbonates. This strict taste in soil type is particularly evident along route 4, which crosses the border between limestone and schist soils.

Riverine forest

Riverine forests are a natural jewel of streams and rivers, where a luxuriant, jungle-like forest of old Oriental Plane trees prevail. The fresh green forest that snakes through the countryside forms a sharp contrast, particularly in summer, with the adjacent dry slopes.

The noble Oriental Plane

There is almost no village on Lesbos without a huge plane tree spreading out its majestic crown gracefully over the main square. For centuries, the noble Oriental Plane has been treasured for its full canopy, providing cool and deep shade. Many of these trees have grown into natural monuments, under which tavernas arrange their tables. These are the best places to enjoy a good meal after a full day in the field.

Plane tree tavernas are a great feature of Lesbos – some of our favourite 10 tavernas are in the welcome shade of a superb plane tree (see page 197). In the wild many of the thickest trees are hollow, some are even big enough to provide room for a convenient shelter. An excellent example is found at the spring of Karini, where the painter Theophilos called a massive hollow tree his home (route 2 and box on page 44).

Three beautiful old plane trees provide shade for the tables of tavernas and cafeneons on Andissa's main square. An excellent spot to enjoy great food and the relaxed island's atmosphere (route 13 and 14).

LANDSCAPE

OLIVE GROVES, ARABLE LAND AND FIELDS

The scarcity of permanent water flows on Lesbos does not limit the distribution of riverine forest. Even in dry river beds, the groundwater will nourish the thirsty trees during a hot summer.

The riverine forest is regarded as one of the most natural forest types on the island. In many places it consists of majestic Oriental Plane trees. The long-lived Oriental Plane is equipped with a vigorous and deep root system to withstand the periodic, extreme water flows. In less dynamic, damp places, such as in shady gorges and springs, these trees are able to attain a height of up to 30 m and develop a mossy trunk of massive proportions. There are few – if any – trees in Europe that develop trunks of such formidable girths as the Oriental Plane. There are some great specimens found along the Evergetoulas river and near Lepetimnos (routes 2 and 10).

White Poplar and White Willow are two other trees frequently found in riverine forest, together with shrubs like Oleander and Vitex that grow along stony riverbeds. All take advantage of the available water and nutrients. Climbing plants like Black Bryony, Silk-vine and Ivy use the trees as substrate in the pursuit of sunlight.

Olive groves, arable land and fields

> The most interesting olive groves with orchids and wildlife feature on routes 2 and 3 and sites C, D, E, G, H and I. Many routes lead through arable land and fields, but the (for naturalists) more attractive arable land is found on route 8, 13 and site V, to explore fields visit route 5, 6, 7, 8, 10, 13, 15 and sites O, Q and R.

Almost 40% of the land surface of Lesbos is cultivated, making farmland – in the widest sense of the word – the dominant habitat on the island. Within this wide category, olive groves and arable fields are dominant, the latter usually lined by stone walls and hedgerows.

The number of people on Lesbos has fluctuated strongly during the course of history. This has had a great impact on the landscape. A huge population increase, directly followed by an exodus in the middle of the 20th century, led to abandonment of cultivated terraces. The result is still visible – many former cultivations are now being grazed and covered by steppe-like, shrubby grasslands. Many olive groves are little managed.

The agricultural landscape of Lesbos can roughly be divided into three zones, based on geology and rainfall. The first is the relatively damp and base-rich region in the east, around the Gulf of Gera. This region is dominated by terraced olive groves and small stone walls to support individual

OLIVE GROVES, ARABLE LAND AND FIELDS

trees. Second are the grazing lands mixed with phrygana on dry, poor volcanic soil in the west. Third, in the centre, a combination of arable land, olive groves and grazing land with oak woodland is found.

Fortunately, many cultivations on Lesbos are still small-scale and extensively managed, hence forming a true agro-ecosystem rich in plants and wildlife.

Olive groves

Large parts of Lesbos are covered by numerous olive groves with millions of olive trees, but many, long abandoned, are so wild that they would be more aptly described as an olive forest. The east, in particular, is covered with a grey-green blanket of olive trees growing on ancient dry stonewall terraces. These groves have a long history and play an import role in island life. Since the Middle Ages, the slow but steady conversion of vineyards (due to vine diseases) and arable land into olive groves marked a huge landscape transformation, changing the habitat conditions for plants and animals.

The olive groves of Lesbos are among the oldest, the most traditionally managed and beautiful in the entire Mediterranean basin. They are unploughed and therefore a hotspot for orchids and wildflowers – especially those on calcareous soil (page 63). A close inspection reveals a surprising diversity within groves. There are patches of maquis vegetation,

Besides offering a habitat rich of wildflowers and wildlife, the traditionally managed olive groves on Lesbos produce high quality, organic olive oil (top; route 3). Both are inextricably linked and mutually dependent. This baby Spur-thighed Tortoise feels at home in such olive groves (bottom).

LANDSCAPE

OLIVE GROVES, ARABLE LAND AND FIELDS

Irrigated arable land in an otherwise barren landscape, as here near Skala Eresou, attract many migratory birds (especially in autumn).

rocks and small cliffs, patches of pine trees and streams with damp riparian vegetation. A variety of woodland birds such as Masked Shrike, Olivaceous Warbler and Middle-spotted Woodpecker breed in the older stands. Persian Squirrels venture through the branches, while Three-lined Lizard and Spur-thighed Tortoise are often spotted along cobbled paths. With a little luck you may even stumble upon Sand Boa or Ottoman Viper, especially where the groves are open and there is water and some scattered shrubs.

Arable land and fields

Only flat or gently sloping areas are suitable for crop growing. As a consequence most arable land is found in the fertile coastal and inland plains. Arable land shows a mix of all kinds of crops, such as potatoes, courgettes, aubergines, tomatoes and legumes. The largest fields on the coast are irrigated and generate the highest yield of crops (e.g. those at Kalloni, Skala Eresou and Chrousos). In autumn, these are the sites that attract many migratory birds.

The deep and loose soil along the edges of fields provides the secretive Lesser Mole Rat with a habitat in which it builds its burrow. Waste places with rough vegetation and rubble are excellent snake habitat, while striking wildflowers such as the Dragon Arum are also found here.

Pastures for grazing cattle are found throughout the island, but they are in nothing like the manicured grassland pastures of northern Europe. Crooked solitary trees, patches of scrub and messy hedgerows give these sites a more natural look and provide habitat for wildflowers and birds (see page 85). Stone walls and sheds offer hiding places for reptiles like Starred Agama, Snake-eyed Skink and Three-lined Lizard.

The grazing lands, brackish fields, larger dry arable fields and the Anise cultivations on the eastern shore of the Gulf of Kalloni (for ouzo production) have a steppe-like allure. The centuries of grazing and the thin soils favour the growth of steppe herbs and grasses. It is here that you can find the migrating steppe birds, like Red-footed Falcon, Pallid Harrier and a variety of larks.

Cliffs, rocky outcrops and screes

> Cliffs and rock outcrops are prominent along routes 2, 6, 13, 16 and sites U and V. Screes are found on route 2. The most impressive coastal cliffs feature on route 13 and sites G, H and J.

Exposed rocks, cliffs and scree fields, shaped by millions of years of geological forces, form a distinct habitat on Lesbos. Two forces are responsible for carving out these rocky landscapes: on the one hand geological processes (tectonic uplift and volcanic eruptions) to provide the raw material, and on the other hand erosion (water, wind and gravity) to selectively sculpt it into fanciful rock monuments. These immense – but usually very slow – forces produced vertical rock faces, rock outcrops, gorges and steep rocky slopes, found scattered throughout the island.

This is the most inaccessible and extreme of all habitats, where life is hard for plants and animals. The shallow soil is prone to desiccation and hard to colonise for plants. Larger animals have a hard time crossing these lands. As a result, competition and disturbance by herbivores and predators is naturally low. It is precisely this feature that gives rise to a specialised flora and fauna which are absent in other locations.

The Lardia gorge (bottom; route 13), with its cliffs and crags, is a good place to find the specialist Rock Nuthatch (top).

CLIFFS, ROCKY OUTCROPS AND SCREES

Flora and fauna of cliffs and steep rock slopes

Cliffs may seem dry and inhospitable, but the flora and fauna is exciting. Virtually only airborne animals and wind blown seeds of wildflowers are able to make their way up here.

Cliff ledges offer breeding sites such as Peregrine and Long-legged Buzzard. The latter often seeks out the cover of a shrub for shade for their hatchlings. A score of other birds is adapted to living on cliffs, such as Rock Nuthatch, Blue Rock Thrush and Chukar. Aerial feeders like Crag and House Martins and Red-rumped Swallow breed here, taking advantage of the crags to build their nests. With one leap they are in the air where they find their food. Impressive coastal cliffs, the result of the endless interaction between sea and rock, are the breeding haunts of Eleonora's Falcon and Lesser Kestrel. They breed predominantly at rocky islets along the coast of Lesbos. The lack of predation and minimal disturbance by humans provide a safe haven.

Like the birdlife, the flora of cliffs and steep rock slopes is very distinct. Such habitats present even more challenges to wildflowers, as they only offer a sun-baked and weather-beaten environment with just small pockets of impoverished soil. In order to survive in this harsh environment these specialised plants are equipped with vigorous and thick roots for strong anchorage as well as to maximise water uptake. To preserve as much water as possible, they often sport small leaves or grow in dense cushions. The benefits of growing on dry steep rocks – there must be at least one – is the provision of a safe retreat, inaccessible to grazing animals and excluded from competition from other wildflowers which cannot grow here. When searching for wildflowers of exposed cliffs, take into account the local growing conditions like bedrock (volcanic, calcareous or ophiolite), exposure to the sun and the proximity to the sea (see page 70). The wildflowers found on the marble screes and rocks high up Mount Olymbos are the most remarkable. At first glance, the summit area seems completely devoid of any vegetation, but closer inspection reveals a rich flora with unique species (see route 2).

The secretive Chukar is more often heard than seen.

CROSSBILL GUIDES • LESBOS

History

Like many other regions in Greece, Lesbos has a rich and often turbulent history. The early records date back to prehistoric times and although Lesbos lacks major archaeological sites such as those at Knossos or Delphi, there are traces in the landscape of all major periods. Some may be still undiscovered, or have simply disappeared in the succession of habitation, through building layer on layer. New archaeological finds are regular. There are frequent articles about people finding remains of ancient monuments on their land. A naturalist may even see reused pieces of ancient buildings in a stone wall while scanning for Starred Agamas. The island possesses a strong identity, different from neighbouring islands and mainland, and is strongly determined by a sequence of rulers over the course of history. Lesbos was the birthplace of many artists and philosophers and is famous for the first appraisal of lesbian love and affection (the word lesbian is a direct derivative of Lesbos – see box on page 44). It is also famed for being the birth place of Ouzo – the well known Greek spirit. Consequently, the mark of all these influences is now seen in Lesbos's rich culture and traditions. A list of ancient monuments and buildings is found on page 198.

Prehistorical and ancient times

Archaeological excavations near the village Thermi, north of Mytilini, have brought to light that Lesbos has been inhabited by different tribes since about 4000 BC. During the Middle Bronze Age, about 2000 BC, an advanced civilization with numerous small settlements developed, characterised by the use of metals and a well-defined social organisation. The island was quite densely populated for that time. The Pelasgians were the main tribe. They inhabited also areas on mainland Greece and other coastal areas of the Aegean Sea. The people lived mainly off fishing and trade. These cultures were strongly influenced by the nearby ancient city of Troy (which was situated in what today is Turkey).
Things changed drastically around 1400 BC when the Mycenaean culture, originating from mainland Greece, spread over the Aegean Sea, including Crete and Lesbos. It represented an advanced civilization consisting of several states. The Mycenaean culture flourished roughly between 1600 and 1100 BC and is known for having the earliest form of the ancient Greek language. They brought forth famous mythical figures like the hero Achilles and Agamemnon, the king of Mycenae. Both feature in Homer's Iliad, describing the legendary Trojan War between

HISTORY

> **Philosophers, poets and painters of Lesbos**
>
> Lyric poetess **Sappho** (625?-570? BC) she was the first to write poems regarding personal emotions, affection and concerns of daily life. Until then the subjects of hymns were gods and heroic acts. Sappho is best known by the fact that she accounts for naming gay women lesbians, after the island of Lesbos (although the word was not coined until early 20th century). Although much lauded as one of the great lyric poets in the ancient world, only a few of her complete poems survived (the best known being *Ode to a beautiful girl*, which is about women's passion and sensuality). Historians assume Sappho established a school to teach women poetry and with the students she had a close relationship. She was born in ancient Eresos. Therefore, in the 1970's, nearby Skala Eresou became a meeting place for gay women all over the world.
>
> Botanist, physicist and philosopher **Theophrastos** (372-287 BC) was also born in ancient Eresos. Theophrastos is considered to have established the foundations of modern botany and is regarded as the 'father of botany'. Some of his writings survived through the centuries. He was the first to conduct scientific and philosophical investigation to the nature of plants. The most important are two large botanical studies which constitute the first systematic works on plants. He also studied geology, and was the first to express the basic rule that rocks consist of minerals. He was a friend of Aristotle, with whom he studied the natural world – Aristotle focussing on the classification of the fauna and Theophrastos of the flora.
>
> Folk painter **Theophilos** (1870-1934 AD) was an eccentric artist, famous for his colourful representations of daily life and nature. He often painted outside on walls of houses, tavernas and shops, in return only of a small fee or a plate of food. Many of his murals didn't survive, as they faded over time or were painted over. During his life he was ridiculed for wearing the traditional Greek kilt on the streets. For some time he lived in the huge hollow Plane tree at Karini, where a faded painting of his hand can still be seen on the wall of the adjacent taverna (route 2). The best preserved painting on the island is found inside a former bakery in Skopelos (ask the owner of the guesthouse Xenonas on site E).

the Mycenaens and the rulers of Troy (1260 and 1240 BC), which took place at the doorsteps of Lesbos.

After the capture of Troy, another tribe called Aeolians arrived from the Greek mainland around 1000 BC. The Aeolians settled peacefully next to the Mycenaeans and Pelasgians. Their language and culture blended with those of the other tribes, effectively resulting in the merging into a single new civilization. The belief in the Olympic gods was established and the Aeolic dialect of Greek became the dominant language. Lesbos developed rapidly into an important cultural centre of the eastern

HISTORY

Aegean. From here the coast of Asia Minor was colonised, which made it a political and cultural part of the Greek world of that time.

City states of Lesbos

Around 900 BC six small city states were founded on the island: Mytilini, Mithimna (modern Molyvos), Pyrra (near Achladeri), Arisvi (near Kalloni), Andissa and Eresos. Some of the old cities are archaeological sites today, for example Ancient Andissa (route 13) and Pyrra – due to an ancient earthquake, the latter lies submerged beneath the Gulf of Kalloni (route 6). The remains of a watchtower belonging to the Eresos city state can be seen at site V. The Aeolic sanctuaries of Klopedi and Mesa (page 198) were founded in this time too and still visible today.

Between the 800 and the 500 BC, the population grew steadily and the island became an important economic centre where artistic and philosophical activities flourished. The poems of Sappho were written in this period (see box on opposite page). Lesbos further developed as a maritime power, increasingly controlling large areas in Asia Minor. These centuries forged the ethnic identity and unity among Greek speaking tribes of the eastern Mediterranean. Increasingly this included the sharing of a common culture: the Hellenic period had begun.

The Persians and Peloponnesian wars

After a prosperous and relatively stable time, trouble started around 500 BC. The Persian Empire invaded Asia Minor from the east and many Greek cities came under their rule. Lesbos was invaded in 492 BC, but the Persian victory was short-lived. As early as 479 BC the Persians were defeated by a coalition of Greek armies and the island became an ally of the city state of Athens. The island was allowed to retain its independence from the Athenian power and its oligarchic government. During the Peloponnesian civil war (429-404 BC) between Athens and Sparta, nearly all city states on Lesbos choose the side of Sparta, with the exception of Mithimna. When Athens was able to assert its

Between the 7th and 2nd century BC the Mesa sanctuary, dedicated to the Gods Zeus and Dionysos, was an important place of worship. Then it was part of the city state of ancient Pyrra. A visit is recommended for both the interesting archaeological finds and tranquil rural setting.

HISTORY

Two impressive sections of the Roman Aqueduct still remain on Lesbos, of which this example near Lambou Mili (route 2) is one. In addition to the sections with arches to span valleys, the aqueduct mainly flowed through underground ducts and channels carved in rocks. The downward inclination over its 26 km course provided a steady flow, boosted by secondary springs, to drinking fountains and baths in Mytilini.

control over the island, all other city states were suppressed and harshly punished. In the following decades the island switched its allegiance various times, bouncing back and forth between Athenian and Spartan rule.

Macedonian empire

Around 335 BC Lesbos joined in coalition with Alexander the Great, king of the Greek city state of the Macedonia, against the resurgent Persians. After definitively breaking the power of the Persians, Alexander extended his Macedonian empire eastwards into India. The years following the death of Alexander the Great in 323 BC, the power of the Macedonian empire declined through civil wars and the rise of the Roman Empire. Nevertheless, Lesbos remained Macedonian territory until 167 BC. These were centuries of prosperity, with the construction of monuments like Mesa sanctuary (still visible today) and the ancient theatre of Mytilini. Intellectual life was blooming again, as represented by the work of philosopher Theophrastos (see box on page 44).

Roman and Byzantine Empires

The Romans seized control of the island in 84 BC. This was not a peaceful transition. In particular the city state of Mytilini resisted fiercely and its inhabitants were harshly punished by the Romans, who plundered and demolished large parts of the city.

Lesbos became part of the Roman province of Asia, but was granted a degree of autonomy and retained its privileges. In 58 AD, the Apostle Paul came to Lesbos to preach Christianity. Nevertheless, it took until the 2nd century AD before Christianity gained ground on the island.

The Romans left their mark on the island with the construction of a 26 km long aqueduct, around 200 AD. It took water from springs around Agiasos to Mytilini. The best preserved section contains some impressive arches and stands near Moria and Lambou Mili (site A and route 2).

In 395 AD, after the division of the Roman Empire into eastern and western parts, Lesbos was incorporated into the predominantly Greek speaking

HISTORY

eastern empire. Its capital city was Constantinople (now modern-day Istanbul), founded by Constantine in 324 AD on the site of Byzantium. During this period, Christianity became common practise, replacing the Olympian Gods. After the fall of the Western Roman Empire in 476 AD the eastern part continued to exist as the Byzantine Empire for 1000 years. Although Lesbos was still part of this empire, dark times came in the centuries after 600 AD. There were frequent raids of pirates, Slavs and Saracens. The life of inhabitants was harsh and island's intellectual life stagnated. Lesbos gradually became isolated from the rest of the empire and was a place of exile for unwanted influential people from the empire (e.g. Empress Irene in 802 AD).

Genoese times and Ottoman rule

As the power of the Byzantine Empire shrank, new players emerged on the scene, both from the east and west. The western forces were first to arrive. In 1355, Lesbos fell into the hands of the powerful family *Gattilusio* from the Italian city state of Genoa. A treaty granted them commercial and religious privileges over the inhabitants, but at least their rule was peaceful. Thanks to the Genoese, the island emerged out of the dark centuries and began their trading activities and invigorated their agriculture. During this time the Gattilusi renovated and extended the castles of Mytilini and Molyvos into the state in which they are today.

The Genoese hold on the island was short-lived. as, in 1462, they were overthrown by the Ottoman Turks. Their predecessors, the Seljuk Turks, started their conquest of Asia Minor in the 11th century and steadily pushed westwards ever since. During the first centuries of the Turkish occupation, the island´s cultural and economic wealth declined. The islanders tried to keep their Christian faith, language and identity by turning monasteries and churches into clandestine intellectual centres and schools.

The Ottoman Empire surged deep into Europe, but the tide turned with their defeat at the gates of Vienna in 1683.

Build in the 14th century by the Genoese, the Kremast Bridge is a remarkable feature of medieval architecture on Lesbos (sites Q and R). In those days the bridge served as an important connection between the eastern and western parts of Lesbos.

LANDSCAPE

HISTORY

Over the centuries, the Ottoman Empire declined, but it wasn't until the 19th century that large areas of mainland Greece (and many Aegean islands) gained independence from the Ottomans. Although Lesbos was still part of the Ottoman Empire, life for the Greek population eased during this period. With room for trade and cultural expression, business on the island flourished again.

Benefiting from the island's favourable position on the Mediterranean – Black Sea trading routes, Lesbos's economy improved rapidly and was, by the end of the 19th century, even booming. The increase of olive oil production in combination with the high international olive oil prices boosted profits. The areas Mytilini, Polichnitos and the Gulf of Gera were the main centres of olive cultivation and production. The numerous historic mansions still found here are a testimony of those wealthy times. Other developments were huge leather processing factories, mainly around Perama, where these impressive, now empty, buildings still stand.

The 20th century

Lesbos was liberated peacefully from the Turks in 1912, during the First Balkan War. After the defeat of the Ottoman Empire following WWI, modern borders were established by the Treaty of Lausanne in 1923. The treaty involved a drastic population exchange between Greece and Turkey. In the centuries of Ottoman rule, many ethnic Turks moved to Greek territory, while many ethnic Greeks still lived in Asia Minor. Half a million Turks that lived in Greece were forced to move to the newly founded Republic of Turkey, while vice versa, 1.5 million Greeks had to pack up and leave their villages in Asia Minor to settle in Greece.

Due to its geographic location, Lesbos was overwhelmed by more than 23,000 Greek refugees from Turkey. The total population of Lesbos exceeded 140,000 for a short while. This immediately threw the island into a major economic crisis. Almost all industrial and trading activities came to a grinding halt and many islanders moved to the other parts of Greece.

Lesbos's economy did not recover before WWII broke out, which had in Greece a nasty encore in the form of a civil war between the communists and pro-capitalist monarchists. Although the epicentre of this political turmoil lay far from Lesbos, it prevented the island from recovering from its problems. By the 1950s unemployment continued, and the island experienced a major population exodus. Australia and South Africa in particular, were popular. In the last few decades, many of the these emigrants have moved back to their mother island, so don't be surprised that some of the elders in remote villages speak fluent English!

HISTORY

Traditional landuse and rural life through the centuries

As we described in the habitat chapetr on page 38 traditional land use is still common practise on Lesbos. However, what 'traditional' entails, varied greatly over the course of history in keeping with the changes in population size and economic developments. During ancient and early medieval times, agriculture was self-supporting and in close proximity to the villages. The plots of land were small. Their use and the crops grown varied greatly. Small groves with vines, olive and figs were combined with vegetables. According to historical sources great parts of the island consisted of extensive mixed forests.

Later, during Genoese times in the 14th century, the first olive groves were established for commercial use. Interestingly, trees from this era can nowadays be found in olive groves on the island, mainly around Plomari and Asomatos. To make the land more suitable, the first terraces were constructed to retain soil and water. Next to groves, sheep and goat herding also became a profit-making activity, but the numbers of livestock were far less than those of today. Many of the stone walls that still snake over the hills found in the western part of the island, originate from this time. They marked the boundaries of the grazing land.

In the first centuries of Ottoman rule the population size slowly increased, finally doubling to about 80,000 inhabitants. Lesbos was a densely populated island for that time and there was an increasing demand for products. Cereals, pulses and cotton were all cultivated on terraces and coastal flats. Many villagers actually had two houses: one near the sea to grow crops in summer, and winter a quarters in the hills above the village to harvest and maintain the olive groves. Some of these small houses are still found hidden in the landscape (e.g. route 4).

Since cereals were extensively cultivated, many watermills were built to grind them, for example the Ligonas valley on route 10 and the Kanatsi watermill (site F). In the 19th century, the landscape transformed even further, when forests on the higher hill slopes were cut to make way for a considerable expansion of olive groves.

In the early 20th century, the streams of immigrants following the Treaty of Lausanne, the subsequent economic 'meltdown' and emigration of the islanders greatly affected the landscape. Almost all cultivations except for olives groves declined. Cereals, pulses, vineyards and groves of fig trees disappeared completely from the landscape as did the mixed farming of arable land and livestock. Due to the abandonment of arable land, the cover of oak woodland increased, for example around Filia. However, animal husbandry increased. The international demand for dairy products grew

LANDSCAPE

NATURE CONSERVATION

and in the 20th century, the island's herd of sheep tripled and grazing land extended greatly. Nowadays, with shrunken population size, numerous olive groves are either abandoned or continue with minimal care. Only half of the olive crop is collected and little management is practised.

Despite all the changes over time, the traditional land use persists to this day on the island. Now, the small fields, scattered pieces of arable land and old olive groves offer the perfect landscape for a wildlife holiday – a recent but important motor of Lesbos's economy. Along with mainstream 'sunseekers', naturalists and birdwatchers flock in from western Europe, creating a new, modest but growing economic potential for Lesbos. That is, when the island's nature is cared for properly.

Nature conservation

In the previous chapter we described centuries old olive groves, pristine river valleys, ancient chestnut woodlands and enthused about their harmonious nature. The wonderful balance between nature and traditional land use, creating so many habitats for so much wildlife, summarises the attraction of Lesbos. This image that we have sketched is not untrue, but it is a little one sided. Lesbos is facing a number of conservation issues, of which the following are the most important.

Desertification and overgrazing

In the 18th and 19th century, Lesbos experienced a great shift in land use, which has had a marked influence on the natural world. Before this time, agriculture was oriented towards supporting their own community. Characteristic was the integration of small scale husbandry with mixed cultivation using cereals, pulses, figs and olive trees. Sheep and goats were herded only in mountainous, barren or inaccessible terrain where they roamed freely over a wide area. During the last century, sheep herding gradually became the focal point of the local economy. The number of sheep and goats grew, from 100,000 in the beginning of the 20th century to more than 350,000 nowadays. This problem is further aggravated by the EU system of subsidising agricultural practises, in which the farmers are paid per sheep.

Sadly, to accommodate the large herds, fields and woodlands were converted into grazing lands, resulting in a loss in biodiversity. The overgrazing halted the rejuvenation of oak forest, while the scrubland set in a degradation to a scant vegetation of thorny dwarf shrubs (see page 32). This

NATURE CONSERVATION

Overgrazing is one of the environmental problems of Lesbos

has made the land susceptible to erosion by wind and water, and cleared the path to desertification. This is not the same as literally turning into a desert, rather it is a type of extreme degradation resulting in the removal of most of the vegetation, nutrients and all available surface water. The dry and hot western part of the island is very sensitive to desertification, which is much in evidence as you travel through it. This is precisely the area with the highest number of sheep. Desertification is a destructive environmental phenomenon and forms a serious threat to the flora and fauna of Lesbos.

Wind turbines

The threat of climate change and reliance on polluting fossil fuels has stimulated investments worldwide in the development of alternative energy. In the scramble for producing renewable energy, the Greek government has approved the construction of a huge wind farm on the western part of the island by 2017 which will consist of 153 wind turbines 67 metres in height. This plan also includes Chios and Lemnos – the latter even has to accommodate 400 new turbines!

There is fierce criticism on this project. Apart from doubts about the sustainability of wind turbines in general, this case is specifically sensitive, as it causes habitat destruction, disruption of breeding grounds of

In addition to the already existing wind turbines (route 16), the proposed wind farm in the western part of Lesbos will have a huge impact on the plants and wildlife. Through habitat destruction, but also by intruding into migration flyways of birds and bats.

NATURE CONSERVATION

rare birds and intruding into migration flyways. The huge impact is not solely due to the turbines themselves, but also from flattening hilltops and the building of 97 km of new roads to support the windfarm.

The benefits for the local community are questionable too, since it is a Spanish company that will build and exploit the windfarm. Besides, the capacity far exceeds that of the island's needs. Ironically, this energy is not even used on the island, which will still have to make do with its polluting power plant. The energy generated by the turbines will be transported to the mainland! What remains for the people is a huge and unrepairable scar on Lesbos's fine landscape.

Road construction

New road construction projects on Lesbos arise from the need for convenient links between villages and towns. Many of the current roads are rather long and winding, as they follow the natural topography of the island. To meet the wishes of the local communities, some existing roads have been broadened and upgraded over time, usually with low impact on the environment.

Recently, this has changed drastically. The most damaging is the huge project to connect Kalloni to Sigri by a major road (partly funded by the Spanish wind turbine company – see above). For this plan large areas of land are being cleared, affecting the rare flora and fauna, including populations of the endemic Lesbos Orchid* (*Ophrys lesbis*). At the time of writing, also the road through the Evergetoulas valley to Agiasos is partly upgraded and relocated, perhaps changing the tranquil atmosphere of the site of Karini forever (see route 2). The impact on nature lies in the fact that these new roads cause habitat destruction and form barriers for animals. Convenient roads also stimulate fast driving causing, disturbance and environmental pollution. The most frustrating part is that often these projects remain unfinished after the damage is done, damaging the landscape, without any benefit for anyone.

Although local communities understandably benefit from the reconstruction of roads, it has a serious impact on the environment. For example here in the Evergetoulas valley near the village Keramia (route 2).

NATURE CONSERVATION

Pollution and drainage of wetlands
It is unavoidable: the visitor to Lesbos will sooner or later be confronted with illegal fly tipping and littering along rivers and in wetlands. These areas are of low agricultural value and therefore 'ideal' places to dump rubbish. This is particularly sad because such areas remain otherwise unspoilt spots – the kind of places of low intensity use that have disappeared from northern Europe in the last century on such a huge scale. Wetlands are also under threat by the construction of ill-planned tourist facilities and encroachment of agriculture. To this end, wetlands are drained and the water is used for irrigation elsewhere, or to supply the new tourist resorts. Several marvellous freshwater sites have disappeared in recent times. The Charamida brackish marsh on Amali peninsula, has been greatly affected by the extraction of water for irrigation in the past (see route 1). Fortunately, it looks like these practises have taken a step back here and the marsh is slowly recovering.

Nature conservation efforts
It is clear that many challenges lie ahead for Lesbos if it is to preserve its rich landscapes and nature. Fortunately, for the conservation and restoration of habitats and species, several sites were designated as a part of the European network of nature protection areas – *Natura 2000*. Together they cover both Gulfs and about 25% of the land surface. This has helped the recognition and protection of Lesbos's natural heritage a great deal, although effective domestic legislation is often still missing. The hands-on work for the protection of Lesbos's environment is conducted by various local and national nature organisations. The Friends of Green Lesbos are campaigning for policies and actions to protect the island's environment. The Ecologist Greens are a Greek political party also active on Lesbos, with a member at the regional council of North Aegean since 2010. They conduct actions for protected areas, such as wetlands, and push local nature conservation efforts. The Hellenic Ornithological Society runs several volunteer programs on the protection of birds and habitats.
These organisations are still facing a daunting task in convincing local (and national) authorities of the importance of nature conservation. One of their ways of doing this is showing the (economic) value of nature for ecotourism. You, dear visitor, play an important role in promoting nature conservation on the island by being visible and thereby showing that visitors from all over Europe are drawn to Lesbos to enjoy its splendid nature. On page 191 you can see what you can do to support nature conservation.

FLORA AND FAUNA

Lesbos is a splendid destination for any kind of naturalist. It boasts a fascinating and diverse flora and fauna in a relatively small area. Although famous amongst birdwatchers and dedicated naturalists, it is just as much a place for those with a more relaxed approach to nature, as there are plenty of interesting and conspicuous species in a pleasant landscape with a benign climate. Many of the attractions can be found with ease during leisurely walks or hikes.

Above all, Lesbos is famous for birdwatching. Next to a profusion of migrating birds, there is a rich breeding bird community that include such star species as Cinereous Bunting, Olive-tree Warbler, Krüper's Nuthatch and Masked Shrike.

A much less known fact is that the flora is equally exciting. There are countless orchids in spring and many other wildflowers which are difficult to find elsewhere. Botanists will be able to find (with the aid of this book) Komper's Orchid and Pontic Azalea, but anyone will have little difficulty in finding a veritable sea of anemones, arums, orchids, fritillaries and tulips. If you explore rocky terrain or scrub, you will encounter an impressive number of reptiles, with many goodies like Sand Boa, Ottoman Viper and the dragon-like Starred Agama. Dragonflies too, are represented in good numbers and variety, with rare species like Black Pennant, Turkish Clubtail and Blue-eyed Goldenring.

Scops Owl is common throughout the island. Its presence is evident by its typical call consisting of long sequences of single flute-like notes.

INTRODUCTION

Unsurprisingly, the flora and fauna of Lesbos is dominated by Mediterranean species. In addition to widespread ones, like Sardinian Warbler, Kermes Oak and Montpellier Snake, Lesbos has a large number of eastern specialities. They are proverbial cherries on the cake! Birdwatchers will enjoy the presence of east-Mediterranean species like Sombre Tit, Western Rock Nuthatch, Olive-tree Warbler, Rüppell's Warbler and Black-headed Bunting. Other birds have such an oriental distribution that Lesbos is at the western edge of their range – e.g. Krüper's Nuthatch, Masked Shrike, Isabeline Wheatear and Cinereous Bunting.

Situated at the gates to Asia, this bias towards eastern species on Lesbos is present in other groups as well – Starred Agama and Ottoman Viper, Persian Squirrel, Komper's Orchid and False Hemp are all of oriental origin, found from Lesbos further east into Asia Minor.

Apart from the Mediterranean species, there are also Balkan and some temperate-European ingredients that add to the flavour. In particular the mountains in the east, with their cooler climate and higher precipitation, give rise to flora and fauna with many 'northern' elements. A few temperate European wildflowers grow on Lesbos on their southern edge of their range. For this reason, they are very rare here. Yellow Centaury and Royal Fern are perfect examples. Balkan Lizard Orchid and Snake-eyed Skink are more typical of the Balkan peninsula, but have important outposts on the island.

Finally, there is the Pontic region – the area of steppes and forests around the Black Sea area. Of this region, just a pinch is added to finalise the flora and fauna of Lesbos. Typical 'pontics' are Isabelline Wheatear and the smashing, yellow-flowering Pontic Azalea.

Both Peacock (with entire stem leaves as on the photo) and Crown Anemones (with deeply lobed stem leaves) come in in a wide variety of colours. The drifts of red, pink, violet anemones in spring are a spectacular sight in olive groves and chestnut woodland.

INTRODUCTION

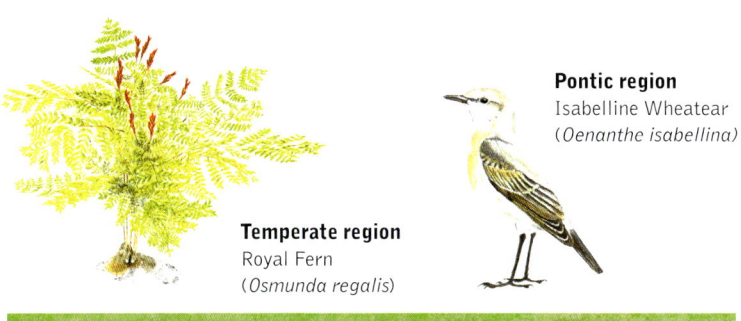

Temperate region
Royal Fern
(*Osmunda regalis*)

Pontic region
Isabelline Wheatear
(*Oenanthe isabellina*)

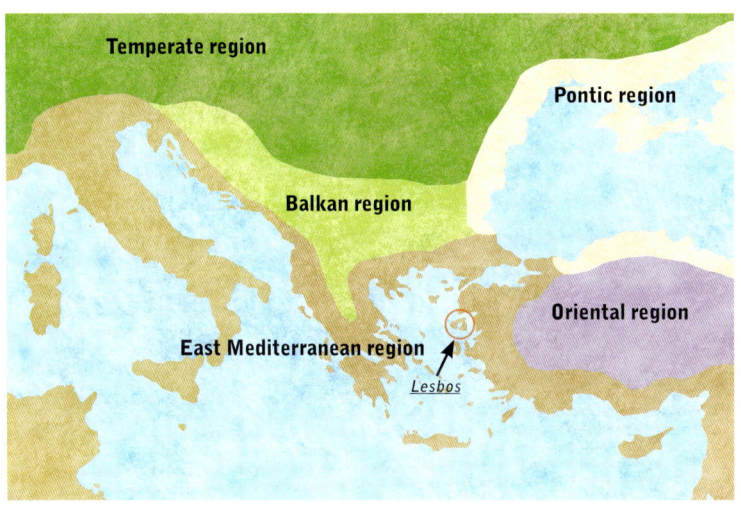

Balkan region
Snake-eyed Skink
(*Ablepharus kitaibelii*)

Oriental region
Persian Squirrel
(*Sciurus anomalus*)

East Mediterranean region
Odalisque
(*Epallage fatime*)

FLORA AND FAUNA

FLORA

Flora

> Excellent scrubland flora is found on routes 9, 11, 13, 14, 16, 17 and sites B, G, and U. Superb flora of olive groves is found on routes 1, 2, 3 and sites C, E, G, H and I. Attractive wildflowers of pine forest feature on routes 1, 4 and sites E, L and T. Flora of chestnut woodland is found on route 3, 4 and site K. Routes 5, 7, 13, 15 and site V are most rewarding for flora of fields and arable land. Cliff flora is best explored on routes 2, 11, 13, 16 and site J. The better routes for dune flora are 5 and 13. Plants of saline wetlands are found on routes 6, 7 and site O, while plants of freshwater coastal wetland features on route 2 and site D. For orchids routes 1, 2, 3, 4, 9, 14 and sites B, C, D, G and H are most rewarding.

Among botanists, the Mediterranean region is celebrated for its rich flora. Lesbos is no exception. With more than 1600 species recorded, the flora is all you could hope for on a Mediterranean island. To put this in perspective, this is about the same number of species found in the whole of The Netherlands, but on a surface 23 times smaller! Compared to the UK, the figures are even more dramatic: Lesbos has two thirds of the number of species recorded in the entire UK, but is less than 1% of its size. And new wildflower species are regularly discovered on Lesbos.

Between March and May the island will treat you to an exuberant wildflower display, featuring every colour and shape imaginable. Countless orchids, anemones and herbs form drifts of flowers in the olive groves, chestnut forests and scrubland. You can stroll through pine woods and along lush streams and encounter one botanical treasure after the other.

This diversity in a relatively small area is caused by three main factors. Firstly, the geology is very diverse. The many different rock and soil types found on Lesbos suit the needs of a wide spectrum of species. For instance, orchids are mainly found in limestone areas in the southeast and northwest, whilst the pretty Pontic Azalea grows exclusively on volcanic rock. Secondly, there are many different habitats in a small area (a result of variation in microclimate, hydrology and human activities). And thirdly, the geographical position of Lesbos in a contact zone of different biogeographical regions explains the presence of plants from temperate Europe, the Pontic or Black Sea region and even the *Irano-Turanian region* (the Orient), next to the obviously well represented East-Mediterranean species. The flora of the most important habitats is described in the following paragraphs. At the very end of this chapter we present the orchids, which are particularly well represented on the island.

Some of the key wildflowers of Lesbos

These attractive plants are either rare, have a limited distribution range or are remarkable oriental species here at the western edge of their range.

Komper's Orchid (*Himantoglossum comperianum* - route 2, 3 and 4) is both one of the rarest and one of the most spectacular plants to look for on Lesbos. It is a tall orchid (up to 70 cm) with large pink flowers, decorated with long, curly ribbon-threads. It usually starts to flower in the beginning of May – lagging a little behind most other orchid species. It occurs very locally throughout its entire range, which stretches from the eastern Aegean islands to Iran. In many places it also frequently fails to flower, making it a very difficult species to find. Lesbos, though, is one of the few places where it can be found in flower every year with relative ease. The best places to search are the chestnut and pine forests around Agiasos, where both the number of 'available' plants and precise flowering period depends on the season. In Turkey, the Komper's Orchid was once widespread and common, but today it is under serious threat from commercial harvesting of the root, which is an ingredient for drinks (salep) and desserts.

Lesbos Orchid* (*Ophrys lesbis*) - route 14) is a rare orchid, exclusively found on Lesbos, Samos and a small area on the nearby Turkish mainland. On Lesbos, it occurs only in the northwest, around the village of Andissa. It is sometimes regarded as full species, or as a subspecies or variety of the Bridled Orchid (*Ophrys argolica*). In any case, it is a true beauty. The flowers have a velvety red-brownish lip, decorated with a horse-shoe shaped marking. The orchid is usually found on calcareous soils in scrubland and oak woodland. Search for it from March to late April.

Pontic Azalea (*Rhododendron luteum* - sites T and U). Lesbos harbours one of only two native European populations of this essentially Asian species (the second is, curiously, in Slovenia where it survived as a Tertiary relict). Its yellow flowers produce a sweet and heavy scent with narcotic properties, so high concentrations of plants can make you feel woozy when you stay around them too long. The pollen and nectar are poisonous, so better not stick your nose inside the flowers! Researchers think that the honey obtained from this plant poisoned whole armies in Ancient Greece. It grows exclusively in Parakila Forest on humid acid volcanic soil.

FLORA

White-flowered Rue* (*Haplophyllum megalanthum* - site U). Until recently this very rare plant was only known from a small area near Izmir in Turkey, but botanists have found it on Lesbos too. This small shrub with white flowers is a member of the citrus family and grows only near the village Agra, in dry rocky *phrygana* scrub. It is amazing that this species was overlooked for so many years, as it grows conspicuously besides a track. But like so many places on Lesbos, this area is hardly explored. It flowers in June and July.

False Hemp (*Datisca cannabina* - site I). The main distribution of this impressive two-metre high plant with its Canabis-like leaves stretches out from West Turkey to the Himalaya. The plant belongs to the very small family of the *Datiscaceae*, consisting worldwide of only two species. Lesbos has, together with Crete and Samos, the only populations in Europe. It is found along damp streams in the area of Mount Parakila, and the hills around Plomari and east of the Gera Gulf.

Flora of scrubland

The scrubland boasts one of the greatest variety of wildflowers on Lesbos, both in numbers of species as well as in growth forms. To appreciate this habitat to the fullest, you should visit it in spring, when the scrub is like a fair ground, with all sorts of colours competing for your attention. The plants take advantage of this short period in which water is abundant and temperatures are relatively low. A thorough exploration can be a challenge

With both the shape and spikiness of a hedgehog, the Spiny Knapweed is perfectly equipped to protect itself against grazing. In contrast to most other knapweeds it is a small shrub, found in phrygana, maquis and dunes.

FLORA

though: not only are the spiny plants densely packed, the sun can be relentless, even in spring. A special feature of this habitat is the large variety of small trees and shrubs which are often aromatic, edible or medicinal (and sometimes all three). Examples of such species are Mastic Tree (anti-sceptic), French Lavender (aromatic) and Myrtle, Three-lobed Sage, Rosemary and Thyme (all kitchen herbs). The open patches between and underneath the prickly shrubs are full of wildflowers, which take advantage of the protection from goats and sheep provided by an umbrella of thorny or unpalatable plants. Composites (plants related to the dandelions), labiates (the mint family), vetches and clovers as well as orchids are frequently found in such places. It is an impossible task to mention all the wildflowers found in scrublands, so we restrict ourselves to the most attractive and recognisable species.

One should make a distinction between the flora of *maquis* and that of the *phrygana* (see also page 30). Typical maquis is composed of taller evergreen shrubs (dominated by Kermes Oak) and stout, perennial herbs. Conspicuous species are Carob or Locust Tree (the flour of the seeds and pods are used as a substitute for cocoa powder), Judas Tree (with pink flowers that grow from the branch), Eastern Strawberry Tree (with reddish-brown bark that flakes off in thin scales), Turpentine (with strong resinous smell) and Mastic Trees, Tree Heath, Broad-leaved False Olive (a relative of the olive, with opposite, dented leaves), Prickly Juniper and Giant Fennel. Also typical is the occurrence of many cistuses like Cretan (large pink flowers) and the smaller, Sage-leaved Cistus (with white flowers). They are the hosts of the peculiar parasitic Pink and Yellow Hypocist, growing like bright red pillows underneath the shrubs.

The scrublands host numerous orchids (e.g. Holy, Long-lipped Tongue, Pyramidal and Sicilian Orchids) as well as other bulbous plants, like Tassel Hyacinth and the bluebell *Scilla hyacinthoides*. In September and October, these are the spots to find Greek Cyclamen and Autumn Squill.

The delicate Sicilian Orchid (top) is difficult to spot in maquis scrubland. Its close relative Eastern Yellow Bee Orchid* (*Ophrys phryganae*) grows here too, but is rarer. The latter is distinguished by two conspicuous knee-like protrusions at the base of the flower's lip. In contrast, the big flowers of Cretan Cistus are hard to miss (bottom).

FLORA

The prickly phrygana grows in the driest parts of the island suitable only for plants with special adaptations to drought. The ultimate species of this land of thorns is Thorny Burnet, a rounded shrub with dense, grey, fiercely spiny branches that give the impression of chicken wire. Other conspicuous thorny phrygana shrubs are the greenweed *Genista acanthoclada*, Spiny Knapweed and Spiny Broom.

Between all this viciousness you find a rich flora with defenceless plants that profit from shelter, like Persian Clover (with its pink flowers upside down!), Button Medick (notice the spiral shaped seed pots), One-flowered Clover, Prickly Caterpillar Bean, *Coridothymus capitatus* and Ground-pine.

Typical species of scrubland
Maquis trees and shrubs Kermes Oak (*Quercus coccifera*), Carob Tree (*Ceratonia siliqua*), Judas Tree (*Cercis siliquastrum*), Eastern Strawberry Tree (*Arbutus andrachne*), Turpentine Tree (*Pistacia terebinthus*), Mastic Tree (*Pistacia lentiscus*), Tree Heath (*Erica arborea*), Broad-leaved False Olive (*Phillyrea latifolia*), Prickly Juniper (*Juniperus oxycedrus*), Cretan Cistus (*Cistus creticus*), Sage-leaved Cistus (*Cistus salviifolius*), Rosemary (*Rosmarinus officinalis*), Almond-leaved Pear (*Pyrus amygdaliformis*), Myrtle (*Myrtus communis*), Spanish Broom (*Spartium junceum*), *Thymus zygioides*, French Lavender (*Lavandula stoechas*), Common Smilax (*Smilax aspera*)

Maquis herbs Giant Fennel (*Ferula communis*), Yellow Star-thistle (*Centaurea solstitialis*), *Echinops spinosissimus*, Narrow-leaved Lupin (*Lupinus angustifolius*), Spiny Asparagus* (*Asparagus acutiofolius*), Three-lobed Sage (*Salvia trilobata*), *Dorycnium hirsutum*, Spotted Rockrose (*Tuberaria guttata*), Mirror Orchid (*Ophrys speculum*), Holy Orchid (*Orchis sancta*), Long-lipped Tongue Orchid, (*Serapias vomeraceae*), Pyramidal Orchid (*Anacamptis pyramidalis*), Sicilian Orchid (*Ophrys sicula*), Tassle Hyacinth (*Muscari comosum*), *Scilla hyacinthoides*, Greek Cyclamen (*Cyclamen graecum*), Autumn Squill (*Scilla autumnalis*), Pink Hypocist (*Cytinus ruber*), Silver Sage (*Salvia argentea*)

Phrygana trees and shrubs Thorny Burnet (*Sarcopoterium spinosum*), *Genista acanthoclada*, Spiny Knapweed (*Centaurea spinosa*), Spiny Broom (*Calicotome villosa*), *Anthyllis hermanniae*, *Erica manipuliflora*, Mediterranean Buckthorn (*Rhamnus alaternus*).

Phrygana herbs Persian Clover (*Trifolium resupinatum*), One-flowered Clover (*Trifolium uniflorum*), Woolly Clover (*Trifolium tomentosum*), Button Medick (*Medicago orbicularis*), Prickly Caterpillar Bean (*Scorpirius muracatus*), Ground-pine (*Ajuga chamaepitys*), Wild Clary (*Salvia verbenaca*), Yellow Star-thistle (*Centaurea solstitialis),* Pink Hawk's-beard (*Crepis rubra*), *Coridothymus capitatus*, *Ballota acetabulosa*, *Phagnalon graecum*

FLORA

Facing the elements in scrubland
Imagine being a plant and having to survive in a harsh environment like Mediterranean scrubland facing a continuous challenge from drought, poor soils and the relentless grazing of goats. Rather than competing with each other over scarce resources, plants face a common struggle against the elements which are set against them. These plants have developed key survival strategies.

Hide underneath your spiny neighbour Wildflowers, like orchids and small herbs which lack defence mechanisms against grazing, protect themselves by growing close to or underneath plants with thorns. Successful growth is facilitated by this protective umbrella.

Avoid unfavourable conditions Many species avoid coping with drought and high temperatures, by spending the summer period as seed, and completing their life cycle of germination, growth, blooming and seed formation within the few months of spring (the so called annuals). In this period there is an abundance of water and pollinators.

Store your energy and water safely underground To keep the precious resources away from goats, some plants developed bulbs, tubers to store them (orchids, tulips, crocuses, hyacinths). Some bulbous plants have an extra feature: they flower and have leaves very early or very late in the year when the temperatures and drought are not so severe. Examples include Winter Daffodil, *Colchicum* species, Autumn Squill (all flowering in autumn) and Stalked Star-of-Bethlehem and Alpine Squill (flowering early spring/winter). Growth occurs mainly in spring when lack of water is less of a limitation. Summer is the period with a minimum activity.

Winter Daffodil flowers in autumn to avoid unfavourable conditions of the hot and dry summer.

Flora of olive groves

Some of the best wildflower sites are not far from the airport. The olive groves around the Gulf of Gera, just a few kms from Mytilini, in the south-eastern part of Lesbos are without doubt amongst the best places for a spectacular display of colourful spring flowers, in which orchids take a lead role. Olive groves are not restricted to this area, but those in other parts of the island are mostly on non-calcareous soil, which limits the number of orchids.

FLORA

The old olive groves that haven't seen a plough for a long time are particularly good. In general the more heavily grazed and ploughed the groves are, the more the diversity declines and the more common weeds of fields take over. The dominance of Summer Asphodel is a clear clue of overgrazing and a reason for botanists to stay away.

The botanically richest olive groves are all governed by low impact agriculture. Man-made structures like the small stone walls around the olive trees (built to retain water) are a good place to look for Four-spotted, Homer's and Small Horned Orchids. In the open grassy parts between the olive trees, the huge stands of Long-lipped Tongue and Bergoni's Tongue Orchids are hard to miss, but it is quite difficult to tell them apart. The colourful anemones draw the attention as well. Both Peacock and Crown Anemones occur, often side by side, in various shades of red, pink and violet. The Peacock Anemone has stem leaves that are entire, while those of the Crown Anemone are deeply lobed, which is the best way to distinguish between them. They often grow together with the daisies Corn Chamomile and *Anthemis chia*, which form patches of white amidst the intense colour of the anemones – an unforgettable sight. Here and there, Green-winged and Naked Man Orchids can be found, elsewhere there are specimens of Larger Venus's-looking-glass or the larkspur *Delphinium peregrinum*, Cretan Catchfly with its bright pink flowers, and the umbellifer *Orlaya daucoides*, which like all *Orlayas* is recognisable by the fact that the outer petals of the outer flowers are much larger. Then there are also many bulbous plants like Grecian Star-of-Bethlehem (which because of its white instead of yellow flowers, doesn't directly remind of a *Gagea*) and

Two frequent flowers of olive groves: Barbary Nut in spring (left), and Greek Cyclamen in autumn (right). The latter often forms pink drifts around the olive trees of old groves.

Stalked Star-of-Bethlehem, Barbary Nut (a small, violet iris), Common Grape-hyacinth and Hairy Garlic (which has white flowers with red stamens). On top of that, there are large numbers of broomrapes, vetches, toadflaxes, clovers and daisies in the grassy spots.

Another type of site to keep an eye out for are small tracks and cobbled roads that run through the groves and are often carved into the dry rocks, providing perfect micro habitats for plants of rocky substrates, like Rock Bellflower (one of the few bellflowers on the island), Yellow Leek and Felty Germander. In contrast, on rocky spots that are moist and shady, you can find Navelwort, Yellow-wort, Shining Crane's-bill, and Greek Saxifrage. Abandoned olive groves shift towards a maquis vegetation where the flora is made up of associated species, like Cretan Cistus. In the rough parts, some 'goodies' to look for in these partially overgrown groves are Bull-headed and Horseshoe Orchids, Italian Gladiole and Eastern Bugle.

Typical species of olive groves

Peacock Anemone (*Anemone pavonina*), Crown Anemone (*Anemone coronaria*), Green-winged Orchid (*Anacamptis morio*), Three-toothed Orchid (*Neotinea tridentata*), Naked Man Orchid (*Orchis italica*), Four-spotted Orchid (*Orchis quadripunctata*), Bull-headed Orchid (*Ophrys bucephala*), Homer's Orchid (*Ophrys homeri*), Small Horned Orchid (*Ophrys minutula*), Horseshoe Orchid (*Ophrys ferrum-equinum*), Long-lipped Tongue Orchid (*Serapias vomeracea*), Bergoni's Tongue Orchid* (*Serapias bergonii*), Anthemis chia, Corn Chamomile (*Anthemis arvensis*), Larger Venus's-looking-glass (*Legousia pentagonia*), Venus's-looking-glass (*Legousia speculum-veneris*), Delphinium peregrinum, Ziziphora taurica, Micromeria juliana, Cretan Catchfly (*Silene cretica*), Centaurium maritimum, Orlaya daucoides, Fumana arabica, Thyme-leaved Rockrose (*Fumana thymifolia*), Italian Gladiolus (*Gladiolus italicus*), Eastern Bugle (*Ajuga orientalis*), Southern Red Bartsia (*Parentucellia latifolia*), Jersey Toadflax (*Linaria pelisseriana*), Hippocrepis ciliata, Grecian Star-of-Bethlehem (*Gagea gaeca*), Stalked Star-of-Bethlehem (*Gagea peduncularis*), Ornithogalum narbonense, Ornithogalum gussonei, Common Grape-hyacinth (*Muscari neglectum*), Barbary Nut (*Gynandriris sisyrinchium*), Hairy Garlic (*Allium subhirsutum*), Neapolitum Garlic (*Allium neopolitanum*), Rock Bellflower (*Campanula lyrata*), Yellow Leek (*Allium flavum*), Felty Germander (*Teucrium polium*), Navelwort (*Umbilicus rupestris*), Horizontal Navelwort (*Umbilicus horizontalis*), Yellow-wort (*Blackstonia perfoliata*), Shining Crane's-bill (*Geranium lucidum*), Saxifraga hederacea, Meadow Saxifrage (*Saxifraga granulata*), Greek Saxifrage (*Saxifraga graeca*), Greek Cyclamen (*Cyclamen graecum*) Autumn Squill (*Scilla autumnalis*), Winter Daffodil (*Sternbergia lutea*)

FLORA

All this is an image of the olive groves in springtime. After the dry and flowerless summer, the shortening of the days initiate the flowering season of the Greek Cyclamen (with thick pen-roots for anchoring in rocky terrain), Autumn Squill and the beautiful winter Daffodil.

Chestnut woodland

The woodlands of Sweet Chestnut around Agiasos are the island's next wildflower haunt. It is cooler and moister here, hence the flora has more species that favour temperate conditions. The most common wildflowers in the undergrowth are Perfoliate Alexanders and Drooping Star-of-Bethlehem, which grow together with the less common Eastern Aegean Corydalis* (*Corydalis integra*) and a high variety of broomrapes.

The lovely Balkan Peony is not only found along streams in chestnut woodland (route 4), but also in damp pine forests and grassy slopes (site E, T and U).

Perhaps the most attractive flowers here belong to bulbous plants. The local tulip is the red-flowered *Tulipa orphanidea*, which grows here and there in clumps. The endemic Lesbos Fritillary* (*Fritillaria theophrasti*) can be abundant in spring in some places. In winter and early spring, its place is taken by the Two-flowered Crocus* (*Crocus biflorus*) and Persian Cyclamen and Greater Snowdrop.

The chestnut forests also form yet another orchid paradise, with some highly sought-after species like Komper's, Holmboe's Butterfly and Reinhold's Orchids. As there is plenty of light in the forest, orchids that are more widespread on the island, like Provence and Three-toothed Orchids and Narrow-leaved Helleborine, find good conditions here as well. There are also plenty of anemones and you can find the odd and evocative Hairy Birthwort. It looks like an old man's pipe with a hairy inside. The tube traps flies that are seduced by its scent. The inward curved hairs makes it hard for the fly to escape and during its struggle to get out, the fly gets completely covered with pollen, constituting an effective pollenisation strategy.

Where mountain streams run through the forest, the shady, cool and moist conditions offer a place of refuge for plants of temperate Europe. They are generally rare on Lesbos, but in places you may come across familiar plants like Common Twayblade and Horse Caraway.

The big and lovely pink flowers of Balkan Peony are found along tracks near streams, together with the impressive Elongated Arum* (*Arum elongatum*), which' repulsive scent attracts flies. Its big purple flower-like spathe (up to

FLORA

Typical species of chestnut forest
Komper's Orchid (*Himantoglossum comperianum*), Holmboe's Butterfly Orchid (*Platanthera holmboei*), Reinhold's Orchid (*Ophrys reinholdii*), Provence Orchid (*Orchis provincialis*), Three-toothed Orchid (*Neotinea tridentata*), Green-winged Orchid (*Anacamptis morio*), Narrow-leaved Helleborine (*Cephalanthera longifolia*), Perfoliate Alexanders (*Smyrnium perfoliatum*), Drooping Star-of-Bethlehem (*Ornithogalum nutans*), Eastern Aegean Corydalis* (*Corydalis integra*), *Tulipa orphanidea*, Lesbos Fritillary* (*Fritillaria theophrasti*), Two-coloured Crocus* (*Crocus biflorus*), Persian Cyclamen (*Cyclamen persicum*), *Ornithogalum sphaerocarpum*, Hairy Birthwort (*Aristolochia hirta*), Pea-cock Anemone (*Anemone pavonina*), Crown Anemone (*Anemone coronaria*), Common Twayblade (*Neottia ovata*), Horse Caraway (*Laser trilobum*), Balkan Peony (*Paeonia mascula*), Elongated Arum* (*Arum elongatum*), *Arum rupicola*, *Colchicum variegatum*, *Colchicum bivonae*, Ivy-leaved Cyclamen (*Cyclamen hederifolium*), Greek Cyclamen (*Cyclamen graecum*), *Loranthus europaeus*

Hairy Birthwort (left) and Lesbos Fritillary* (*Fritillaria theophrasti*; right) are both found in chestnut woodland. The latter is endemic to the island.

30 cm high) usually doesn't exceed the leaves in length, which is how you tell it apart from its relative, the *Arum rupicola*, whose main distribution is in the mountains of the Middle East. Fortunately, this one is odourless. In season, the autumn crocuses *Colchicum variegatum* and *Colchicum bivonea* grow in abundance on the forest floor and by the road side. The first has wide open flowers (like a trumpet), while the latter has a broad cup-shaped flower. They grow together with Ivy-leaved Cyclamen and, in more rocky exposed sites, Greek Cyclamen. Finally, notice the parasitic mistletoe-like plants growing on the branches of many chestnut and oak trees. This is *Loranthus europaeus*, which, in contrast to the true Mistletoe, sheds its leaves in winter.

FLORA AND FAUNA

FLORA

Flora of pine forest

The flora of the Turkish pine forest varies greatly in diversity and attractiveness, depending on the age of the forest and the bedrock it grows on. Typical species to find in almost any stand are *Jurinea consanguinea* (a pink flow-ered thistle on high stalks) and the nearly leafless Violet Bird's-nest Orchid, which has a symbiotic relationship with fungi.

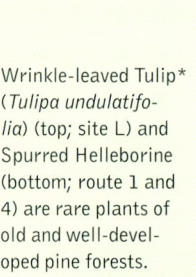

Older and more undisturbed forests on calcareous soils (e.g. near Agiasos and the Gulf of Gera) or volcanic rock (as in Mesa, Parakila Forest and Klapados) support more interesting species, like Roman Orchid and the delicate Autumn Lady's-tresses. These woodlands often have an undergrowth of shrubs and herbs that are also commonly found in the maquis, such as cistuses, Kermes Oak and Eastern Strawberry Tree. Although these forests are no match for the botanical wealth of scrubland and olive groves, some emblematic species can be found in Turkish pine forests, like Komper's Orchid (only in the area of Agiasos), Spurred Helleborine (Agiasos and peninsula of Amali), Pontic Azalea (Parakila Forest) and Wrinkle-leaved Tulip* (*Tulipa undulatifolia*; Vrisa).

Wrinkle-leaved Tulip* (*Tulipa undulatifolia*) (top; site L) and Spurred Helleborine (bottom; route 1 and 4) are rare plants of old and well-developed pine forests.

The extensive pine forest dominating the central part of Lesbos grows on serpentine bedrock and is rather dull from a botanical point of view (see page 33). Drought and the naturally high concentrations of nickel and cobalt in these rocks, create a stressful environment where only plants able to tolerate metals can grow. The forest here is almost devoid of shrubs. The endemic Lesbos Alison* (*Alyssum lesbiacum*) is confined to such environments. On the peninsula of Amali, a much smaller forest on serpentine rock exists, but here the variety of plants is higher due to the maturity of the forest, including some interesting Helleborines (see route 1).

FLORA

> **Typical species of pine forest**
> Jurinea consanguinea, Violet Bird's-nest Orchid (Limodorum abortivum), Roman Orchid (Dactylorhiza romana), Autumn Lady's-tresses (Spiranthes spiralis), Komper's Orchid (Himantoglossum comperianum), Balkan Lizard Orchid (Himantoglossum caprinum), Spurred Helle-borine (Cephalanthera epipactoides), Pontic Azalea (Rhododendron luteum), Wrinkle-leaved Tulip* (Tulipa undulatifolia), Lesbos Alison* (Alyssum lesbiacum), Galium divaricatum, Genista acanthoclada, Thlaspi ochroleucum, Felty Germander (Teucrium polium), Micromeria nervosa, Ziziphora taurica, Acinos rotundifolius

Flora of wastelands, fields and arable land

Wastelands are great areas to look for wildflowers. Although many species here are generally common and widespread, they are nonetheless striking and beautiful. One of the most impressive plants is the Dragon Arum, with a deep purple, leaf-like bract that envelops a spike with tiny flowers. It doesn't flower every year, which is why you encounter its peculiar leaves much more often than flowering plants.

Vitex is a common shrub with lilac flowers in long spikes, which is an important nectar source for insects in summer and autumn. The same goes for the thistles, of which Milk, Yellow Star and Syrian Thistles are particularly common. A curious autumn-flowering plant is the Squirting Cucumber, with a peculiar, yet not unfamiliar, mechanism to spread its seeds. When the ripened fruit is touched, the seeds and juice are squirted up to 6m away.

The most exuberant flora on Lesbos in spring is found in fields. The deep red masses of flowering poppies, alternate with a yellow wash of Crown Daisy and Corn Marigold, and hues of blue from the Cornflowers and gold speckles of Common Marigold. A close inspection reveals a range of wildflowers, like Hypecoum, Scarlet Pimpernel (both red and blue flowers) and countless daisies and vetches. In damp fields near the coast the stunning Oriental Iris is found.

The gorgeous Oriental Iris flowers in brackish marshes and damp fields near the coast.

FLORA

The marble rocks of the summit area of Mount Olymbos hosts a special flora, with rare species like Silene urvillei (top; route 2). Oddly, this species is also found on a small area with calcareous rocks on the west side of Pithariou reservoir (route 16).

Typical species of wastelands, fields and arable land
Dragon Arum (*Dracunculus vulgaris*), Vitex (*Vitex agnus-castus*), Milk Thistle (*Silybum marianum*), Yellow Star-thisle (*Centaurea solstitialis*), Syrian Thistle (*Notobasis syriaca*), Rayless Chamomile (*Anthemis rigida*), Berger's Bastard Toadflax* (*Thesium bergeri*), Squirting Cucumber (*Ecballium elaterium*), Mediterranean Lineseed (*Bartsia trixago*), Italian Viper's-bugloss (*Echium italicum*), Purple Viper's-bugloss (*Echium plantagineum*), *Heliotropium hirsutissimum*, *Thapsia garganica*, Salsify (*Tragopogon porrifolius*), Common Poppy (*Papaver rhoeas*), Crown Daisy (*Glebionis coronarium*), Corn Marigold (*Glebionis segetum*), Common Marigold (*Calendula officinalis*), Field Marigold (*Calendula arvensis*), Hypecoum (*Hypecoum procumbens*), Cornflower (*Centaurea cyanus*), Scarlet Pimpernel (*Anagallis arvensis*), Small Sainfoin (*Onobrychis arenaria*), Red Pea (*Lathyrus cicera*), Oriental Iris (*Iris orientalis*)

Flora of cliffs and rocks
The exposed rocks with their crevices, ledges, steep slopes and vertical rock faces form another excellent habitat to look for wildflowers. Only specially adapted rock-dwelling plants (*chasmophytes*) can grow on these seemingly inhospitable places, which lack proper soils, nutrients and water. It is surprising to see how these wildflowers manage to survive in these cracks, no matter how narrow and small they are.

Summit areas
Although barely reaching 1000 m elevation, the summit areas of Mount Lepetimnos and Mount Olymbos have a harsh climate, with blistering winds, extreme summer drought and intense solar radiation. Only plants with very specific adaptations are able to survive here and these traits make it impossible for them to grow elsewhere. Some unique plants are found (especially on Mount Olymbos which consists of poor and porous marble rocks), such

FLORA

as the cushion-forming catchfly *Silene urvillei* and Turkish St. John's-wort, which are restricted to the mountains of Lesbos and West-Turkey. A commonly encountered wildflower is the ground-hugging Shrubby Milk-vetch* (*Astragalus angustifolius*), a spiny dwarf shrub with small white flowers, forming large colonies. It grows together with the pink-flowered crucifer Aubretia (an ornamental plant in northern Europe), the ironwort *Sideritis sipylea*, the sandwort *Minuartia anatolica* and the chamomile *Anthemis cretica*. The Mountain Cherry is a small but eye-catching shrub, often found growing in crevices. It has beautiful bright, rose-like flowers in spring and, later in the year, red berries. In the deeper shady cracks, relatives of the stonecrops are found, like *Rosularia serrata*.

Coastal cliffs

In contrast to the summit areas, the flora of coastal cliffs lack endemic species. This habitat doesn't develop under conditions that are unique or far away from distant similar environments, hence the cliff coasts lack the isolation required for populations to evolve into new and local species. Many wildflowers here have wide distributions, occurring throughout the Mediterranean or even the Atlantic coasts. Noticeable species on rocks close to the sea are the edible Rock Samphire, with thick and fleshy leaves, and Winged Sea-lavender, which stands out by its contrasting cream with purple flowers. Higher up on the cliffs, the Curry Plant grows together with the striking umbrella shaped daisy *Cardopatium corymbosum*, with bright blue flowers and spiny leaves. Less conspicuous is the delicate sand crocus *Romulea linaresii*, which grows on the upper cliffs. In summer and autumn keep an eye out for the impressive, up to 2 metres tall Sea Squill, with an asphodel-like spike of white flowers. The Hottentot-fig is a mat-forming succulent plant with big pink flowers and fleshy leaves. It is an invasive species native to South Africa, that poses a threat to plant life on cliff coasts.

Rock Bellflower is common on old stone walls.

Rocky slopes

Wherever you go on the island, rocky areas are a constant and flowery companion. The best patches are often found right alongside the

FLORA

road on rocks and old walls. A typical wildflower here is the Caper Bush, which edible flower buds or capers are widely known and appreciated, is readily recognised by its big white flowers with bundles of bright pink stamens. It grows together with the widely occurring Rock Bellflower, Silver-leaved Samphire* (*Inula heterolepis*) and Annual Buckler-mustard, with odd fruits consisting of paired disks, looking like spectacles. The joint-pine *Ephedra foeminea* has distinctive pink fleshy berries in autumn, while the impressive Sclary Sage grows along bare rocks along tracks.

> **Typical species of cliffs and rocks**
> **Summit areas** *Silene urvillei*, Turkish St. John's-wort (*Hypericum aviculariifolium*), Shrubby Milk-vetch* (*Astragalus angustifolius*), Aubretia (*Aubrietta deltoidea*), *Sideritis sipylea*, *Minuartia anatolica*, *Anthemis cretica*, Mountain Cherry (*Prunus prostrata*), *Rosularia serrata*, Balkan Harebell* (*Asyneuma limonifolium*), *Torilis webbii*, *Iberis acutiloba*
> **Cliff coasts** Rock Samphire (*Crithmum maritimum*), Winged Sea-lavender (*Limonium sinuatum*), Curry Plant (*Helichrysum stoechas*), *Cardopatium corymbosum*, *Romulea linaresii*, Sea Squill (*Drimia maritima*), Sweet Alison (*Lobularia maritima*), Fringed Rue (*Ruta chalepensis*), Common Leadwort (*Plumbago europaea*), *Dianthus glutinosus*, *Senecio bicolor*, Grey Bird's-foot-trefoil (*Lotus cytisoides*), Eastern Sand Stock* (*Malcolmia flexuosa*), Tree Medick (*Medicago arborea*), *Sedum litoreum*, Pale Stonecrop (*Sedum sediforme*), Hottentot-fig (*Carpobrotus edulis*)
> **Rocky slopes** Caper Bush (*Capparis spinosa*), Rock Bellflower (*Campanula lyrata*), Silver-leaved Samphire* (*Inula heterolepis*), Annual Buckler-mustard (*Biscutella didyma*), *Ephedra foeminea*, *Ephedra nebrodensis*, Sclary Sage (*Salvia sclarea*), *Dianthus anatolicus*, *Cymbalaria longipes*, *Convolvulus elegantissimus*, Lesbos Alison* (*Alyssum lesbiacum*), *Sedum pallidum*

Flora of dunes and coastal wetlands

The coastal areas of Kambos and Vatera have a rich dune flora. The high tide line on the beach is reserved for familiar pioneer plants like Sea Rocket, Sea Stock and Prickly Saltwort. A little further from the sea, where the first dunes have formed, look for Sea Medick, Cottonweed, Dune Carrot, Yellow horned-poppy and Sea Spurge. The latter's scientific name *paralias* is in fact the Greek word for beach – handy if you want to ask for directions. In summer and autumn, this is also the site to look for the beautiful Sea Daffodil. Often, plants from *phrygana* scrub blend in with the dune plants, like Spiny Knapweed.

The saline coastal wetlands which are mostly found along the Gulf of Kalloni support only few plant species. This habitat is dominated by

FLORA

Sea Spurge, like here on the beach of Kambos (route 13), is perfectly adapted to the wind, high temperatures and drought of dune habitat. It has well-developed extensive rhizomes (root-like underground stems) to anchor itself in the sand, and to reach the deeper sand layers which are cooler and damper.

glassworts like Common Glasswort, that give the plains a distinctive purplish-brown colour. The attractive South-African Bottonweed is frequent too. Other species found here are Winged Sea-lavender, Button Glasswort, Hairy Sea-heath and the summer-flowering Sea Aster.
A special type of freshwater wetland is found along the Gulf of Gera. In May the soaking wet meadows are a hotspot for marsh orchids (see route 2 and site D), Yellow Bartsia is also found here.

> **Typical species of dunes and coastal wetlands**
> **Dunes and beaches** Sea Rocket (*Cakile maritima*), Sea Stock (*Matthiola sinuata*), Prickly Saltwort (*Salsola kali*), Sea Medick (*Medicago marina*), Cottonweed (*Otanthus maritimus*), Dune Carrot (*Pseudorlaya pumila*), Yellow Horned-poppy (*Glaucium flavum*), Sea Spurge (*Euphorbia paralias*), Sea Daffodil (*Pancratium maritimum*), Spiny Knapweed (*Centaurea spinosa*), Three-horned Stock (*Matthiola tricuspidata*), Shore Medick (*Medicago littoralis*), Sea-holly (*Erynchium maritimum*), Woolly Ironwort (*Sideritis lanata*), Sea Bindweed (*Calystegia soldanella*), Dune Galingale (*Cyperus capitatus*), Greek Tamarisk* (*Tamarix hampeana*) *Trigonella coerulescens*, *Anthemis tomentosa*, *Anthemis rigida*
> **Coastal wetlands** Common Glasswort (*Salicornia europaea*), *Salicornia fruticosa*, Annual Sea-blite (*Suaeda maritima*), Buttonweed (*Cotula coronopifolia*), Winged Sea-lavender (*Limonium sinuatum*), Narbonne Sea-lavender* (*Limonium narbonense*) Loose-flowered Orchid (*Anacamptis laxiflora*), Marsh Orchid (*Anacamptis palustris*), Elegant Marsh Orchid (*Anacamptis elegans*), Yellow Bartsia (*Parentucellia viscosa*)

FLORA

> **Splitters and lumpers**
>
> Due to many ongoing changes in taxonomy, it is impossible to provide a definitive number of orchid species on Lesbos. Orchids exhibit hopeless morphological variations through hybridization, which, having been studied thoroughly for a long time, have given rise to many 'invented' species, subspecies and variations. New genetic analytical techniques don't really make things any clearer, but just reflect a different kind of variation. This goes especially for the charismatic group of the bee orchids (*Ophrys*), making the taxonomy of this group a minefield with complicated complexes of species. Like drawing some overlapping coloured circles with many shades of colours in between, it is not always possible to find a 'true' species. Defining the colours within the circles seems to be a matter of taste. There are two ways to deal with such slippery slopes. The first is to split all different groups of individuals into seperate species. The splitter is a precise observer eager to define species by even the smallest aberration in colour or shape. This may result in an endless list of species, with which it is difficult to work. The other position is that of the lumper, who accepts variation within orchid species shoehorning them into manageable groups. But sometimes, by squeezing many former species into fewer groups, they overlook the variation as a result of evolution and geographical patterns.

Orchid paradise

Lesbos is a superb destination for orchid lovers. Depending on the literature you use, there are from 40 to over a 100 species on the island. The huge difference in number does not reflect inadequate exploration, but different opinions regarding where to draw the line between varieties and species (see textbox below).

Although Lesbos attracts its share of true orchid fanatics who like to solve complex taxonomic puzzles, this shouldn't deter more casual wildflower lovers from enjoying the sheer abundance of orchids.

It is not just the overwhelming number of species that attracts, but also the fact that many orchids occur in such profusion that you could almost consider them, in some areas at least, as weeds. The first thing you should know if you want to look for orchids, is that they are very unevenly distributed over the island. Some areas abound in them (both in numbers and species) while in other places they are thinly spread. Incidentally, the best areas for birdwatching are those that are rather poor in orchids, so if your trip is solely focused on birds, chances are you will miss the spectacular display of orchids.

The calcareous east and the small pockets of marl in the west harbour the most orchid species (see map on page 201). On the rest of the island,

FLORA

consisting mainly of volcanic rock or serpentine rock – you have to search harder, although there are special species here too. To help you to get to grips with the most complicated group, the bee orchids (*Ophrys*), we've included a guide to the main groups of bee orchids on Lesbos. It is a starting point, a practical guideline to point you in the right direction. Be aware that, depending on the weather conditions, the flowering time of orchids can shift up to a few weeks.

Main groups of *Ophrys*

Group 1: Flowers have a 'boxing glove' shape and bluish parts on the lip
Ophrys iricolor – Bright blue colour, lip purplish-red underneath (mid March – early May)
Ophrys fusca – See photo. Downcurved lip, dull blue. Variable species with many forms described (mid January – late April)
Ophrys blithopertha – Flat lip, conspicuous yellow margin. Robust and short plant. (mid March – late April)
Ophrys cinereophila – Small, spirally arranged flowers with strongly downcurved lip. Very rare (February – mid April)

Group 2: Slender, erect plant (up to 1 m) with small and narrow flowers carrying 'horns'
Ophrys cornuta – Long horns (mid March – mid April).
Ophrys minutula – See photo. Shorter horns and reflexed sepals. (April – early May). Special for Lesbos
Some specialists refer to the whole group as *Ophrys scolopax*

Group 3: Robust plant with greenish sepals, from which the upper sepal forms a roof.
Ophrys umbilicata – See photo. Less compact than the next species. Sepals white to pink (mid March – late April)
Ophrys bucephala – Bigger flowers in a denser spike. Sepals green to white, rarely pink (March – late April). Special for Lesbos

Group 4: Erect plant with big, dark lip with colourful shiny spot
Ophrys lesbis – Photo on page 59. Lip velvety red. Sepals pink (mid March – mid April)
Ophrys ferrum-equinum – See photo. Black lip, with spot often shaped like a horseshoe. Sepals pink (mid March – late April)
Ophrys mammosa – Black lip with pronounced protrusions Sepals green to brownish (mid March – late April)

MAMMALS

Mammals

> There are no routes particularly suitable for finding small mammals, although on some passing through scrubland or woodland (routes 2, 4, 10, 16, 17 and sites R and V) you have a higher chance. On route 2 you may spot Otter. Most promising for spotting sea mammals are routes 5, 12, 13 and site J.

Although Lesbos is the only place in Europe where it occurs, Persian Squirrel is one of the most easily spotted mammals on the island.

As lesbos is a small island, its mammal fauna is not particularly rich, but nevertheless holds a number of species of interest. The most eye-catching is undoubtedly the charming Persian Squirrel: easy to spot and found in almost any terrestrial habitat. Its most active during early morning and late afternoon. This animals are a real joy to watch as they are playing and jumping around in the shrubs and olive trees. It has a rusty-red belly with a beautiful silver-grey back. With a natural distribution from Lesbos and Turkey to Iran, its occurrence here is unique in Europe. In contrast to areas on the mainland, the population density on Lesbos is quite high – a typical 'island effect' caused by the scarcity of natural enemies.

The local hedgehog is the Northern White-breasted Hedgehog. It is mostly found in gardens, fields and scrubland. Other small inconspicuous rodents and insectivores are Günther's Vole, Lesser White-toothed Shrew, Bicolored Shrew and the odd Lesser Mole Rat. The latter looks like it just crawled off the set of an Alien movie: a shapeless, hairy body with four pronounced teeth sticking out. It lives underground in unploughed fields, pastures and olive groves where it is only occasionally spotted crawling around its burrow. Like many other mammals, Hares and Rabbits came on Lesbos via an ancient land bridge and are a staple food for the raptors of Lesbos.

The introduced Wild Boar and Fallow Deer are the only large herbivores on Lesbos (besides some unrestrained goats and horses in semi-natural conditions). Both occupy mainly the wooded areas in the eastern and

MAMMALS

northern part of the island. An encounter is rare, but their presence is generally indicated only through signs of digging, footprints and rubbing on trees. Wild Boar occurs in increasing numbers on the island. It is hunted all over the island, not just for sport but also to control damage to agriculture. If you are in Lesbos in autumn (the hunting season) and up for it, try some of the excellent local Wild Boar dishes which are served in good tavernas (e.g. route 3).

The most common carnivore is the Beech Marten. Sadly, it is mostly found dead on the tarmac. Red Fox is the largest predator and frequently seen in scrubland and olive groves. The Otter is much harder to spot, but occurs in the rivers in the Gulf of Gera. Presumably, it swims across the channel from populations on the Turkish coast.

With a coastline of approximately 320 km, it is no surprise sea-dwelling mammals are a big draw for naturalists. The Aegean Sea holds the largest populations in the world of the very rare and critically endangered Mediterranean Monk Seal, once distributed through the whole basin, but now confined to the Aegean Sea in the east and the Atlantic waters of Madeira in the west. Century-long commercial hunting for skin and fat, together with a gradual habitat destruction led to an almost complete eradication of the species. Beach tourism also took a heavy toll on the seals, driving them away from the beaches where they gave birth to the young. Over time, they changed their behaviour and now seek refuge in inaccessible caves along remote coasts. In the waters of Lesbos there still is a small population, but catching a glimpse of these animals requires a lot of luck.

Few people are unmoved by the sight of graceful dolphins. Watching them playfully leaping out of the sea is an unforgettable experience. Although not easily spotted, Bottlenose, Striped and Common Dolphins all occur in the seas around Lesbos. The latter species is most often seen, especially around headlands and remoter parts of the coastline.

The subterranean Lesser Mole Rat is completely blind, its tiny eyes are covered with a layer of skin. The solitary animal lives in a burrow containing a wide network of tunnels and chambers. To communicate with neighbouring mole rats, the animal will thump its head rhythmically against the top of tunnels to send subtle signals over long distances.

FLORA AND FAUNA

Birds

> Birds of cliffs are best encountered on routes 2, 10, 13, 16, 17 and site J. For birds of woodland and forests, head for routes 2, 4, 6 and 10. Scrubland birds are particularly abundant on routes 8, 10, 11, 12, and sites Q and R. The better routes for species of dry rocky habitat are 9, 16, 17, and sites U and V. Routes 5, 6, 7, 15 and sites O, P and V are most rewarding for birds of coastal areas and fields.

Lesbos is among the premier birdwatching destinations of Europe, competing in popularity with such birding hotspots as Extremadura and Andalusia. There are two main attractions that make the island such an exciting place to look for birds. First is the presence of a large number of attractive Mediterranean species. Widespread beauties like Bee-eater, Roller, Short-toed Eagle and Subalpine Warbler are complemented with a good number of rare and localised birds of the eastern Mediterranean, such as Rock and Krüper's Nuthatches, Masked Shrike and Cretzschmar's and Cinereous Buntings. Many of them are nowhere easier to see than on Lesbos.

The second avian perk is Lesbos's position on a major migration route (see box on page 88). From mid-April to mid-May, there is a bonanza of hundreds of thousands of migrating birds that pass over the island on their way to the breeding sites in eastern and northern Europe. They return in September, strengthened in numbers after the breeding season.

The peak in activity and visibility of most of the breeding birds coincides with the mass spring migration. It is hence this blessed period – mid-April to mid-May – that Lesbos is truly magical. Songbirds are almost dripping from the branches and a steady stream of raptors pass along the island's valleys. A week of dedicated birding in this prime time may easily produce a list of 160 species.

Confusing diversity

Usually the habitat is a good way to predict the potential birdlife present in a specific spot. However on Lesbos, transitions between habitats are often gradual – birds of woodlands seamlessly merge into assemblies of scrubland birds and those belonging to steppes and *phrygana* scrubland. To complicate this image even further, the waves of migrating birds often appear in areas you would never expect them – woodland birds like flycatchers suddenly occupy low shrubs and steppe birds like Red-footed Falcons appear in coastal marshes. Warblers of all sorts may drop down to rest in the hedgerows. We've seen Subalpine, Wood,

BIRDS

> **Bird names**
> Until recently, eastern and western populations of a number of similar birds were regarded as 'subspecies', but are increasingly seen as 'full' species. In practical terms, as ranges largely don't overlap, it is usually clear which sibling species is meant. So, to avoid cumbersome names (e.g. Eastern Olivaceous Warbler), they are referred to in the main body of the text by their familiar, and simpler, names.

Olivaceous, Reed and Cetti's Warblers and Common Whitethroat in a single hedgerow, half of which would never in their right mind choose such a site as breeding habitat. This all makes Lesbos both a terribly exciting as well a bit of a confusing place to go birding.
To get a bit of grip on the birdlife of Lesbos, in this section we've done something you would not be able to do so easily when you're in the field – we separated the breeding birds from the migrants and discussed them in different chapters.

Breeding birds – the eastern delights

There is a good diversity of breeding birds on Lesbos, dominated by species of the Mediterranean realm. Several eastern Mediterranean species occur on the island which are the highlights for visiting birders, like Black-headed Bunting, Isabelline Wheatear, Rock Nuthatch and Long-legged Buzzard. Since the Mediterranean migrant birds are forced to choose between either the eastern or western migration routes, west and east Mediterranean bird populations became separated and evolved into a western and eastern (sub)species, which differ usually subtly in plumage (see box on page 88). For example the Orphean, Subalpine, Olivaceous and Bonelli's Warblers and Rufous Bush Robins of Lesbos all belong to the eastern forms. There is also a set of remarkable birds with an oriental distribution, reaching their western limit here, like Krüper's Nuthatch, Cinereous Bunting, Masked Shrike, Rüppell's Warbler, Cretzschmar's Bunting and Chukar. The latter two occur on Peloponnesos too.

Spur-winged Lapwing is one of the star species found in coastal wetlands.

BIRDS

10 top breeding birds of Lesbos

Cinereous Bunting Route 16, 17, site U
Breeding range: East Aegean to southeast Turkey.
Attractive because: rare, endangered and nowhere easier to find than here.

Krüper's Nuthatch Route 2, 4, 6
Breeding range: Lesbos and Turkey to the Caucasus.
Attractive because: attractive bird with very small range.

Masked Shrike Route 2, 5, 6, 8, 9, 10, 11, 13, 15, 16, sites C, O, Q, R
Breeding range: southeast Bulgaria to Iran.
Attractive because: beautiful bird with a small distribution range.

Rüppell's Warbler Route 10
Breeding range: Peleponnesos to south Turkey.
Attractive because: beautiful bird with small distribution range.

Olive-tree Warbler Route 5, 8, 14, site O, Q, R
Breeding range: coast from Croatia to Turkey.
Attractive because: fairly small distribution range and generally rare.

Eleonora's Falcon Route 6, 10, 11, 15, 16, site O, V
Breeding range: Mediterranean and Canary Islands.
Attractive because: graceful falcon, rare and declining with an odd specialisation of hunting migratory birds.

Cretzschmar's Bunting Route 9, 10, 11, 12, 14, 16, 17, site R, T, U, V
Breeding range: coast from Corfu to Israel.
Attractive because: fairly small distribution range.

Western Rock Nuthatch Route 6, 8, 10, 11, 13, 16, 17
Breeding range: Croatia to Iran.
Attractive because: unusual to see a nuthatch in rocky habitat.

Sombre Tit Route 5, 8, 10, 14, 16, 17, site Q
Breeding range: southeast Europe to Iran.
Attractive because: one of the few European tits with a fairly small distribution range.

Rufous Bush Robin Route 7 9, 15, 16, site V
Breeding range: Morocco to Iran.
Attractive because: beautiful bird of semi-desert areas, rare in Europe.

Three sought-after breeding birds on Lesbos: Cinereous Bunting (top), Krüper's Nuthatch (middle) and Olive-tree Warbler (bottom).

Birds of cliffs and rock outcrops

The community of rock-dwelling birds forms one of the most distinct, well-defined groups on Lesbos. Many rock-dwelling species are only found on cliffs and amongst rocks, while a few widespread birds also find ideal nesting sites in a rocky environment. Any one of the larger cliffs will typically house Blue Rock Thrush, Rock Nuthatch and Crag Martin, often joined by the more widely occurring Black-eared Wheatear and Chukar. For Crag Martin and Alpine Swift, the cliffs – or more precisely the crags between them – are only a place to nest. Their real habitat is of course the air, where they catch insects on the wing. The agile Alpine Swift is considerably larger than its close relative the Common Swift. Rocky overhangs and bridges close to water surfaces are the nesting sites for Red-rumped Swallow.

The Rock Nuthatch is the most sought-after bird of this habitat. This large, pale nuthatch runs along cliffs agilely. It has the perfect camouflage jacket, but it is nevertheless quite easy to find because of the excited movements and loud calls (reminding very much of Common Nuthatch, which is rare on Lesbos). Rock Nuthatches are resident birds on Lesbos and don't migrate in winter. They are widespread but never common.

More level, rocky terrain attracts different birds, a lot of which are also found in *phrygana* scrubland. Such terrain makes for very exciting birdwatching with 'goodies' like Cinereous and Cretzschmar's Buntings, Rock Sparrow, and Chukar. We describe these birds in more detail on page 84.

Blue Rock Thrush is a common bird on cliffs.

BIRDS

Birds of forests

Roughly three kinds of forests are found on Lesbos: deciduous oak and chestnut woodland, stands of Turkish Pine and riverine forest.

The cool and shady chestnut forests around Agiasos have a temperate feel and harbour a familiar birdlife for the visitor from northern Europe. This is the breeding realm for Robin (uncommon on Lesbos), Hawfinch and Song Thrush. Bonelli's Warbler breeds here too, but can also occasionaly be found in oak forest elsewere.

The deciduous woodlands are also the place to look for Lesbos's only resident woodpecker, the Middle-spotted Woodpecker. It is quite common in open, old woodlands with oak and chestnut, but also in old olive groves.

Wherever woodlands are more open and mixed with tall shrubs, Mediterranean songbirds appear. Subalpine Warbler is perhaps the most common one and also appears frequently in woodlands.

The pine forests have quite a poor birdlife. There is only one bird specifically adapted to living here, but that one makes this habitat more than worth exploring: the Krüper's Nuthatch. This small, smart-looking nuthatch with its brick-red breast is a species with a very limited distribution, being mainly restricted to the Turkish coast, and just extending into Georgia and with an isolated outlier in Russia (thus largely coinciding with the range of the Turkish Pine). Lesbos is the only Greek island where it occurs. The nuthatch shares its domain with a number of much more widespread birds like Short-toed Treecreeper, Mistle Thrush, Coal Tit and Spotted Flycatcher. The more open, park-like stands of pine, attract Masked Shrike, although the forest clearly is a secondary habitat for the species. Patches with large pine trees may act as migrant traps, where anything may turn up.

Finally, in riverine forests Golden Oriole, Nightingale and Cetti's Warbler are the typical birds along with the more common woodland species. The planes and poplars of the riverine forest are also favoured by migrants. Especially where surrounded by dry *phrygana* scrubland, the forest forms a safe haven in an otherwise barren landscape.

Maquis and open woodlands

Maquis scrubland is the haunt of the *Sylvia* warblers: small songbirds well adapted to living in dense shrubs. Sardinian Warbler is mainly found in coastal scrubland, but rarely further inland. This bird is unexpectedly picky on Lesbos (in the western Mediterranean, Sardinian Warbler is widespread and the most indiscriminate of all the *Sylvia* Warblers). On Lesbos, it is the Subalpine Warbler that is found throughout, while the

BIRDS

beautiful Rüppell's Warbler is confined to one known breeding area in the north (see route 10). The striking males can be separated from the similar looking Sardinian Warbler by the black head and throat, separated by a moustache-like white streak. Orphean Warbler prefers open woodland with shrubby underbrush, where it lives in the canopies of tall trees. During migration, these four *Sylvia* warblers are joined by three others: the familiar Common and Lesser Whitethroats, and the stout Barred Warbler of Eastern Europe.

Rüppell's Warbler (top) and Sardinian Warbler (bottom) are breeding birds of maquis scrubland in coastal areas. The first is very rare, the area south of Molyvos being the best place to look for it (route 10) and the second is more widespread, but scarce.

The maquis and open oak woodlands support many more small songbirds. The drab, greyish-brown Olivaceous Warbler is very common. Its frantic song greets you from almost any bush or olive tree. Much less common is its large cousin, the Olive-tree Warbler, which is mostly found in open woodland mixed with olive trees. Maquis and open woods are also the key habitat of the Sombre Tit, another sought-after south-east European bird.

Most raptors breed in trees and rocky spots in woodlands. In contrast to the mainland, they are rather sparse on Lesbos. The limiting factor is not so much the lack of suitable habitat, but rather the availability of suitable prey puts the numbers down. But still there are plenty of species to search for, including Peregrine, Lesser Kestrel, Short-toed Eagle and Long-legged Buzzard.

FLORA AND FAUNA

BIRDS

The area of Agra (site U) supports a wide variety of habitats: plane forest, oak woodland, stony fields and phrygana. This is an important factor explaining the higher bird diversity here.

Middle-spotted Woodpecker is common in oak woodland and olive groves throughout the island. Oddly, Syrian Woodpecker is absent despite being common in nearby Turkey.

Birds of *phrygana* and stony fields

Perhaps the habitat which harbours the most elusive birds is *phrygana*, a dry rocky form of scrubland with sparse vegetation found in western and central part of the island. It is the domain of Cretzschmar's and Cinereous Buntings, the most heat-and-drought loving buntings. Lesbos harbours the largest population in Europe of the very rare Cinereous Bunting. The best place to find it is the Ipsilou monastery where it is often found singing from the top of a tree or high boulder (route 17). A more widespread *phrygana* specialist is the elegant Black-eared Wheatear, often seen from the car on your way in the west, on the watch for prey from a perch (usually a rock or stone wall). Rock Sparrow prefers rocky slopes and gorges with *phrygana* vegetation. Rocky fields with old stone buildings support Little Owl.

Generally speaking, the birds of *phrygana* prefer habitat with some variation, like grassy and stony fields, alternating with thorny bushes. Where grassy patches dominate look out for Isabelline Wheatear, which is essentially a steppe bird. Finally, Rufous Bush Robin is mainly a bird of drier areas in the southern part of the Mediterranean and Middle East. On Lesbos, it generally favours shrubby areas near the coast, along shallow valleys with solitary trees and dry, sparsely vegetated olive groves. The bird is often spotted between the low shrubs or on a low perch, where it raises and spreads its distinctive rusty coloured and white-tipped tail.

Birds of olive groves and fields

The cultivated areas on Lesbos are usually small in scale and managed in a traditional manner. They provide both food and breeding habitat for birds. Olive groves are abundant and in contrast to many other Mediterranean areas, managed extensively, leaving plenty of room for herbs and shrubs. They form a key habitat for Middle-spotted Woodpecker and Sombre Tit. Where olive groves merge with patches of oak woodland, highly prized birds like Masked Shrike and Olive-tree Warbler can be found.

Small fields and arable land with weedy edges form a mosaic within the landscape and provide a great diversity of birds. Olivaceous Warbler is found in shrubby areas near olive groves, occurring together with Lesser Grey and Woodchat Shrikes. The latter two frequently perch on electricity wires. Fields surrounded by old fences with wooden poles provide posts for hunting Lesser Kestrel and migratory Red-footed Falcons. Hedgerow-lined fields and arable land hold Black-headed Bunting, Roller and flocks of Bee-eaters. Small coastal plains with irrigated farmland, providing excellent feeding sites for hungry migrants (routes 7, 15, and sites O, V) has some splendid fields that are alive with birds during migration).

Man-made constructions like troughs and water tanks for livestock are a vital sources of water during the hot summer months. These are interesting places to check throughout the year for birds that come down here to drink (especially in the early morning or the evening).

Saline wetlands and salt pans are of great importance for birds like Greater Flamingo (route 6, 7 and site O). Its flashy bright pink plumage can be spotted from afar.

Birds of wetlands

Coastal wetlands and inland lakes provide excellent habitats for birds on Lesbos. Due to the temporary desiccation of wetlands in summer, there is only an abundance of food in spring when water levels are high. Saline wetlands attract thousands of migrant birds that profit from the favourable feeding conditions. A typical migration bird of saltpans is the Greater Flamingo, of which fairly large numbers are found in spring and autumn. They originate from the nearby breeding colony in the Gediz Delta in Turkey and come to Lesbos to feed.

BIRDS

Although the wetlands of Lesbos primarily attract passing migrants, there are a number of breeding birds too. In the saltmarshes, Little and Common Terns, Stone Curlew, Black-winged Stilt, Avocet and Kentish Plovers breed. The saltpans of Kalloni and Polichnitos consist of many small lakes with varying water levels that provide the perfect breeding habitat.

The beautiful rusty brown Ruddy Shelduck is also found in saline wetlands and breeds in the area of the clay pits near Palios and river mouths like Tsichliondas (see routes 9 and 16). The dry grasslands and fields bordering the saltmarsh have a steppe-like appearance. This is the place to look for Black-headed Wagtail, Greater Short-toed and Crested Larks, Black-headed Bunting and Lesser Grey and Woodchat Shrikes. With luck you may also find a Stone Curlew, or harriers during migration.

Inland freshwater wetlands, such as Metochi Lake, have a dense vegetation where Little Grebe and Cetti's, Sedge, Reed and Great Reed Warblers breed. Again, these habitats are a magnet for migrants in spring, including the likes of Little Crake, Little Bittern and Night Heron.

Sea birds

The seas surrounding Lesbos are shallow and harbour a lot of fish. They are the haunt of Cory's and Yelkouan Shearwaters which can be seen from coastal headlands. Both have a typical flight, flipping along the bird's axis, alternatively pointing the one and then the other wing downwards, as being pulled by ropes like a stunt kite. Yelkouan is the smaller

Shags are sometimes spotted perching on a jetty.

and more elegant of the two. Cory's has a much bigger head, giving it a stocky shape that can often be made out from a distance. Shag is rather frequent as well. Look for it ooff shore on rocks and islets.

In general, these rocky islets provide important nesting sites as they are largely free of human disturbance and predators. The most common breeding bird is the Yellow-legged Gull, but the much rarer and more sought-after Audouin's Gull also breeds on islets off the northern coast (route 9). Eleonora's Falcon breeds exclusively on cliffs on islets. It nests very late in season (July-August), taking advantage of autumn migration when young songbirds, on their first journey south, are an easy prey for the falcons, with which they feed their chicks.

Birds on migration

The main eastern migration flyway follows the Turkish coast and passes right over Lesbos (see box on next page). Being a green island with a fair number of wetlands, it is a preferred stopover on the way north (and in autumn back south).

The migrating birds that pass Lesbos are those that breed in eastern and northern Europe. They include arctic birds (e.g. Red-throated Pipit, Temminck's Stint and Wood and Curlew Sandpipers), birds of temperate Europe (like Black Stork and Red-backed Shrike), steppe birds (like Rosy Starling and Long-legged Buzzard), and Mediterranean birds like Bee-eater and Black-headed Bunting. The latter groups involve birds that also breed on Lesbos. They arrive in large waves on the island, the majority of them continuing further north, while only a smaller number remains to breed, making these birds much more common on Lesbos than in most other parts of the Mediterranean – during the migration at least.

On passage, birds use the habitat rather differently than they do when on their breeding grounds. Since field guides describe only the breeding habitat, it pays to imagine yourself in the position of a bird on migration, arriving, after an undoubtedly exhausting trip over the sea, on the island. In spring, there is a constant trading off between the need to find food and shelter, and the urge to get to the breeding site early in order to occupy the best territories. Small songbirds just arriving on the island drop down onto headlands with bushes or small trees, where they find some shelter. In good weather conditions, the birds work their way along north-south orientated valleys and coasts, searching for food. With a head turned by hormones, many male birds are already singing and courting. Some species even mate before moving further north – all to the confusion of the birdwatcher who sees

BIRDS

birds establishing territories that aren't on the list of breeding birds. Migratory birds have a tendency to congregate in patches of trees and vegetated valleys (so called migrant traps), until the wind and weather conditions are favourable for them to continue their journey. During spring migration, these habitats constantly fill up with birds and empty when conditions are right, like a heart pumping to the rhythm of wind and weather.

The situation for migrating wetland birds is no different, although they are more strongly tied to specific sites like coastal marshes and lakes.

Migration routes

Migration is, of course, a good way to escape the winter cold and scarcity of food, but it remains a risky enterprise. As they head south they have to negotiate the Mediterranean Sea before having to cross the vast Sahara desert with its unavoidable shortage of both food and water.

Because of the Sahara, European birds face more intense hardships than their East Asian or American counterparts. For most birds, the Sahara represents an almost unsurmountable barrier – much more difficult to defeat than either the Mediterranean Sea or the mountains of central Europe. The Nile valley and the coastal strips on the Atlantic and the Red Sea with a short hop across the Strait of Gibraltar or Bosphorus are the only migration routes that substantially reduce the risks. Hence, most of the European migrating birds follow one of two main migration flyways: a western one (over Gibraltar) or an eastern one following the Turkish and Israeli coasts then crossing the Red Sea at Eilat or heading along the Nile valley (other routes across to Italy or along the eastern shores of the Black Sea are less important). The East Mediterranean route runs right over Lesbos. The island certainly isn't the only hotspot along this route, but it is an attractive stopover for birds because it is green with some marshland providing plenty of food for refuelling. Furthermore, it is an easy and comfortable place to visit for birdwatchers.

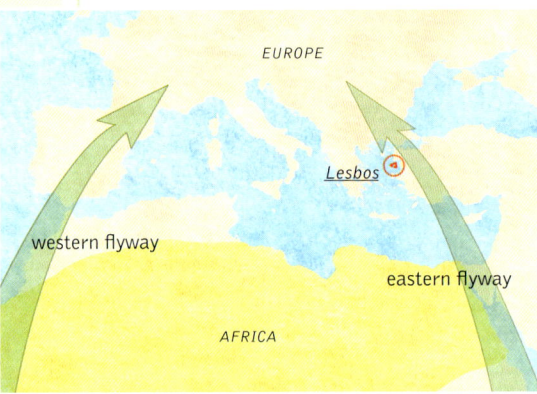

Simplified overview of the two main migration routes of birds in Europe and North Africa.

BIRDS

These birds tend to stay a little longer to take advantage of the abundance of food. Raptors and other broad-winged birds like storks do the same, but for them, the rising air – the result of the sun heating rock faces – is important, which is why in the morning, they often follow south-facing valley slopes where the air warms up first.

What really counts for migrant birds is not so much finding their optimum habitat, but a convenient place to make landfall and quickly refuel. The central and western part of Lesbos is on the main migration route so it attracts many more birds than the east.

6 top migrating birds

Little Crake Route 5, 8
Breeding range: central Europe.
Attractive because: not nearly as difficult to see here as in breeding range.

Pallid Harrier Route 7, 15, site P
Breeding range: far eastern Europe and west Asia.
Attractive because: rare elsewhere in Europe.

Levant Sparrowhawk Route 1, 5, 11, 15, 17, site Q
Breeding range: south-east Europe.
Attractive because: small range in Europe where it can be seen.

Barred Warbler Route 10
Breeding range: Eastern Europe.
Attractive because: common on Lesbos but not often seen in western Europe – hard to see except for short period in spring.

Broad-billed Sandpiper Route 7, site O
Breeding range: Scandinavia and north-west Russia.
Attractive because: very hard to see in breeding area and rare on western migration route.

Red-footed Falcon Route 6, 7, 15, 16, site O
Breeding range: Steppes from Hungary to Ukraine.
Attractive because: there are few areas in Europe where this species is easily seen.

Top notch migrating birds on Lesbos: Little Crake (top) and Red-footed Falcon (bottom).

FLORA AND FAUNA

Reptiles and amphibians

> Reptiles can be found along all routes. Routes 4, 6, 10, 12, 14, 16, 17 and site S support the greatest variation of species. Any route which includes lakes, rivers and streams will support amphibians, especially route 8, 9, 16.

Anyone who takes the time to observe the Three-lined Lizard, of which there are so many on Lesbos, cannot fail to be impressed. The slender body, the long and agile tail and the bright green scales on the back contrast wonderfully with the intense yellow throat. It is no wonder that the lyrics "I can't get your body out of my mind…" of the famous 90s rockband Presidents Of The United States Of America were not written for a beautiful girl, but were an ode to the reptiles. It could have been written on Lesbos, as with 22 species of reptiles, including several highly attractive and visible ones, this island is a heaven for reptile lovers. With a little experience and some dedication, many species are found with relative ease.

The variety of habitats and the proximity of Asia Minor accounts for a very interesting blend of species, although – unlike on some other Greek islands – there are no endemics.

Balkan Terrapin, easy recognisable by its striped neck, is common in all kinds of freshwater wetlands.

Tortoises and terrapins

The charming tortoises are a delight to watch. On Lesbos they are quite common. The rustling of leaf litter in the woods is the usual sign these friendly ramblers are around. Spur-thighed Tortoise is the only species that occurs naturally on the island. It is found in olive groves, scrubland, open woodland and forests. They are peaceful creatures, except during the mating season (spring), when the males become aggressive towards rivals (never to humans). We once found a dominant male violently banging the carapace of a rival in an attempt to turn the intruder upside down.

The presence of the Marginated Tortoise is supported by only few records. If it is present, it is most likely introduced from mainland Greece.

This species is distinguished from the Spur-thighed by the colouration and the bell shaped end of the carapace.

Terrapins (small freshwater turtles) are also common. There are two species on Lesbos. The first is the Balkan Terrapin, which needs but a small puddle to feel at home. Most lakes, ponds, ditches and coastal marshes have their population of this terrapin with its characteristic, yellow striped neck. The animals are easily observed when basking, yet difficult to approach since they disappear in the water at the slightest disturbance. In some places, though, they are fed by tourists and cautiously paddle towards you if you approach carefully (e.g. route 6). The second species of terrapin on Lesbos is the European Pond Terrapin, distinguishable by the spotted, rather than striped neck pattern. It often coexists with the Balkan Terrapin, but is much less common, most probably due to its limited resistance against summer drought.

Snakes

For the naturalist who has an appetite for finding snakes, Lesbos is without doubt an excellent destination. Of the 24 species of snake found in Greece, no less than 12 are found on the island. Most common are probably the Caspian Whip and Montpellier Snakes, which are both active during the day. Both are impressive snakes reaching up to 2 metres in length and, when approached, are intimidatingly aggressive, even though neither of them have a dangerous venom. Both occur in a wide array of habitats. Montpellier Snake is distinguished by the V-shaped, eyebrow-like ridges above its large eyes, while the adults of Caspian Whip Snake have typical yellowish scales with a dark lining, resembling the pattern of fishnet stockings. Sadly, these beautiful creatures are often found as roadkill, reflecting their unhealthy habit of wandering onto roads.

Two other snakes that are easy to see and both live in the water are Dice Snake and Grass Snake. With some practice, it is not difficult to spot them in rivers, lakes and coastal marshes. The best way to find them is to look down from a bridge or river bank and check the shallow parts on the edges of the water.

The other snakes are more secretive and it will take more luck or effort to spot them. The remarkable Sand Boa, the only European relative of the boas, is often found in olive groves. Just like its exotic family members, it uses constriction to kill its prey, which consists of small rodents and lizards. Sand Boas are active during the early morning and late evening and only then will it show itself above ground. Otherwise it hides in rodent burrows and under rocks.

REPTILES AND AMPHIBIANS

Another snake with a subterranean lifestyle is the odd Worm Snake: a pink, up to 30 cm long, primitive snake, strongly resembling an oversized earth worm. It prefers rocky habitats with soft soils, in which it is protected from predators. We were lucky to find it above the ground after rainfall in a riverbed, but otherwise your best chance is near ant nests – its main prey.

A special species on Lesbos is the Dwarf Snake, a small, usually unmarked grey to light brown snake with black blotches on its head. In Europe it is only found in some east Aegean islands, where it is quite common. This species seems not to be picky about its habitat and can be found in maquis, woodland and olive groves where it mainly feeds on small invertebrates found under rocks.

The slender, agile and beautiful Dahl's Whip Snake (unmarked brown body with typical black spots in the neck) is found in a wide range of habitats as well, but is has a preference for stony oak woodlands and old stone walls. You might catch a glimpse of it in the hot hours of the day, speeding away typically with its head and neck raised. Cat Snake (so named because of the vertical, cat-like pupils) is mostly found in dry landscapes with sparse vegetation, generally in the central and western part of Lesbos. Due to its strictly nocturnal lifestyle it is more common than the infrequent observations indicate.

Arguably the most beautiful snake of Europe is the Leopard Snake, which looks like as if an artist carefully painted its body with black-bordered, red

Sand Boa is fairly common in olive groves and sandy areas on Lesbos, but difficult to find. It hunts by lying in ambush beneath the surface, catching passing prey.

spots, on Lesbos often merged to form two parallel lines. This harmless snake is found in open woodland, olive groves, gardens and cultivated fields, and frequently shows up in old sheds and even in houses. No surprise the Greek name is *spitofido*, meaning house snake. This name is not, as you may think, meant in a negative way as a snake that unwantedly enters houses. On the contrary, it is a much appreciated guest because it keeps the mice in check. In spite of its habitat choice, it is uncommon, secretive and not often seen. Your best chance on finding one is in the limestone region in the southeastern part of Lesbos, where it is somewhat more common. Recently, the Coin Snake has been discovered in the central part of the island.

The Ottoman Viper is the only viper on Lesbos. It is an eastern species, which reaches its western limit on the east Aegean islands. It is the only snake on Lesbos with a venomous bite – although Cat Snake and Montpellier Snake also produce a mild venom in their rear fangs, it is only injected when devouring prey, not in attack or defence.

The Ottoman Viper is considered to produce the most potent venom of any snake in Europe. Fortunately, the risk of getting bitten is small – the Ottoman Viper is a shy snake and will avoid any contact with humans when possible. The viper is readily distinguished from the other snakes on Lesbos by a broad head, plump body and dark brown zigzag pattern on the back.

Lizards

Without doubt, the main attraction among the lizards is the heat-loving Starred Agama, which can be seen soaking up the sunbeams on stone walls and rocky places all over the island. Like the Ottoman Viper, the Starred Agama is an Asian element in the fauna of Lesbos. In fact, it is the only species of agama lizards (which have a typical dragon-like look) in Europe. All other species occur either in Asia or Africa. In contrast to the Agama's fierce appearance and size, it is actually quite a shy animal, never wandering far from its network of holes. When disturbed it disappears rapidly into a crevice and if caught, it expands its body to prevent being dragged out of its hideout. Although sightings of Starred Agama on stone walls and rocks are nearly guaranteed to anyone who spends some time on Lesbos, it is difficult to photograph them. As soon as you stop and pick up your camera they dash off.

There are only a handful of other lizard species on Lesbos. The Three-lined Lizard – the largest and most brightly coloured lizard on the island – is very common. Any walk in well vegetated terrain will reveal at least a

REPTILES AND AMPHIBIANS

The Starred Agama covered in rough scales and plates resembles a small dragon.
Although less distinct than with chameleons, it is capable of changing colour by becoming lighter when the temperature rises.

Snake-eyed lizard has an eastern distribution, in Europe only found on the Eastern Aegean islands and in Thrace.

few of these stout (up to 40 cm), bright green lizards. The only other 'conventional' lizard is the tiny Snake-eyed Lizard. The small size is enough to tell it apart, although the main feature of this species is the staring, lidless eye which gave it its name. It will cross your path frequently in places where volcanic bedrock dominates, which means mostly in the western and central part of the island. If you find one, observe it closely and you'll see they often display a curious hand waving gesture! It is believed to be a form of communication, perhaps to avoid a challenge with a potential rival.

The small, bronze Snake-eyed Skink lacks eyelids as well. You may spot it crawling in leaf litter and on dry stone walls. The legless European Glass Lizard is a stout Mediterranean relative of the Slow Worm, which grows up to a metre or more! The eyelids and deep lateral groove which runs down each side of its body distinguishes it from the snakes. It is generally first heard then seen, as it noisily makes its way through the leaf litter.

Last but not least, there are the geckos – charming lizards of tropical origin, of which two species occur on the island. The nocturnal Turkish or Mediterranean House Gecko is common and can often be spotted on walls of buildings, or even inside houses. The darker coloured Kotschy's Gecko lacks the 'sticky' toe pads, being a lesser climber than its relative. It is usually found on rocks and stone walls, from which it emerges to pursue insects.

Amphibians

Only 5 species of amphibians are known to occur on Lesbos (out of a total of 23 in Greece). This low number is probably due to the fact that sea water is a barrier to amphibians. In addition, sparseness of suitable habitat limits the number of amphibians. Nevertheless, Lesbos holds some interesting species you don't easily encounter elsewhere in Europe.

Spring is the period when amphibians are easily found; the rest of the year they generally live a secretive life. Like in many other areas with limited surface water availability, amphibians have a short period in which to complete their reproduction circle. The most common species is Green Toad, which can be found at night all over the island, including in villages. Expect to find it wandering around the garden of your hotel too. Like on many other Mediterranean islands, the Common Toad is surprisingly rare, but it does occur. Like its Green cousin, it frequents fairly dry habitats, except in early spring when toads migrate to small pools or streams to mate and lay their eggs.

The secretive Eastern Spadefoot, with its characteristic vertical pupils, is most often seen during breeding season in spring.

In spring and early summer the prominent croaking of Tree Frogs is the typical sound of a warm Lesbos night. It accompanies you even when sipping your drink at a seaside taverna. In one case we even found them clinging to a wooden frame on a terrace! They are most common on the eastern and central part of the island, with high numbers in coastal marshes and reedbeds along the Gulfs of Kalloni and Gera.

In spring, the Levant Water Frog is found in many streams and ponds. This species is a Marsh Frog to the untrained eye, but there are genetic differences and the call is distinct. But since there is only one water frog present on the island, you don't have to take a DNA sample or wait until it croaks to identify it. In Europe, the Levant Water Frog only occurs on some Aegean islands and in Thrace.

Finally, there is the Eastern Spadefoot. Within Europe it is confined to the Eastern Aegean islands, Thrace and the Black Sea coast. It is fairly common on Lesbos, if rarely seen. During the day this nocturnal master of concealment digs deep into the soft sandy soils. It burrows itself backwards, using sharp-edged 'spades' on the hindlegs. Only during breeding

REPTILES AND AMPHIBIANS

season (March-May) Eastern Spadefoots are active during the day too. During this period they are found migrating to riverbanks and (seasonal) pools to spawn. With luck you might stumble upon one during an evening stroll along muddy ponds, especially after rain. In contrast, the tadpoles are easily found. They are big bronze creatures, much bulkier than any other tadpoles, and are common in all kinds of pools.

> **Human impact on the reptiles and amphibians of Lesbos**
> Since ancient times humans have had a huge impact on the ecosystems of the East Mediterranean region. Lesbos, with its long and rich history, is no exception. In contrast to popular belief, this human impact did not have a negative impact on the diversity of reptiles.
> It is fair to say that compared to mammals, reptiles are relatively resilient to unfavourable environmental impacts. During the late Pleistocene (roughly 12,000 years ago), climate change and other major events caused a wave of extinctions resulting in the loss of a third of all mammal species in Europe. But in the case of reptiles, almost no extinctions occurred, supposedly due to advantages conferred by their low metabolic rates, small size and long hibernation periods.
> It has been assumed that before the arrival of ancient tribes (pre-Neolithic times) fewer reptile species occurred on Lesbos than in the present-day. From about 2000 B.C. increased human activity resulted in the accidental or deliberate introduction of reptiles. The early voyagers in the Aegean Sea carried materials (like marble and pottery) that offered excellent hiding places for small-bodied species or their eggs. On Lesbos examples of this process may include Mediterranean House Gecko and Starred Agama. Introductions possibly also took place as a means of pest control (e.g. Leopard Snake).
> In addition to the introduction of new species, human activities also had major influence on habitats which favoured reptiles. As in many other areas in the Mediterranean much of the original forest cover has been removed or has degenerated through felling, fires and grazing. The change of landscape was gradual, so reptiles could both adapt easily and benefit from the new open habitats.
> On Lesbos, many species are now more or less confined to traditional agricultural landscapes like olive groves. They provide the essential open space for basking as well as vegetation to take shelter. The great extent of stone walls in the western part of Lesbos offer ideal hiding places and support thriving populations of reptiles of scrubby and arid landscapes. During your stay on the island, you will find that these are excellent places to look for reptiles.

REPTILES AND AMPHIBIANS

Species	Occurrence	Preferred habitat
Lizards		
Snake-eyed Skink (*Ablepharus kitaibelii*)	Frequent	Scrubland, open woodland
Kotschy's Gecko (*Cyrtopodion kotschy*)	Common	Stone walls, rocky sites, scrubland
Turkish Gecko (*Hemidactylus turcicus*)	Common	Houses
European Glass Lizard (*Pseudopus apodus*)	Common	Scrubland, rocky sites, arable land
Three-lined Lizard (*Lacerta trilineata*)	Common	Any terrestrial site
Snake-eyed Lizard (*Ophisops elegans*)	Frequent	Open rocky sites, volcanic rock
Starred Agama (*Laudakia stellio*)	Common	Stone walls, rocky sites, stony terrain
Snakes		
Caspian whip snake (*Dolichophis caspius*)	Common	Any terrestrial site, prefers rocks
Dahl's Whip Snake (*Platyceps najadum*)	Common	Scrubland, open woodland, olive groves, stone walls
Montpellier Snake (*Malpolon monspessulanus*)	Common	Any terrestrial site, prefers rocks
Grass Snake (*Natrix natrix*)	Common	Aquatic habitats
Dice Snake (*Natrix tessellata*)	Common	Aquatic habitats
Coin Snake (*Hemorrhois nummifer*)	Very rare	Rocky sites, scrubland
Cat Snake (*Telescopus fallax*)	Local	Rocky sites, scrubland
Dwarf Snake (*Eirenis modestus*)	Frequent	Scrubland, open woodland, olive groves
Leopard Snake (*Zamenis situlus*)	Frequent	Olive groves, arable land, scrubland
Sand Boa (*Eryx jaculus*)	Frequent	Olive groves, scrubland
Worm Snake (*Typhlops vermicularis*)	Frequent	Rocky sites and streambeds with deep and soft soils
Ottoman Viper (*Vipera xanthina*)	Frequent	Scrubland, olive groves
Tortoises and terrapins		
Spur-thighed Tortoise (*Testudo graeca*)	Common	Open woodland, scrubland, arable land
Balkan Terrapin (*Mauremys rivulata*)	Common	Lowland ponds, lakes, marshes, estuaries
European Pond Terrapin (*Emys orbicularis*)	Rare	Lowland ponds, ditches, slow flowing rivers
Frogs and Toads		
Tree Frog (*Hyla arborea*)	Common	Reedbeds, ponds, streams, rivers
Levant Water Frog (*Pelophylax bedriagae*)	Common	Any water body
Eastern Spadefoot (*Pelobates syriacus*)	Frequent	Muddy and sandy areas, brackish and freshwater waters
Common Toad (*Bufo bufo*)	Local	Scrubland, meadows, gardens
Green Toad (*Pseudepidalea virides*)	Common	Throughout

INSECTS AND OTHER INVERTEBRATES

Insects and other invertebrates

> Basically any route is good for butterflies of flowery scrubland, but are particularly abundant on routes 1, 10, 11 and 12. For species of woodland and forests head for routes 3, 4, and 10. The better routes for butterflies of dry rocky habitat are 2, 16 and 17. For dragonflies and damselflies of coastal areas routes 1, 2, 6 and 9 are most rewarding. For river species try routes 2, 8 and 13, while special dragonflies and damselflies of streams are best found on routes 2, 3, 4, 10 and site N. Great routes for species of small standing waters and lakes are 9, 10 and site M. Along route 13 you can find several species of praying mantis

Among birdwatchers and botanists Lesbos constitutes a top notch area that should be visited at least once. But for naturalists with interest in insect life, the island is a relatively unknown. Now that finding butterflies, dragonflies and damselflies is beginning to gain in popularity this is gradually changing. Although both mainland Greece and Turkey have a lot more to offer, there is still a lot to see on Lesbos. In particular the dragonfly fauna is quite rich. As the island is under-watched, particularly in summer, it is quite possible to find new butterflies and dragonflies for the island. Besides these popular groups of insects, Lesbos has a number of other invertebrate attractions.

False Apollo is another eastern speciality on Lesbos on the wing in early spring. The best locations for it are olive groves in the eastern and central parts of the island, but we also found the caterpillar on the lava dome of Ipsilou Monastery (bottom; route 17).

Butterflies

About 76 species of butterflies are known to occur on Lesbos, which are on the wing between March and October. The main period is from late May until July, while in spring and autumn – when most naturalists visit the island – the numbers are lower. Lesbos hosts a mix of typical Mediterranean and Balkan species, most of which are fairly widespread.

Early spring kicks off with the remarkable False Apollo, only found in the east Mediterranean region and Turkey. It flies from March until mid-April in olive and chestnut groves, where its host-plant Hairy Birthwort grows (e.g. route 4).

CROSSBILL GUIDES · LESBOS

INSECTS AND OTHER INVERTEBRATES

The scaling of the wings of older specimens has worn off, so the wings have become transparent allowing you to see what the butterfly is resting upon.
In the first half of April more butterflies start to emerge. The eye-catching Eastern Festoon is usually found in open woodland and olive groves near streams and damp places, together with the flashy Cleopatra and Southern White Admiral. On a typical spring day in the scrublands you should be able to find Lesser Spotted and Aegean Fritillaries, Eastern Dappled and Balkan Marbled Whites, Clouded Yellow, Eastern Baton and Green-underside Blues, Ilex Hairstreak and Oriental Marbled and Orbed Hungarian Skippers. A good place to find (and photograph!) these species are in patches with flowering Oregano.

An attractive butterfly is the thinly distributed Southern Swallowtail. With the dark tiger stripes on its yellow wings, it resembles somewhat the common Scarce Swallowtail.
Late spring and summer generally bring more species of a different sort. Different habitats each have their own specific species of interest. Open woodlands are good butterfly haunts with Great Banded Grayling and Black-veined White, Nettle-tree Butterfly, Lang's Short-tailed Blue and the striking Cardinal all being abundant. Open areas within these woods, in particular those with damp grasslands and flowery edges, are the places to look for Amanda's Blue and Purple-shot Copper.
Good sites with this habitat are present in the area of Agiasos, which is an interesting area for butterflies in general. Fruit orchards in the same area provide good habitat for Large Tortoiseshell. A localised species for Lesbos and one found in rocky habitats is Krueper's Small White, which is confined to Mount Olymbos (see box on the next page). Along the northern flanks of Mount Lepetimnos and around Filia, Marbled Fritillary occurs in spots where Woolly Blackberry grows.

Eastern Festoon is a common spring butterfly (top). Amanda's Blue (bottom) is generally scarce on Lesbos, mostly found in woodland edges in the northern and the southern part. Other than Sicily, this is the only island in the Mediterranean Sea where it occurs.

INSECTS AND OTHER INVERTEBRATES

The dense Turkish pine forests in the central part of Lesbos have few butterflies. Typical is the Eastern Rock Grayling, which is common here, locally accompanied by Green Hairstreak. The latter is a rare find on Lesbos. Among the more widespread butterflies is the Lattice Brown, with its typical, yellow circled eye-spots underneath its hindwing. It is usually found in shady gullies and dry streambeds. When disturbed, it has the strange habit of flying into the dense vegetation, where it later may be observed resting on trunks and branches.

Hot and dry rocky habitats like *phrygana* scrubland and cliffs are home to Balkan, White Banded and Freyer's Grayling (all during summer), Large Wall Brown, Inky Skipper and Levantine Skipper. They are best located near patches with some high shrubs and trees. The Levantine Skipper is a rare species in the eastern Mediterranean region. It resembles 'our' Small Skipper which also occurs on Lesbos, but is slightly bigger and has a greenish underside. The Mediterranean Southern Comma shares the same habitat, but can also be common in villages and on stone walls. It is easily distinguished from Comma by the brighter orange colour of the upper wings and the small white letter gamma (γ) instead of a 'c' underneath.

Finally, Mediterranean and Millet Skippers are specialists of hot coastal areas where they fly in gullies and dunes (see routes 9 and 13). These highly territorial species take off at incredible speed to chase away intruders, but regularly return to rest at a fixed spot where it can be observed.

Krueper's White occurs in rocky areas from the southern Balkan peninsula to central Asia.

White butterfly of white rocks

The summit area of Mount Olymbos is home to Krueper's Small White, a species that is restricted to areas with limestone and marble rocks. The caterpillar feeds exclusively on Golden Alison, which occurs high up on Mount Olymbos. The butterfly strays a bit further from these sites to find nectar, for example to the flowery edges of nearby woodlands. At first glance, the butterfly looks like just an ordinary White, but closer inspection reveals a delicate green underside. Krueper's Small White is on the wing throughout spring and summer.

INSECTS AND OTHER INVERTEBRATES

Browns and Graylings
Lesbos is home to a number of eastern specialities, which are difficult to identify but great for butterfly enthusiasts to encounter. Turkish Meadow Brown and Persian Meadow Brown are related to our familiar Meadow Brown. They look alike and both are widespread on the island but more common in the western and northern part. They are mostly found around Oregano and yellow crucifers. You can tell them apart by the number of eye spots on the hindwing, Persian Meadow Brown has several small ones, while Turkish only has two.
The graylings need a specialist's eye to identify them. Eastern Grayling resembles the Aegean and Balkan Grayling closely, but almost lacks the white spots on the hind underwing of the other two. Aegean and Balkan Grayling can only be seperated by genital examination. All these graylings occur on rocky slopes on Lesbos. A good place to find them is Ipsilou Monastery (see route 17).

Dragonflies and damselflies

With 44 species to encounter, Lesbos is an excellent place for watching dragonflies and damselflies. The list includes some very interesting species (see box on page 103). At first glance this richness seems strange. In comparison with northern Europe, Lesbos has few permanent rivers and wetlands. However, the seasonal abundance of water in spring is sufficient to support a good number of dragonflies and damselflies especially adapted to surviving periods of drought.
Most species start to emerge from mid-April and are found until September. To give some practical guidelines for finding dragonflies and damselflies, we grouped them in relation to four major dragonfly habitats on the island.

Coastal wetlands
A good place to start your search for dragonflies is on the coastal wetlands. This is good habitat for damselflies like Eastern Willow Spreadwing, Common Winter Damsel and Blue-eye. There are also three species of skimmer here: Epaulet, Southern and Small. The outlet of small rivers to the coast form pools that are on one side less vegetated. These places are home to Red-veined Darter, Blue-eyed Hawker, Broad-bodied Chaser, Vagrant Emperor and Southern Darter. Some of these species can also be found at inland lakes.
An odd wetland is the freshwater reedbed of Dipi (route 2), because it is the only marsh on Lesbos that is fed by calcareous water. It is one of only two spots that supports Yellow-spotted Emerald (late May to September) and the only site for the sought-after Black Pennant (mid-May

INSECTS AND OTHER INVERTEBRATES

to early August). The latter is a rather small black dragonfly, identified by an =-marking near its front wingtips.

Green-eyed Hawker and Blue Chaser are scarce species, which also prefer the water type and rich riparian vegetation this marsh has to offer. Lesser Emperor and the rare Hairy Hawker are also found here earlier in the season, from April onwards.

Brackish marshes, such as those of Charamida on route 1, and the Kalloni saltpans of route 7 are home to Dark Spreadwing – the only damselfly that prefers slightly saline waters.

Rivers

Although the majority of the rivers that drain the hills of Lesbos are seasonal, the middle and lowland sections of the larger streams rarely dry up completely. The vegetated sandbanks form nurseries for the Turkish Clubtail. The mature dragonfly often wanders from the river and is frequently found higher up on the slopes bordering the river. This spectacular and rare dragonfly is recognised by its blue eyes.

The striking Violet Dropwing (top) is a very common dragonfly in summer. Odalisque (bottom) is a robust damselfly found along streams. The abdomen of males are a dull blue colour, while females have a striped pattern.

Small Pincertail, Blue Featherleg and Black-tailed Skimmer are common in the riverbed itself, frequently resting on the rocky and sandy shores. More densely vegetated pools which sometimes form along the larger rivers, may hold species of standing water like Blue-eye and Small and Southern Skimmers.

Small rivers and streams

The seasonal streams and upper sections of rivers in forests host different species which are absent in coastal areas. An eastern speciality like Odalisque is common and widespread on Lesbos, often seen resting near the water with its wings spread. It is usually in the company of Keeled Skimmer and Banded and Beautiful Demoiselles. Other typical species of small streams are Eastern Spectre and Turkish Goldenring, but they

INSECTS AND OTHER INVERTEBRATES

are dependent on permanent small streams with sandy substrates. They are regularly seen over tracks near such streams.

The spectacular Blue-eyed Goldenring is recently discovered on the island, along the small mountain streams of Mount Olympos (route 4). It prefers slow water flows with sandy substrate.

Lakes, flooded quarries and small standing waters

There is a wide variety of standing waters, which form good dragonfly and damselfly haunts. Only few larger inland natural lakes exist on Lesbos, namely Mikri Limni and Metochi lake (site M on and route 8). Both have well vegetated shores supporting Blue Chaser, Vagrant and Lesser Emperor and Green-eyed Hawker. Mikri Limni is the better site, spiced up with elsewhere rare or absent species like Common Winter Damsel, Small Spreadwing and Hairy Hawker. Artificial sites like reservoirs, quarries and clay pits are inhabited by Violet Dropwing, Dainty Bluet, Small

Special dragonflies and damselflies of Lesbos

Odalisque	*Epallage fatime*	Southern species, widespread along shady streams	Early April-August
Dark Spreadwing	*Lestes macrostigma*	Rare species of brackish marshes	March-August
Dainty Bluet	*Coenagrion scitulum*	Scarce species, near standing waters like clay pits and reservoirs	April-August
Eastern Spectre	*Caliaeschna microstigma*	Balkan species, frequenting shady streams	Late April-September
Turkish Clubtail	*Gomphus schneiderii*	Rare southern species, on middle sections of rivers	Mid April-July
Turkish Goldenring	*Cordulegaster picta*	Southern species, along sandy forest streams	May-early August
Blue-eyed Goldenring	*Cordulegaster insignis*	Rare southern species, along small mountain streams	Late April-July
Yellow-spotted Emerald	*Somatochlora flavomaculata*	Temperate species, rare on Lesbos in reedbed marshes	May-August
Epaulet Skimmer	*Orthetrum chrysostigma*	Southern species, on lowland rivers	April-October
Small Skimmer	*Orthetrum taeniolatum*	Southern species, on lowland rivers	Mid April-September
Black Pennant	*Selysiothemis nigra*	Rare Mediterranean species of reedbed marshes	Mid May-mid September

INSECTS AND OTHER INVERTEBRATES

Bluetail, Blue Emperor and, perhaps the most typical of such habitats, Broad Scarlet, the males of which have strikingly red abdomens. Large puddles along tracks attract rapid colonisers like Common Bluetail, Violet Dropwing and Black-tailed Skimmers.

Old flooded quarries are excellent places to look for dragonflies and damselflies, for example this one along the road between Skopelos and Tarti (site H).

Other invertebrates

Besides butterflies, dragonflies and damselflies, Lesbos is crowded with a large variety of spineless flyers, jumpers and creepy crawlers. Some of them don't require a thorough search, they'll cross your path sooner rather than later. Here follows a selection of the more conspicuous and easily en-countered species.

Ascalaphids or Owlflies are striking insects found in flowery scrubland and grassland. They combine the fast and straight flight of a dragonfly with the colourful wings of a butterfly, but are closely related to neither. Instead, they belong to the antlions. The most frequent species are Yellow-veined Owlfly* (*Libelloides longicornis*) and Eastern Owlfly* (*Libelloides macaronius*) - the first has a marbled black and yellow wing pattern, while the latter has solid black dots on its yellow fore-wings.

Other eye-catching members of this group, flying in the same habitat, are the graceful streamertails. Their excessively long wingtails give it an exotic appearance. Two species are found on Lesbos, Grecian Streamertail and *Nemoptera sinuata*, which differ in wing pattern.

Beautiful moths, such as the Cream-spot Tiger Moth and Striped Hawk-moth may be found during the day resting on the vegetation. Hummingbird Hawk-moth is a fast day-flying moth, hovering like a tiny hummingbird while draining flowers of their nectar with its long tongue. Other moths encountered during daytime are Blood Droplets and White-collar Burnets. Two brightly red moths often seen resting on flowerheads.

Grasshoppers and crickets can be encountered anywhere. A remarkable species in summer is Long-nosed Grasshopper. Several species of brightly coloured bush-crickets are common and widespread in summer, crawling on thistles and thorny bushes. One of them is *Poecilimon mytilenensis*, one of the few endemic species of Lesbos.

INSECTS AND OTHER INVERTEBRATES

Praying mantises are other remarkable insects to find. Like the aforementioned species, the adults are mostly seen in summer. They stake out their prey and grab it with their big forelegs. European Mantis and Conehead Mantis are frequent species in shrubs. The latter species has a striped appearance with a conspicuous crest on its head.

Among Lesbos' spiders, there are some very handsome species. Time has come to overcome your arachnophobia and admire the small, bright-red *Philaeus* jumping-spiders, which live in rocky terrain and jump from rock to rock. In the same habitat you may be lucky enough to come across the rare Giant Ladybird Spider* (*Eresus walckenaeri*). The males have a flashy bright orange back with four large black spots (hence the reference to ladybird). The females are much larger and black (see photo). This spider builds a pink coloured tube-like web under rocks or in crevices. We found them crawling around in the area of Pterounda (site T). None of these spiders bite, nor do any others on the island.

With some luck, you might find the European Oil Beetle, recognisable like all oil beetles by the worm-like abdomen that protrudes from underneath the short wing cases. It has a fascinating life-cycle, in which the larva climbs on a plant and attaches itself to a passing ground-nesting solitary bee. After entering the nest they feed on the eggs and nectar of the bee.

An encounter with a suspicious European Mantis on the cobbled streets of Sigri (top). The female of the amazing Giant Ladybird Spider* (*Eresus walckenaeri*) can have a body length of more than 4 cm.

Turning stones might reveal a Mediterranean Checkered Scorpion or an agile Megarian Banded Centipede. Both can inflict a painful sting or bite. This in sharp contrast to the harmless millipedes that you'll encounter frequently. The yellow spotted millipede *Melaphe vestita* is very common on damp soils and feeds on dead plant material. It can be distinguished from centipedes by a double pair of legs for each body segment.

FLORA AND FAUNA

PRACTICAL PART

If you've read the previous sections and browsed the photos, then no doubt you want to explore the flora and fauna, enjoy the wonderful landscapes, marvel at the geological features and admire the historical remains for yourself! This part of the book will help you to experience the full flavour of this marvellous island.

In this chapter we describe 17 detailed routes and 22 sites all over the island, starting in the southeast (routes 1, 2, 3, 4; sites A, B, C, D, E, F, G, H, I, J, K), then continuing towards the Gulf of Kalloni (routes 5, 6, 7, 8; sites L, M, N, O, P) and followed by the north (9, 10, 11, 12; sites Q, R, S) before finally discussing western Lesbos (routes 13, 14, 15, 16, 17; sites T, U, V). Combined, these offer the maximum diversity in landscape and optimises your chances of finding the island's birds, wildlife and attractive wildflowers.

The south-eastern part of the island is the greenest, characterised by picturesque olive groves, flowery deciduous woodlands and shady rivers. The routes will take you to the calcareous Olympos massif and scenic areas around the Gulf of Gera, painted with wildflowers.

The central part around the Gulf of Kalloni covers Lesbos's coastal wetlands, which are famous for their breeding and migratory birds. This section of the island also harbours superb river valleys, old pine forests and maquis scrubland full of wildlife.

The northern part is dominated by Mount Lepetimnos, covered in wild oak woodland and maquis. The routes take you to the slopes of the massif with lush streams, beautiful valleys and impressive rugged coasts.

The volcanic west, the driest part of Lesbos, is predominantly covered in phrygana scrubland. The barren land is interspersed with fields, patches of woodland and riverine forest snaking down towards the estuarine wetlands, all offering excellent bird and wildlife watching.

After the routes, from page 172 onwards, we describe a large number of sites, which encompass hikes, short routes and singular spots of interest. The selected routes and sites fulfil all different kinds of interests and activities like birdwatching, wildflower hunting and hiking, covering all the island's habitats. The routes should not be viewed as a rigid framework to organise your field trip, but as an invitation to discover and explore the encountered scenery. On your way you come across many small traditional villages, which offer excellent opportunity to sit down and enjoy great food and the relaxed islands' atmosphere after a day of hard 'work' (see page 197).

Lesbos offers great opportunities to explore interesting habitats off the beaten track. This photo is taken near Liota along route 14.

ROUTE 1: AMALI PENINSULA

Route 1: Amali Peninsula

FULL DAY, 45 KM
EASY

Little visited part of Lesbos with something for all naturalists.
Excellent orchid hunting.

Habitats scrubland, olive groves, coastal marsh, Turkish pine forest
Selected species Mammose, Horseshoe, Fan-lipped and Roman Orchids, Broad-leaved, Turkish and Spurred Helleborines, Winter Daffodil, Sardinian Warbler, Olivaceous Warbler, Middle-spotted Woodpecker, Levant Sparrowhawk, Short-toed Eagle, Dahl's Whipsnake, False Apollo, Dark Spreadwing

Since every visiting naturalist to Lesbos arrives in Mytilini, it is remarkable that the peninsula of Amali, just below the city, is so little visited. It remains a quiet and authentic part of Lesbos, and a splendid one to explore. The peninsula is characterised by its diversity: the combination of limestone and serpentine bedrock makes for a diverse flora and fauna. This route, combining a car trip with short and easy walks, has something to offer for all, but particularly orchidophile botanists! Note that the warm microclimate causes the flowering periods of the orchids to be at least a week earlier than in other parts of the island.

Starting point Koundouroudia

Getting there from the main road Mytilini – Kalloni, take the exit *Loutra* and follow the signs *Koudouroudhia*. Park behind the taverna of the latter hamlet.

1 Continue along the track around the headland on foot. The pretty walk becomes truly interesting after 1500 m when a small islet in the bay is to your left. The olive groves and

CROSSBILL GUIDES · LESBOS

scrubland here are excellent for wildflowers. This is limestone country, with calcareous rocks of some 300 million years old. As in many limestone areas, you can find many species of orchids, including Long-lipped Tongue, Naked Man, Holy, Four-spotted and Pyramidal Orchids, which flower here in April. Earlier in spring you can see the *Ophrys* genus in full glory. Among the many species, look for Mammose, Horseshoe, Mirror, Rainbow, and various species of the Dull Bee orchid group such as *Ophrys attaviria*, *Ophrys blitopertha* and *Ophrys cinereophila*. The flowery slopes are visited by butterflies such as Green-underside, Lang's Short-tailed and Eastern Baton Blues and Ilex Hairstreak. In March and early April this site is promising for False Apollo. In autumn, the crocus-like Sternbergia washes the slopes yellow, while Greek Cyclamen forms pink drifts in the olive groves. The poisonous Sea Squill and the edible Rock Samphire grow on rocks along the seashore.

Return and turn right to Loutra. At the next T-junction, at the bar at the entrance of the village, turn right. After 3,5 km go right signposted *Ag. Ermogenis*. Park in the bend where the tarmac ends.

2 Walk 100 m back and turn left onto an unsignposted trail into pine forest. This is a different orchid habitat, with species such as Roman Orchid, Violet Bird's-nest and Dense-flowered Orchid. We also found Dahl's Whipsnake here. Continue along the trail to the shore, overlooking the mouth of the Gulf of Gera. The bay of Agios Ermogenis (below the car park), in itself a scenic place, is perfect for a swim or for snorkeling.

The olive groves near Loutra are excellent for wildflowers.

Return to the T-junction and continue to Charamida. At the beach, turn right onto a track and park underneath the tamarisk trees. Walk towards the headland and turn right onto a track which leads beside a reedbed that marks the Charamida marshes.

PRACTICAL PART

ROUTE 1: AMALI PENINSULA

3 This is a wonderful and underwatched site with freshwater and brackish marshland, which is sadly threatened with drainage. This is a very good location on the island to find the rare damselfly Dark Spreadwing, together with Eastern Willow Spreadwing. Loose-flowered Orchid grows in the reedbeds.

Here you will have little difficulty (in spring at least) hearing the loud songs of Great Reed and Cetti's Warblers, but you need to search a little harder to find Sardinian and Olivaceous Warblers, Blue Rock Thrush and Middle-spotted Woodpecker in the woods and scrub on the hillside. In the flowery edge you find Persian Meadow Brown and Turkish Meadow Brown. Walk over to the headland and scan the sky for migrating Levant Sparrowhawk, Honey Buzzard, Short-toed Eagle and Peregrine (the latter especially in autumn), and the sea for Cory's and Yelkouan Shearwaters and Shag.

Charamida marsh is home to Dark Spreadwing, a localised damselfly in Europe which is much dependant on saline marshes.

Continue along the tarmac the road. After 4 km, turn left onto track signposted *Monastery* (blue sign), follow the track uphill until you see a chapel on your left. Park here.

4 Explore the area around the chapel. This is a wonderfully quiet, atmospheric place. Note how different it is from the limestone areas of the first and second stops. The mature Turkish pine forest around the chapel grows on green-coloured serpentine rocks (originating from the Earth's oceanic crust, see page 15). It has a well-developed understory with Kermes Oak and many maquis wildflowers. Three species of Helleborines occur here: Turkish (with purple flowers appearing in the 2nd half of May), the familiar Broad-leaved and the east-Mediterranean Dense-leaved Helleborine (both flowering in June). Behind the chapel you'll find Violet Bird's-nest Orchids in a rare form with light pink flowers. Spurred Helleborine has been recorded here too.

Return to the main road and turn left.

5 On your way along the coast, stop at suitable viewing points. A particularly good spot is the small pier (see map), to scan the sea for dolphins. From this deserted stretch of rocky shore, Yellow-legged

ROUTE 1: AMALI PENINSULA

Gull, Shag and Cory's and Yelkouan Shearwaters are frequently seen. You have good views of the Turkish coast in the distance.

Pass the airport and after 3.8 km, turn left to Akrotiri. Turn left at the T-junction and subsequently, after 150 m, right onto a steep tarmac road, signposted Προς Αγιος Βαρθολομαίος. Now follow the signs Loutra. Along the way the road turns into a (well maintained) dirt track.

6 You cross a wide valley with olive groves, which is the geological divide between serpentine rocks on the south side and older limestones to the north. Note the difference in the rock shape – on the lefthand side of the track you see the thin layers of shiny schist and on the opposite side outcrops of paler and more rounded limestone rocks. In season, the divide is also visible in the flora. Half way along the route over to Loutra (roughly at the pass over the mountain), you cross the divide and limestone plants like orchids start to appear. Look for Three-toothed, Horseshoe, Homer's and (early in spring) Mirror and Fan-lipped Orchids. Butterflies don't mind the type of bedrock though – the entire stretch is good for Southern Comma, Aegean Fritillary, Eastern Baton Blue and Large Wall Brown.

Continue down, turn right to Loutra and turn right to the main road Mytilini – Kalloni.

The limestone rocks on the right side of the track to Loutra are much in evidence. Here it hosts an inaccessible cave where prehistoric artefacts were found, which are now visible at Archaeological Museum of Mytilini (see p. 200). Cirl Bunting is easy to find in open woodland mixed with maquis scrub (top).

PRACTICAL PART

ROUTE 2: ALONG EVERGETOULAS RIVER TO MOUNT OLYMBOS

Route 2: Along Evergetoulas river to Mount Olymbos

FULL DAY, 34 KM
EASY TO STRENUOUS

Following Lesbos' largest river From the sea to the highest peak.
Great wildflower and dragonfly route.
Impressive geological and historical features.

Habitats coastal marsh, olive groves, pine forest, oriental plane forest, scrubland, cliffs
Selected species Loose-flowered, Marsh, Holy, Komper's, Horseshoe Orchids, Spurred Helleborine, *Silene urvillei*, Otter, Persian Squirrel, Masked Shrike, Krüper's Nuthatch, Black Pennant, Yellow-spotted Emerald, Turkish Clubtail, Turkish Goldenring, Eastern Spectre, Krueper's Small White

Valley deep to mountain high is a good summary for this route where many different aspects of a Mediterranean river ecosystem come together. The route combines sites and short walks along the course of Evergetoulas river, one of the most important rivers on Lesbos. Starting in the coastal marshes

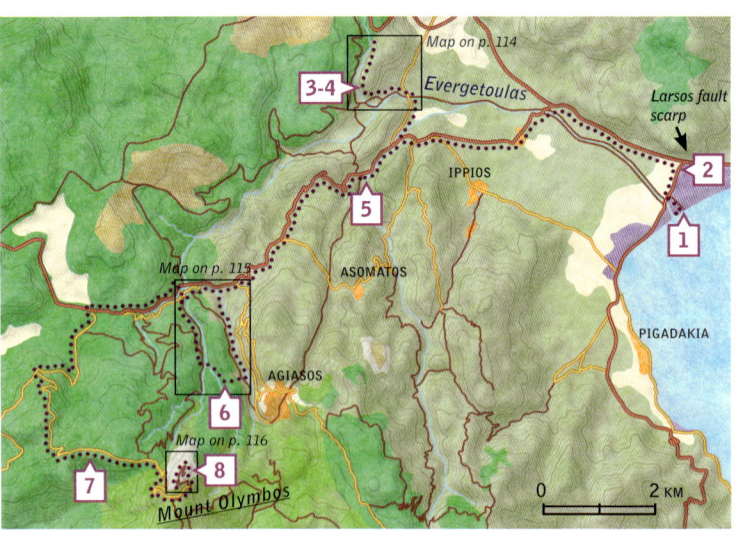

CROSSBILL GUIDES • LESBOS

ROUTE 2: ALONG EVERGETOULAS RIVER TO MOUNT OLYMBOS

of the Gulf of Gera and ending at the summit area of Mount Olymbos, this varied route visits some rare habitats on Lesbos. The wildlife is rich and varied. The dragonfly fauna and the flora is particularly diverse. This route also has some remarkable geological features on offer and brings you to the hidden remains of a Roman aqueduct. Because of its length, we advise to start early in the morning.

Starting point Dipi Larisos marsh

Getting there from the main road Mytilini – Kalloni, take the exit to Plomari and after 600 m park at a parking place on the left opposite a taverna (look for a blue sign with "ΨΑΡΟΤΑΒΕΡΝΑ". Walk a bit further along the road and turn left onto a track. Leave the gate as you find it, either open or closed. The track ends at the shore of the gulf and the river mouth.

1 Depending on the season you'll find brackish and freshwater pools along the track which are superb for finding rare dragonflies like Black Pennant and Yellow-spotted Emerald. Hairy Hawker, Green-eyed Hawker and Blue Chaser are all associated with freshwater marshes, hence rare on Lesbos except here. For a wetland site, the birdlife is surprisingly poor, although Sedge, Reed and Great Reed Warbler, Black-headed Wagtail and Little Ringed Plover can make this site worth a (quick) stop for birdwatchers. Tree Frog is abundant and especially in the evenings, the croaking is deafening. Looking inland you see the impressive Larsos fault scarp, a spectacular geological phenomenon which is the result of a rupture in the earth's crust. Whereas in most places, both sides of a fault move alongside one another, here only one side rose, exposing a massive rock wall. With binoculars you can clearly see the channel of the Roman aqueduct constructed inside the rock face (for reference look for the white sign ΕΟΔ painted on the rock).

Dipi Larisos marsh is home to the sought after Black Pennant.

At the shore, turn right to the mouth of the river. Otter is occasionally seen here, most likely originating from populations on the Turkish west coast.

ROUTE 2: ALONG EVERGETOULAS RIVER TO MOUNT OLYMBOS

The stout inflorescences of pink orchids in the damp meadows of Dipi Larisos marsh are impressive. Plants may even grow up to more than a metre in height. This is the Marsh Orchid, which has a spreading lip, like Elegant Marsh Orchid. The latter has bigger stem leaves which nearly reach the flowers.

Return by car to the main road Mytilini – Kalloni. Just before the T-junction, stop at a small car park.

2 A small trail leads into the (sometimes very) wet reedbed and meadow, where in May huge stands of the striking Marsh, Elegant Marsh and Loose-flowered Orchids grow. These three species are closely related, but there are few places where they all occur together.

At the T-junction turn left. After 2.5 km turn left to the main road to Polichnitos. Ignore the turn to Asomatos and instead, after 3.3 km, turn right to a tarmac road signposted *L.Myloi* and *Kalloni*. After the bridge, turn left onto a track and park here.

3 Walk back to the bridge over the Evergetoulas and go down to the river bed on the right. The shady banks harbour demoiselles, Odalisque and Eastern Spectre. Although on the same river and only 5 kms from the previous sites, the dragonfly fauna has changed completely.

4 Follow the track where you parked your car. After 500 m, turn right through olive groves which are good for Masked Shrike, Olivaceous Warbler, Cirl Bunting and other wildlife like Persian Squirrel. Along the track we found the rare blue eyed Turkish Clubtail. After 300 m turn right, just before the river (with Balkan Terrapin), onto a scenic trail through the valley, marked with red dots. The trail leads to the remains of a Roman aqueduct from the 2nd century AD (see page 46). This stretch is excellent for orchids, including Holy, Homer's, Rainbow and Horned Orchids. Equally interesting is the geology: the valley forms the sharp border of 300 million year old calcareous rocks (recognisable by olive groves) and more recent ophiolitic rocks. The latter is covered with pine forest, as olives cannot grow here (see page 15).

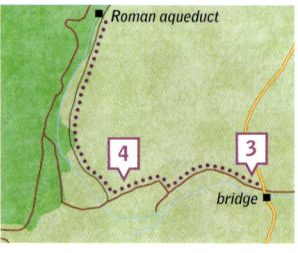

CROSSBILL GUIDES • LESBOS

ROUTE 2: ALONG EVERGETOULAS RIVER TO MOUNT OLYMBOS

Return to your car and go back to the main road towards Polichnitos. After 800 m park along the road near some stalls with local products.

5 The taverna on the other side of the river marks the wonderful green oasis called *Karini*. The painter Theophilos (see page 44) lived here for some time in the huge hollow plane tree, which is hard to miss on the left side of the premises.

Continue along the main road and turn left to a tarmac road signposted *Old Prov. Road to Polichnitos*. Park after 400 m near the house with a veranda and lush orchards, which was an inn for travellers in the 18th century. The springs in the area served as the starting point of the Roman aqueduct all the way to Mytilini.

6 The track behind the wooden house is the start of a marvellous 4.5 km signposted circular route, passing through the valley of the Karkavoura tributary. Scan the cliffs for Crag Martin, Short-toed Eagle and Long-legged Buzzard, all of which breed here. A demanding and steep ascent brings you to an old pine forest, where you may find Krüper's Nuthatch, Serin and Spotted Flycatcher. Along the trail search underneath the pines for Violet Bird's-nest and Roman Orchids. The last 2 km of the route leads through olive groves, with a good number of orchids including Horseshoe, Four-spotted and Three-toothed Orchids. Turkish Goldenring hunts over the track, while Golden Orioles sing their fluty tune in the riverine forest of poplars and Oriental Plane.

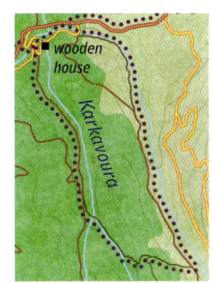

Back at the car, continue on the old road, which rejoins the new road. Turn left. After 500 m turn left again onto a tarmac road signposted *Akrasi* and *Plomari* and take the first tarmac road left signposted *Olymbos*.

7 The road winds up the mountain through pine forest on ophiolitic rocks, hosting mainly wildflowers adapted to this ultra basic environment (see page 68). Violet Bird's-nest Orchid is abundant here. Higher up, there is a section of the road, straight and with mount Olymbos in front of you, where you cross a strict border from ophiolitic rocks to limestone bedrock. It is distinguished by the sudden abundance of of Kermes

ROUTE 2: ALONG EVERGETOULAS RIVER TO MOUNT OLYMBOS

Oak and wildflowers in general, which all prefer the limestone soils. In late May, look for Komper's Orchid and Spurred Helleborine in the pine forest and the side tracks near the wooden gazebo (a little further along on the left). Stop at the damp shady patches of oriental plane forest some 700 m further on where the road bends. This area supports an interesting vegetation, which includes the rare *Arum concinnatum*.

Park your car on the car park beneath the cliff of Mount Olymbos.

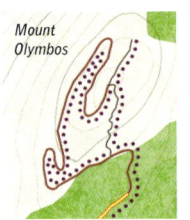

Mount Olymbos

8 Around the mountain a unique woodland thrives of Common Hawthorn (some reaching more then 10 m!), Cretan Maple and stunted trees of Kermes Oak (normally a shrub!).

Black-eared Wheatear, Cirl Bunting and Subalpine Warbler breed here. Follow the track on foot and after the first sharp bend, just where the tarmac ends, turn right onto a signposted trail (red dots on rocks; see map), leading to the east side of the cliff. On your way up, stop regularly to scan for Blue Rock Thrush and Crag Martin. Also keep an eye out for the rare Krueper's Small White (a butterfly), unique on these dry marble slopes. It flies here together with Inky Skipper.

Botanists will enjoy the many rock plants found in the summit area, such as Mountain Cherry, Hypecoum, the crucifer *Aubrietta deltoidea* and the mountain tea *Sideritis sipylea*. The rare Turkish St.John's-wort and the catchfly *Silene urvillei* grow almost exclusively here. At the summit area enjoy the spectacular view on Agiasos, Evergetoulas river valley and Gulf of Gera.

Return to your car via the track starting near the buildings.

Woodland below the summit of Mount Olymbos, where the branches of the trees are covered with lichens.

Route 3: Hiking the olive grove trails

6 HOURS, 9 KM
MODERATE TO STRENUOUS

Superb hiking through old olive groves and along lush streams.
Excellent for finding orchids.

Habitats olive groves, scrubland, chestnut forest, streams
Selected species Naked Man, Three-toothed, Homer's, Horseshoe, Rainbow, Komper's, Horned and Holmboe's Butterfly Orchids, Lesbos Fritillary* (*Fritillatia theophrasti*), Bonelli's Warbler, Middle-spotted Woodpecker, Sand Boa, Ottoman Viper, Spur-thighed Tortoise, Amanda's Blue, Odalisque

This circular route offers superb hiking through the flowery olive groves for which Lesbos is famous. If wildflowers have your interest then this is a route certainly not to miss. We found at least 20 orchid species in mid-April, but maybe even more can be added to the list! The varied landscape of streams and woodland make this a delightful hike in any season. The grand starter for this route is Agii Anargiri, a lush surprise with an abundance of water – especially in spring. The route leads you mainly on old *kalderimi* (cobbled paths). This is a fairly long walk, so to get the most out of it - including some great food in Agiasos – we recommend an early start.

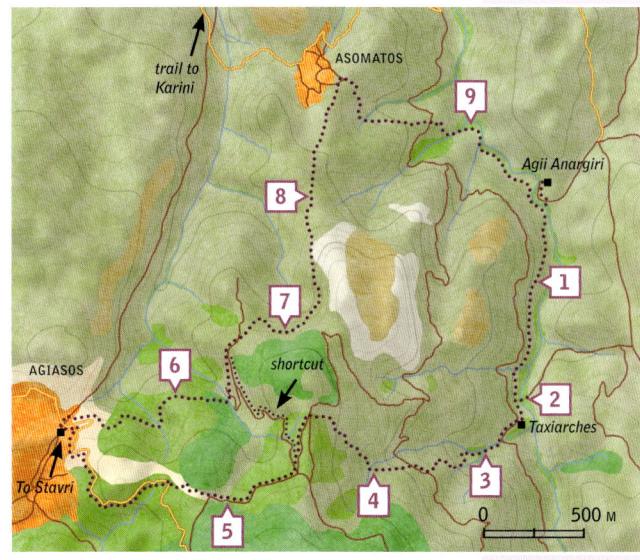

Starting point Agii Anargiri

ROUTE 3: HIKING THE OLIVE GROVE TRAILS

The beautiful old olive groves around Asomatos are unploughed, and therefore jam-packed with orchids and other interesting wildflowers.

Getting there From the main road Mytilini – Kalloni, take the exit to Polichnitos. After 2.4 km turn onto a tarmac road at a sharp bend, signposted *Asomatos*. Take the first turn left, signposted *Ag. Anargyroi*. Continue straight along the tarmac road for 3.2 km following the signs to *Ag. Anargyroi*. The olive groves along this road are full of orchids. Just after a row of pine trees, park at the car park of Agii Anargiri, near a chapel and a small taverna. You can fill up your water bottles at the tap.

Walk 220 m back along the road and turn right onto a track. Take the first turn right and cross a bridge where you turn left onto a trail signposted *Radi-Taxiarxes*. The trail is marked with red diamonds all the way.

1 The old olive groves along the way are excellent for wildflowers in spring – above all orchids like Naked Man, Three-toothed, Green-winged, Bergoni's Tongue, Long-lipped Tongue, Horseshoe, Homer's and Rainbow Orchids. The striking Peacock and Crown Anemones add even more colour to the scenery, growing together with many other typical plants of olive groves, like Larger Venus's-looking-glass, Common Grape-hyacinth and Grecian Star-of-Bethlehem. Further on the terrain becomes more forested, creating a damp and shady environment with Lesbos Fritillary* (*Fritillatia theophrasti*), Drooping Star-of-Bethlehem, Navelwort and Greek Saxifrage. From April on you may, with some luck, come across sought after reptiles like Sand Boa and Ottoman Viper.

After 1.2 km turn left at the T-junction to a wooden bridge.

ROUTE 3: HIKING THE OLIVE GROVE TRAILS

2 From the bridge you have a good overview of the stream that is lined with Black Poplar, Oriental Plane and Bay Laurel. The latter is a relict of laurel forests that once covered much of the Mediterranean region when the climate was more humid. Around 4 million years ago when the region became drier, the laurel forests gradually disappeared (only on the Canary Islands and Madeira, large stands remain). Frequent butterflies here are Southern Festoon, Cleopatra and Southern White Admiral. Keep an eye out for Eastern Spectre, Odalisque and Beautiful Demoiselle.

Return to the junction and turn left. Pass the chapel of Taxiarches (notice the huge, centuries old Kermes Oaks – a species that in many places in the Mediterranean remains a small shrub!) and follow the trail up the slope until you reach a track. Turn left here and after 150 m turn right onto a trail uphill, signposted *Agiasos*. The next stretch is a more strenuous part of the route.

3 The trail runs through olive groves with many old walled terraces, on which typical wildflowers of rocky environments thrive, like Rock Bellflower and the bindweed *Convulvulus elegantissimus*. Four-spotted and Provence Orchid grow underneath the olive trees, while in autumn, Greek Cyclamen and Autumn Lady's-tresses are found. Keep an eye out for Olivaceous Warbler and Middle-spotted Woodpecker.

When you reach a broad track, turn right and after 60 m, turn left onto a trail.

4 The next section continues uphill through more excellent olive groves, similar to those of point 3. Stop every now and then to scan the sky for raptors. While doing so, don't forget to turn around and enjoy the splendid view to the Gulf of Gera. Higher up, chestnut forest starts to take over, which is suitable habitat for Bonelli's Warbler. In the undergrowth you find interesting wildflowers including Violet Bird's-nest Orchid and Narrow-leaved Helleborine. In autumn look for the autumn-crocus *Colchicum variegatum*.

When you reach a track, turn left and go straight, ignoring the side track left leading uphill. Continue straight on (alternatively you can take the track downhill to the right for a shortcut, to reduce the walk to 7 km).

PRACTICAL PART

ROUTE 3: HIKING THE OLIVE GROVE TRAILS

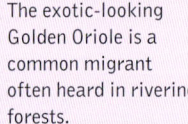

The exotic-looking Golden Oriole is a common migrant often heard in riverine forests.

5 After 780 m you arrive at a spot with walled terraces on your left. In May, look here underneath and around the scrub for the superb and very rare Komper's Orchid. This is a reliable spot for it.

Continue and go straight along a trail which ends on a tarmac road where you turn right (Warning – there is a fiercely barking dog here). After 1 km you reach Agiasos. In the village turn left, just before a concrete bridge, down onto a cobbled road. In case the hike stirred up your appetite, enjoy excellent local dishes here at the taverna *To Stavri* (see page 197). Turn right, pass underneath the bridge and take the ascending trail to the right, marked with a hiker symbol.

6 The trail runs through chestnut woodland mixed with orchards. On the way we found Holmboe's Butterfly Orchid and Small-leaved Helleborine. At the end of this stretch, Amanda's Blue flutters around wet spots on the ground to collect minerals.

The trail crosses a track and a little further arrives at a second, which you follow to the left. After 140 m, turn right onto a trail signposted *Asomatos*.

7 The route brings you back into the olive groves. En route, the area around the obvious tap (beautifully covered in Maidenhair Fern) is a good spot to look for Small Horned and Homer's Orchids. Continue on the trail signposted Ασώματος.

ROUTE 3: HIKING THE OLIVE GROVE TRAILS

8 After the steep slope on your right, the olive groves are mixed with maquis. Underneath the Cretan Cistus shrubs, notice the parasitic Pink Hypocist with red leaves and small white flowers. This area is also good for Sand Boa, Ottoman Viper, Montpellier Snake and Spur-thighed Tortoise.

Keep on the main trail and when you reach Asomatos turn right, signposted *Aghii Anargyri* (for a recommended visit to the traditional village, turn left here). The scenic route leads down to the valley crossing terraced olive groves full of wildflowers. Eventually you cross a track and pass a chapel with an impressive old oak tree, reaching this stature only in sacred places.

The parasitic Pink Hypocist has bright red leaves with white flowers and, grows exclusively underneath the pink flowering Cretan Cistus (see photo). Yellow Hypocist, with yellow flowers, has the same relationship with Sage-leaved Cistus.

9 The lush orchards in the valley are home to the secretive Leopard Snake, perhaps the most beautiful of all the snakes of Lesbos. Look in the small stream along the path for freshwater crabs. From the damp oriental plane forest further on in the valley you hear the songs of Nightingale and Golden Oriole. The stream itself is home to Beautiful and Banded Demoiselles and Odalisque.

Continue on the right bank of the stream until you reach the bridge at the starting point. Turn left to the car park.

The best chance of seeing the striking Leopard Snake is by hiking in the southeast of Lesbos where promising habitats are orchards and chestnut woodland.

PRACTICAL PART

Route 4: Through the heart of the Olymbos massif

!
Plans exist to tarmac this track

FULL DAY, 22 KM
EASY

Scenic route through the highest mountains in the south of Lesbos.
A rare flora and insect life.
Stunning walks through chestnut forests and along mountain streams.

Habitats scrubland, chestnut forest, streams, pine forest, olive groves
Selected species Spurred Helleborine, Komper's, Reinhold's, Holmboe's Butterfly, Provence and Balkan Lizard Orchids, *Tulipa orphanidae*, Balkan Peony, Persian Squirrel, Krüper's Nuthatch, Alpine Swift, Short-toed Eagle, Leopard and Dwarf Snakes, Spur-thighed Tortoise, Snake-eyed Lizard, Blue-eyed Goldenring, Purple-shot Copper, Amanda's Blue, False Apollo

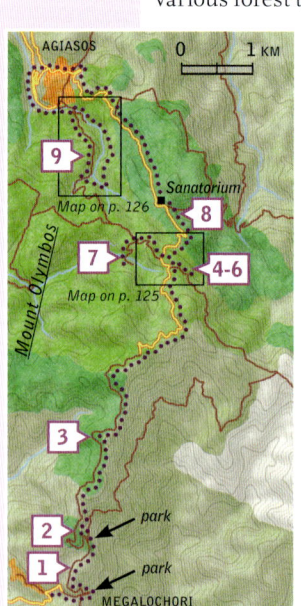

This scenic route through the Olymbos massif is perfect for exploring the various forest types of Lesbos. In several short walks, you'll explore scrubland, pine woodland, streamsides, and the highlight of this route, the lovely chestnut forests and groves where a stunning flora is found. For orchid aficionados this route is almost mandatory. Nearly all the rare and special species of orchid on Lesbos can be encountered, including Spurred Helleborine and Komper's, Holmboe's Butterfly and Reinhold's Orchids. The fauna is also well represented with high profile species like Krüper's Nuthatch, Dwarf Snake and Blue-eyed Goldenring.

Starting point Megalochori

Getting there Megalochori can be reached from Plomari (south) or Akrasi (north). Upon entering the village turn right, signposted *Agiasos*. Soon the tarmac road becomes a track and winds up into hairpin bends.

1 Park at the second bend and walk up the track. In spring, look underneath the shrubs on the right side of the track for Narrow-leaved Helleborine and Mammose, Three-toothed and Reinhold's Orchids. The latter is rather

ROUTE 4: THROUGH THE HEART OF THE OLYMBOS MASSIF

scarce in Greece, but not uncommon in the southeastern part of Lesbos. Towards the end of May this is also a good location to find Balkan Lizard Orchid and Turkish Helleborine. In rocky spots, look for Starred Agama. Walk up to the bend with the first shady patch of pine trees and look for Lesbos Fritillary * (*Fritillaria theophrasti*) and Greek Saxifrage. In autumn, there are many Ivy-leaved Cyclamen.

2 Continue by car and park where the road forks. Follow the left track on foot. Walk uphill for about 1.5 km, exploring side trails. You cross a Turkish pine woodland with a typical understory of Cretan Cistus and Kermes and Downy Oaks. Bonelli's and Subalpine Warblers are frequent, but again the orchids steal the show. At the end of May this is one of the few places on the island you may find a bunch of stunning *Himantoglossum* orchids which are notorious for hybridization: Komper's, Balkan Lizard and Eastern Lizard Orchids. Also the Provence, Violet Bird's-nest and Green-winged Orchids are hard to miss, but flower earlier in the season. Common butterflies here are Great Banded Grayling and Eastern Festoon.

Return to your car and continue along the same track. At the T-junction on a ridge, turn right.

3 From the track you overlook a broad valley with wide vistas over the countryside and Mount Olymbos. During migration, this is a good place for Alpine Swifts and migrating raptors like Peregrine, Honey Buzzard and Short-toed Eagle. Scan the scrubland and olive groves for Bonelli's and Subalpine Warbler. The latter is very common here.

About 2 km after the track becomes a tarmac road, near a military base, turn sharp right onto a steep, concrete track (first gear!). Park on the level stretch further up without blocking the way.

In June several remarkable orchids of the Himantoglossum group can be found. Specialists name this hybrid *Himantoglossum x agiasense*.

PRACTICAL PART

ROUTE 4: THROUGH THE HEART OF THE OLYMBOS MASSIF

4 The majestic trees in this old, open chestnut forest are the result of an ancient cultivation which persists into the present day. It is worth to explore the area thoroughly for wildflowers. The undergrowth shows a lavish display of orchids dominated by Provence, Green-winged and Four-spotted Orchids. Look also for the Holmboe's Butterfly Orchid and the rare Komper's Orchid. Further along the track on the left side there is a population of *Tulipa orphanidae*. Persian Squirrels hop from branch to branch, while Middle-spotted Woodpeckers fly by regularly. Closer to the ground, scrabbling in the leaf litter, you'll find plenty of Balkan Green Lizards and perhaps the much rarer Spur-thighed Tortoise. The track to the left leads all the way to Skopelos. This scenic stretch is well worth exploring (see site E).

Three-lined Lizard is common in scrubland and open woodland.

5 Walk back to the main road and turn left. Walk another 100 m, the open area on the left side hosts a rich flora including again many orchids, *Tulipa orphanidae*, Perfoliate Alexanders, Crown and Peacock Anemones and Hairy Birthwort. The latter is the host plant of the False Apollo, on the wing here in March and April.

6 Return along the main road on foot and take the first turn left onto a concrete road with a small goat farm on both sides of the road. After the first big bend, there is a hole in the fencing with an open patch, excellent for orchids including Holmboe's Butterfly Orchid, Narrow-leaved Helleborine, Three-toothed and Green-winged Orchids. To the left there is a small track leading into the chestnut forest. In the undergrowth look for Nodding Star-of-Bethlehem, Lesbos Fritillary* (*Fritillaria*

ROUTE 4: THROUGH THE HEART OF THE OLYMBOS MASSIF

theophrasti) and Small-leaved Helleborine. This entire area remains excellent for Middle-spotted Woodpecker and Persian Squirrel.

7 A little further on the main track, turn left at a black fence and take the track down into the lush valley. Notice the old buildings, once housing families living off the cultivation of chestnuts. The valley is home to Leopard and Dwarf Snakes. Balkan Green and Snake-eyed Lizards are abundant. Cross the stream in the valley where large stands of the stout *Arum rupicola* occur. Along the stream, keep an eye out for Odalisque, Eastern Spectre and the rare Blue-eyed Goldenring.

Retrace your steps to the car and continue on the main road. After 500 m beyond the last sharp bend, park along the track before the Sanatorium building.

8 The dry flowery grassland here is a good spot for some butterflies that are rare on Lesbos, like Purple-shot Copper and Amanda Blue. Walk back along the tarmac road to the last hairpin bend you passed. In season, this is a good place to look for Komper's Orchid, Spurred Helleborine and Balkan Lizard Orchid. This stretch of pine forest is promising habitat for Spotted Flycatcher and Krüper's Nuthatch. Notice the distinct border between chestnut and pine forest, which shows the sudden shift to calcareous rocks where the calcifuge Sweet Chestnut cannot grow.

Continue to Agiasos and follow the main road through the upper village. At the football pitch, in front of a gate, turn to the left. On the main road, at the bottom of the valley, turn left and park here. Walk up through the village past the tourist stalls and turn right after the library and pass the church *Zoodochos Pigi*. Continue straight to the chapel, where you find the start of a *kaldarimi*.

Elongated Arum* (*Arum elongatum*) is frequent along damp valleys around Agiasos.

PRACTICAL PART

ROUTE 4: THROUGH THE HEART OF THE OLYMBOS MASSIF

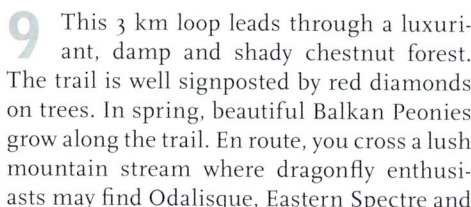

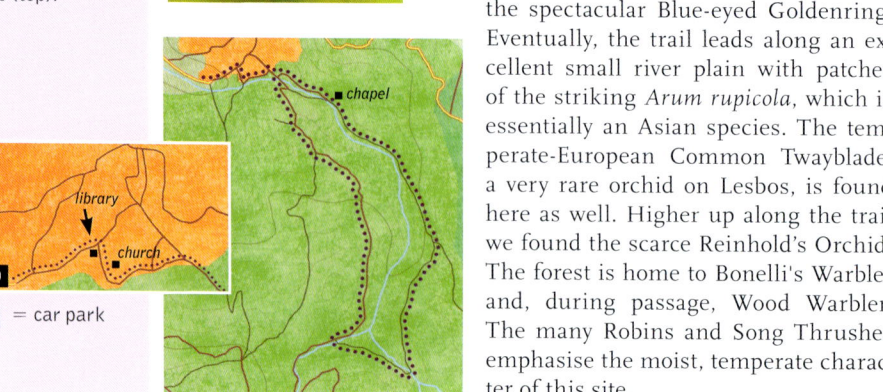

The Agiasos area offers excellent opportunities for walks in chestnut woodlands. Sought-after wildflowers here are Reinhold's (bottom) and Holmboe's Butterfly Orchids (top).

p = car park

9 This 3 km loop leads through a luxuriant, damp and shady chestnut forest. The trail is well signposted by red diamonds on trees. In spring, beautiful Balkan Peonies grow along the trail. En route, you cross a lush mountain stream where dragonfly enthusiasts may find Odalisque, Eastern Spectre and the spectacular Blue-eyed Goldenring. Eventually, the trail leads along an excellent small river plain with patches of the striking *Arum rupicola*, which is essentially an Asian species. The temperate-European Common Twayblade, a very rare orchid on Lesbos, is found here as well. Higher up along the trail we found the scarce Reinhold's Orchid. The forest is home to Bonelli's Warbler and, during passage, Wood Warbler. The many Robins and Song Thrushes emphasise the moist, temperate character of this site.

Route 5: From Ambeliko to Vatera

6 HOURS, 25 KM
EASY

Varied landscape with a diverse geology. Excellent for migrating birds in rather underwatched areas.

Habitats scrubland, olive groves, coastal wetland, dunes, rivers, rocky grassland
Selected species Pink Butterfly Orchid, Sea Daffodil, Monk Seal, Common Dolphin, Levant Sparrowhawk, Long-legged Buzzard, Masked Shrike, Black-eared Wheatear, Orphean Warbler, Olive-tree Warbler, Sombre Tit, Roller, Cory's and Yelkouan Shearwaters, Starred Agama, Epaulet Skimmer

The central-south part of Lesbos sports a diverse geology, from volcanic and calcareous rocks to river deposits. As is to be expected, this translates in a diverse landscape, with a rich flora and fauna. This is somewhat of a backwater, with small tranquil roads with many opportunities to stop and explore. This route combines a number of easy accessible sites, some of which are rather underwatched, hence offering the opportunity of a surprise or two.

Starting point Ambeliko

Getting there From Ambeliko, head 800 m south on the tarmac road, and turn right to a track signposted *Stavros* and *Vatera*.

ROUTE 5: AMBELIKO TO VATERA

1 The first stretch offers beautiful views over the valley with its mosaic of scrubland, olive groves and patches of pine forest. Stop at good viewpoints to scan the sky for migrating Levant Sparrowhawk, Short-toed Eagle, Long-legged Buzzard and Honey Buzzard. Any part of this 7 km dirt road can reveal interesting birds. The olive groves are home to Masked Shrike and Middle-spotted Woodpecker, while Woodchat and Red-backed Shrikes occur in the scrub. Keep an eye out for Starred Agama and Snake-eyed Skink on the rocks and old stone constructions along the way. There are plenty of snakes as well, although you have to search a little harder to find them. The scrublands by the hairpins on the last section of the track are good for birds like Sombre Tit and Olive-tree, Subalpine and Orphean Warblers. Along the whole stretch keep an eye out for orchids including Holy, Pink Butterfly, Province, Green-winged and Small-flowered Tongue Orchids.

Short-toed Eagle feeds on snakes and lizards and is frequently spotted hunting over hills with scrubland.

Further on, the track becomes a tarmac road. After the village of Kato Stavros, you cross a bridge and turn left, but before you continue don't forget to check the river for herons and waders (best in migration periods).

2 Along the road there are a few places to stop. Notice that the olive groves are carpeted with the pale yellow flowers of the endemic Lesbos Alison* (*Alyssum lesbiacum*) – it is a perfect giveaway that ultra basic ophiolitic rocks surfaces here locally (although not in such quantities to prevent the cultivation of olives). Scan the sky for migrant raptors following the valley.

3 Upon reaching the seaside, directly after the road bends right, turn left onto a track and park. Not many birdwatchers explore this area. Search the river mouth, the reedbeds, fields and dry grassland, all of which may hold a good number of migrants in both spring and autumn, particularly egrets, herons, waders and wagtails. In the woods and scrub near the river course, look for Golden Oriole, Roller and Bee-eater. In spring, migrant raptors arriving from the sea include Long-legged Buzzard and Marsh and Montagues Harriers. The ugly and, sadly, impossible-to-miss building is an unfinished hotel, a monument to the unfortunate building frenzy ('development') that has blighted some parts Greece and Turkey.

ROUTE 5: AMBELIKO TO VATERA

4 Continue the coastal road along the longest sandy beach of Lesbos. In places the dune vegetation is well developed with typical species like Sea Spurge, Sea Medick, Yellow Horned-poppy and – in summer and autumn – Sea Daffodil. Vatera and its beach is a favorite holiday destination in summer, as is evident from the bars and hotels along the road, but elsewhere, the sandy coastline is quite intact. The area is also known for another reason: 2 million years old fossils are found in the sedimentary rocks near Vatera (see page 16). Excavations revealed typical 'European' mammals for that time: giraffes, gazelles, rhinoceroses and mammoths! These finding can be seen in the nearby Natural History Museum of Vrisa, just north of Vatera.

Yellow Horned-poppy is a typical dune plant found on the beach of Vatera.

Continue along the coast, ignoring the righthand turns. After Vatera the tarmac road turns into a track. Park on the left at the bend.

5 Walk along the shore to the mouth of the river. Here a narrow pool has formed which is home to Balkan Terrapin, Tree Frog and Levant Water Frog, while Blue Chaser and Keeled and Epaulet Skimmers are the typical dragonflies. Keep an eye out too for Collared Pratincole which is sometimes seen here. During migration, the area near the seahore and reedbeds along the river may produce egrets, herons (including Little Bittern, Purple and Squacco Heron), wagtails, waders, and occasionally Little Crake.

Continue on foot along a path by the river to a bridge, from which you have a good view over the reedbeds. Don't forget to check the surrounding scrubland and fields, which may hold good numbers of birds, including Black-Eared Wheatear and Olive-tree Warbler, but like in many places on Lesbos anything can turn up! In spring notice the fields which are full with bright red poppies and many other 'weeds' of the fields.

PRACTICAL PART

ROUTE 5: AMBELIKO TO VATERA

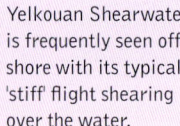

Yelkouan Shearwater is frequently seen offshore with its typical 'stiff' flight shearing over the water.

Retrace your steps and continue by car along the track, cross the bridge and turn left. Stay on main track and turn left at the junction. You pass a military base. At the headland the road bends sharply to the left. Park along the track just before the harbour.

6 Walk up the headland of Agios Fokas. The raised position makes this a good spot for scanning the sea for Cory's and Yelkouan Shearwaters, and checking for migrants coming in from the sea (including raptors, Black-headed Bunting and other passerines). You might spot some dolphins as well and, if you are very lucky, catch a glimpse of the rare Monk Seal, which is occasionally seen here.

Walk back along the same track you took by car, turning left at the junction and continuing by foot for about 2 km.

7 The scrubland is excellent for tracking down Sardinian Warbler and Black-eared Wheatear. The area consists locally of calcareous rocks, making this geological 'island' interesting for orchids. Look in the groves and road verges for Pink Butterfly, Holy, Green-winged, Pyramidal and Long-lipped Tongue Orchids. In early spring (March-April) you might spot members of the Dull Bee Orchid group.

Route 6: Gulf of Kalloni – along the eastern shore

4 HOURS, 10 KM
EASY

Scenic route, excellent for wetland, forest and migratory birds.
Prime location to spot Krüper's Nuthatch.
Variety of aquatic habitats with rich dragonfly fauna.

Habitats coastal wetland, pine forest, scrubland, cliffs, olive groves
Selected species Krüper's Nuthatch, Rock Nuthatch, Red-footed Falcon, Eleonora's Falcon, Ruddy Shelduck, Stone Curlew, Masked Shrike, Roller, Orphean Warbler, Balkan Terrapin, European Pond Terrapin, Dice Snake, Starred Agama, Small Skimmer, Odalisque, Eastern Spectre

This route combines many different habitats, ranging from coastal marshes and rocky terrain to closed pine forests with streams. Birds are the greatest draw of this route, with fine species like Krüper's Nuthatch, Masked Shrike and, during migration, Red-footed Falcon. In spring and even more so in autumn, there is a wide and daily changing range of migrants to be found along this route. But there is much more to discover. The dragonfly and reptile fauna is rich, and several orchids of pine forest can be found. This is a relaxed route with pleasant short strolls through woodlands and marshes.

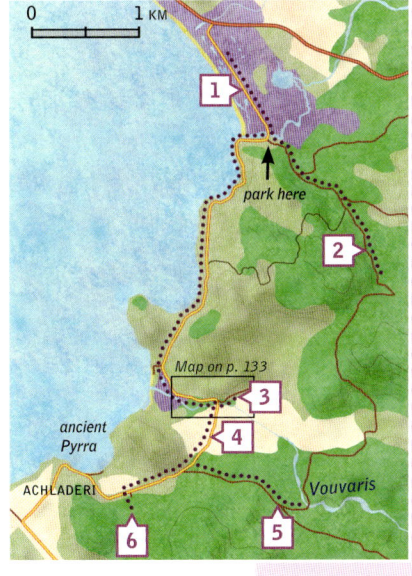

Starting point Mesa wetland on the Kalloni – Mytilini road

Getting there From the main Kalloni – Mytilini road, take the exit south, signposted *Achladeri* and *Polichnitos*. Although tempting, don't start birding straight away as this can be a busy road. Instead, park after 1 km on the left at a parking place at a bend, just beyond the bridge.

1 The best way to explore the wetland is to walk back in the direction from which you came. Along the way, keep an eye out for migrating

ROUTE 6: GULF OF KALLONI – ALONG THE EASTERN SHORE

Although water in saline wetlands is abundant, due to the high salt concentration it cannot be used by plants, hence creating a 'wet desert'. Only specially adapted plants can grow here, like glassworts. But for birds these places offer an abundance of food, attracting many passage migrants like these Black Storks.

Red-footed Falcons, which are common here in spring. They often occur in small flocks resting on fences, overhead wires and shrubs along the way. They are sometimes accompanied by other falcons like Hobby and Eleonora's Falcon. The pools in the saltpans may produce Ruddy Shelduck, Black Stork, herons, egrets, waders and Greater Flamingo. Stone Curlew breeds in the open salt flats but is remarkably well camouflaged. The obvious rocky hill on the right is home to Rock Nuthatch and Blue Rock Thrush – you'll need a telescope to see them well. Closer at hand, Snake-eyed Lizards are shooting away between the rocks at the side of the road.

2 Return, but instead of continuing by car, follow the track into the pine forest of Achladeri on foot. Along the way, keep an eye out for Krüper's Nuthatch which breeds here. The scrub and open patches in the forest are home to Nightjar, Woodlark, Orphean Warbler and Red-backed and Woodchat Shrikes. In autumn, the small but graceful orchid Autumn Lady's-tresses grows beneath the trees. In spring look for Violet Bird's-nest and Roman Orchids, both typical of pine forests. After about 3 km there is a military camp. Don't approach these premises too closely.

Retrace your steps and continue by car for 3 km. Park on the left in one of the small parking places just before a small bridge over the Vouvaris river (recognised by a yellow fence).

ROUTE 6: GULF OF KALLONI – ALONG THE EASTERN SHORE

3 The pines near the bridge are a classic site for Krüper's Nuthatch which come down here to forage. Its relative the Rock Nuthatch, together with Blue Rock Thrush, might also be spotted on the cliffs facing the wetland. If you approach the bridge slowly you'll be gazed at by dozens of curious Balkan Terrapins paddling leisurely in the river or resting on its muddy edge. The rare European Pond Terrapin occurs here too, but in very low numbers. Dice Snake might be spotted from the bridge.

Explore the banks of the Vouvaris river, both upstream and downstream towards the sea (see inset map). Keep an eye out for Kingfisher, which is rare on the island but is occasionally seen here. The slow-flowing water is perfect habitat for dragonflies and damselflies. Look for Eastern Willow Spreadwing, Blue-eye, Beautiful Demoiselle and Southern and Small Skimmers. The latter is basically an Asian species but not uncommon here. You might spot Starred Agama in dry and rocky places as well.

Southern Skimmer is widespread and common on Lesbos in coastal wetlands and along streams and rivers.

Return and continue by car.

4 You'll pass some colourful fields of poppies. This is another excellent site for birdwatching during migration periods. The hedges can be alive with all sorts of warblers and other passerines. In the trees around the fields and on the wire, we frequently spotted Rollers.

Continue. Beyond the fields you re-enter the forest, where the road gradually climbs. In a wide bend, turn left onto a track and park here without blocking the road.

5 Continue on foot. The track leads through another scenic part of Achladeri forest. Autumn Lady's-tresses grows here by the hundreds, while Violet Bird's-nest and Roman Orchids are in evidence in spring. Krüper's Nuthatch may be heard or seen here too.
After 1 km, a track branches off to the left and leads to a stream. This is another excellent spot for dragonflies and damselflies. Likely species are Keeled Skimmer, Small Pincertail, Green-eyed Hawker, Eastern Spectre, Odalisque and Beautiful and Banded Demoiselles.

ROUTE 6: GULF OF KALLONI – ALONG THE EASTERN SHORE

Achladeri forest is a reliable area for the delicate Autumn Lady's-tresses, especially after the first autumn's rains.

Return to the car and continue. After 1.3 km park at the picnic site on the left side of the road near a white building (drive down carefully, especially in a car with limited ground clearance!).

6 This is another very reliable location for seeing Krüper's Nuthatch and is well-known by birdwatchers. The scrubland holds Masked Shrike, Orphean Warbler, Lesser Grey Shrike, Cirl Bunting and Hoopoe. Scan for raptors like Long-legged Buzzard, Peregrine and Short-toed Eagle. The seafloor next to the opposite hill is the site of ancient Pyrra. Once it was the capital of one of the seven city states of Lesbos, but it was swallowed by the sea following an earthquake in 230 BC.

This site marks the end of this route. Time permitting, you can continue on the main road to connect with additional sites M and N.

The picnic site near Achladeri is a good place to see the sought-after Krüper's Nuthatch and Masked Shrike (see photo).

Route 7: Kalloni Saltpans

**3 - 5 HOURS, 4 KM
EASY**

Major arrival point for migratory birds.
A great diversity of both wet and dry habitats.

Habitats coastal wetland, fields, dry grassland, dunes, scrubland
Selected species Greater Flamingo, Audouin's Gull, Marsh Sandpiper, Temminck's Stint, Glossy Ibis, Collared Pratincole, Ruddy Shelduck, Stone Curlew, Tawny Pipit, Greater Short-toed Lark, Rufous Bush Robin, Red-footed Falcon, Grass Snake, Snake-eyed Lizard, Eastern Spadefoot, Dark Spreadwing

For birdwatchers the Kalloni saltpans are a real Mecca – brilliant, impressive and an absolute highlight. Spring is the main season. The area is the arrival point for most migrating birds from the south that enter the Gulf of Kalloni. In particular birds of wetlands and open dry habitats are plentiful. To make the most of this site, share sightings with fellow birdwatchers, plenty of whom will be around. Besides birds, this route supports a variety of wildflowers and reptiles.

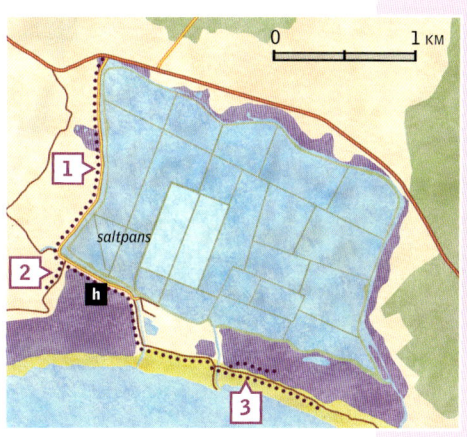

h = bird hide

Starting point Kalloni Saltpans

Getting there Take the main road from Kalloni to Mytilini. After 3.4 km, just before the canal, turn right onto a tarmac road that runs along the canal surrounding the saltpans (note this turn is easily missed).

1 The pool on the right and the canal on the left are very good for waders like Black-winged Stilt, Avocet, Ruff, Wood Sandpiper, and many others, including the occasional Marsh Sandpiper. The Greek and Turkish populations of Spur-winged Plovers are on the rise and this species is seen increasingly frequent at Kalloni.

ROUTE 7: KALLONI SALTPANS

Black-headed Bunting is a common migrant bird, easy to spot in the fields surrounding the saltpans.

A little further, the saltpans harbour egrets, herons and storks. Greater Flamingo occurs in good numbers in both spring and autumn. Whiskered, Little and Common Terns, sometimes joined by migrating Black and White-winged Terns, hunt above the saltpans. Audouin's Gull may be present as well. Directing your attention towards the other side of the track, perhaps encouraged by a passing harrier or by the songs of Corn and Black-headed Bunting and Zitting Cisticola, do take a moment to note the striking Oriental Iris, whose double-toned yellow flowers contrast beautifully with the green of the wet meadows (see page 69).

Continue along the main track along the channel. After the sharp bend to the left there is a building on the right with a good overview of the southern wetlands.

2 During migration, it is worth checking the sky regularly for birds arriving from the south. The fields in this area hold wagtails, Quail, Whinchat, Meadow Pipit, Corn Bunting and Crested Lark in addition to

Glossy Ibis is a star species found in the area of the saltpans of Kalloni.

CROSSBILL GUIDES • LESBOS

ROUTE 7: KALLONI SALTPANS

being a good hunting area for raptors like Red-footed Falcon. Check the electric wires for Woodchat Shrike and Black-headed Bunting. The seasonal pools on the right side past the raised bird hide may hold waders, egrets and herons.

Continue past the entrance to the saltworks. From the concrete bridge you have a good view over the area. Park 300 m further along the track and continue on foot.

3 Across the bridge you enter a diverse area with seasonal wetlands, dry grasslands and small dunes. In the dry areas you may find Stone Curlew, Red-throated (passage) and Tawny Pipits and Short-toed Lark. In late spring the sought-after Rufous Bush Robin is occasionally spotted in shrubby areas near the shore. Scan the seasonal pools, especially the wetter ones more distant from the bridge, for Glossy Ibis, Temminck's Stint, Collared Pratincole and Ruddy Shelduck and rarities like Great Snipe and Broad-billed Sandpiper. The rare Dark Spreadwing (a damselfly) is found here in the brackish pools. This area is also rewarding for reptiles and amphibians. The pools are home to Grass Snake and Eastern Spadefoot, while Snake-eyed Lizard and Caspian Whip Snake are found in the dry grassland. Many typical plants of dunes can be found here as well, including Spiny Knapweed, Hypecoum, Sea Rocket, Sea Stock, Sea Medick and, in autumn, Sea Daffodil. Notice the attractive Buttonweed along the edge of the seasonal pools, an invasive species from South Africa.

Beautiful drifts of Winged Sea-lavender washes the shores of the Gulf of Kalloni pink.

PRACTICAL PART

Route 8: Potamia Valley

3 - 4 HOURS, 7 KM
EASY

Excellent birdwatching and good reptile and dragonfly sites.

Habitats lakes, rivers, fields, scrubland, olive groves
Selected species Little Crake, Night Heron, Little Bittern, Little Grebe, Masked Shrike, Rock Nuthatch, Olive-tree Warbler, Long-legged Buzzard, European Pond and Balkan Terrapins, Grass and Dice Snakes, Turkish Clubtail

After the Kalloni saltpans, Metochi Lake is the most visited site by birdwatchers. The great attraction lies in the fact that many species can be seen up close, among them elusive beauties like Little Crake, Masked Shrike and Little Bittern. Nearby are a couple of other sites where reptiles and dragonflies and a number of other bird species can be seen with ease. This route connects all these sites. Being centrally located on the island and well connected by roads, this route is must for every first time visitor to Lesbos.

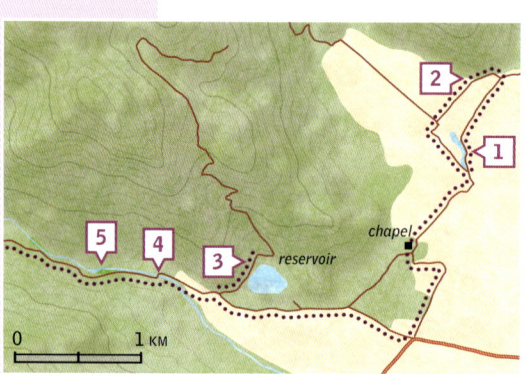

Starting point Metochi Lake

Getting there From Kalloni, take the main road west to Parakila. After 4 km turn right onto a track in a sharp left-hand bend. Immediately beyond, turn right onto a track signposted *Metochi*. At the fork, go left and turn right at the chapel. Just before a concrete bridge, you see a track to the left, signposted *Metochi*. Leave your car at a suitable place without blocking the road – it can be very busy here – and follow the signposted track to the east side of the lake.

1 This site is excellent – even the stretch towards the lake is productive. Little Bittern, crakes and herons can often be spotted in the water channel. They are accompanied by both European Pond (spotted

ROUTE 8: POTAMIA VALLEY

neck) and Balkan Terrapins (striped neck). Metochi Lake is one of the few places on Lesbos where they are found together. Tree Frog occurs too. A bit further on you arrive at the lake. Check the margins for crakes, Night Heron, Little Bittern, Little Grebe and Marsh, Great Reed and Cetti's Warblers. This is one of the few spots where Little Crake can reliably be seen. Note the many swifts, swallows and martins wheeling above the water. In autumn the water level is usually lower, producing good habitat for waders like Green Sandpiper, Kentish and Little Ringed Plover. As always scan the sky for raptors – this site lies on the main migration route over the island. Typical dragonflies along the lake shore are Blue Chaser, Green-eyed Hawker and Violet Dropwing. The males of the latter have a striking violet hue and characteristic red veins. It flies in the second half of spring.

2 On the east side of the lake you can take a 2 km circular hike. Follow the track through olive groves, which are excellent to spot Persian Squirrel and Masked Shrike. After 600 m turn left onto a track parallel to a rocky slope with scrubland. Rock Nuthatch and Blue Rock Thrush occur here, sharing their habitat with Starred Agama and Snake-eyed Lizard. Continue through the fields, keeping an eye out for shrikes and buntings. Oriental Iris grows on the wet places along the track. Turn left at the T-junction and take the first track left along a water channel, where you might find Little Crake.

Return to the car and drive back to the junction with the main road. Just before the junction, turn right onto a track. Two side tracks branch off to the right. Park at the second and follow it to a reservoir.

Little Bitterns roost along the vegetated shores of Metochi Lake and the water channels (top). Red-backed Shrike (bottom) is found in the surrounding fields.

PRACTICAL PART

ROUTE 8: POTAMIA VALLEY

3 The reservoir itself is not a pretty sight, but may hold some species of interest, like Little Grebe. Scan the scrubland for Sombre Tit, Subalpine Warbler and shrikes.

Return and continue, either by car or foot, to the bridge some 500 m further on.

4 From the bridge, Balkan Terrapin, Grass and Dice Snakes are easily observed in the river. Look for Levant Water Frog in the puddles near the river. Tree Frogs are harder to spot as they hide in the river bank vegetation. Explore the tracks either side of the river. The olive groves here are a good location for the rare Olive-tree Warbler, as well as Masked Shrike and Middle-spotted Woodpecker, while Long-legged Buzzard and Honey Buzzard may pass overhead. In late April, notice the yellow 'ribbons' running down the slope on the left – these are actually streams lined with colonies of the Pontic Azalea (see also site T).

5 500 m beyond the bridge you come across some pools, which are good for dragonflies. Look for Turkish Clubtail, Small and Southern Skimmers, Small Pincertail, Broad Scarlet and Banded Demoiselle.

The beautiful valley is worth exploring more thoroughly by foot (the track is rather rough for a normal vehicle), where many of the aforementioned species can be seen.

From the bridge in Potamia river valley you might witness a rare interaction between Balkan Terrapin and Dice Snake, both require convenient basking spots on the rocks in the river.

Route 9: Palios

4 HOURS, 7 KM
EASY

Man-made pools with rare aquatic wildflowers, amphibians and dragonflies.
Archeological site in a remote part of Lesbos.

Habitats pools, scrubland, rocky grassland, pine forest, coastal wetland, dunes
Selected species Yellow Centaury, Eastern Tongue, Roman, Pink Butterfly Orchids, Ruddy Shelduck, Rufous Bush Robin, Cretzschmar's Bunting, Black-eared Wheatear, Masked Shrike, Eastern Spadefoot, Tree Frog, Dice and Grass Snakes, Mediterranean Skipper, Small Spreadwing, Dainty Bluet

During the medieval ages the remote hamlet of Palios was a city and an important port for Christian pilgrims. Today, the remains of the castle, the ancient tombs and the hamlet itself have been almost forgotten. Yet this sleepy backwater forms the backdrop of a great wildlife route – one that is in landscape, history, flora and fauna very unlike any other on the island. This route brings you to man-made pools, dunes and coastal wetlands which are, above all, rich in plants and reptiles. This route will delight the naturalist who likes to go out and discover new things in underwatched sites.

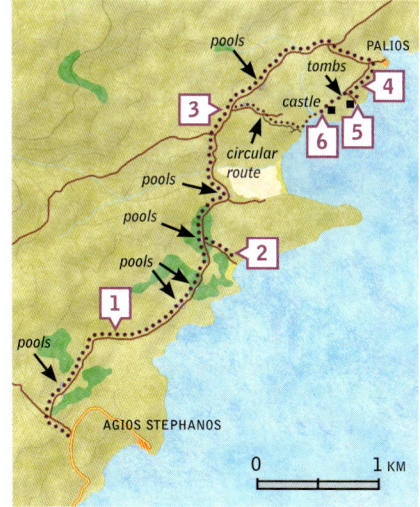

Starting point Agios Stephanos

Getting there From Mandamados, take the main road south to Mytilini and after 5 km turn left to Agios Stephanos. Continue through the southern part of the village. Beyond where the road turns away from the coast, go left onto a track signposted Palios. Then take the first signposted track to the right. On your way, just before the first bridge after turning off the main road the rare Loose-flowered Orchid grows in a meadow.

ROUTE 9: PALIOS

The clay pits near Palios constitute a unique habitat on Lesbos (top). Here the tiny Yellow Centaury is found, at the southern limit of its distribution range.

1 Along the track you'll find various pools, which are the result of clay extraction for the making of pottery – the local craft of the village of Agios Stephanos. Volcanic clay in itself is a very rare soil type on Lesbos, and clay pits with permanent, standing and nutrient-rich water are restricted to this area. This habitat hosts some plant species that are very rare in the region, but are familiar in such habitats in western Europe. We are referring to the diminutive Yellow Centaury, Grass-poly, Small Pillwort and Coral-necklace – all 'dwarfs' that have high and peculiar demands on their environment. No doubt dedicated botanists will find some more small treasures here! On the higher ground between the pools a good collection of orchids is to be found, including Small-flowered Tongue, Long-lipped Tongue and Eastern Tongue Orchids. It's not only the flora that makes these pools a great place for naturalists. Dice and Grass Snakes and Balkan Terrapin are found here and there are a number of interesting dragonflies including Small Spreadwing, Vagrant Emperor and Dainty Bluet. Cretzschmar's Bunting, Subalpine Warbler and Black-eared Wheatear breed in the scrub.

ROUTE 9: PALIOS

After 2.2 km along this track, park at a pool on the left near a clearly visible sign *Ancient tombs 3 km*. On the right side of the road, step over the wall where a track leads to the coast.

2 Along the track in the grassy areas look for Small-flowered Tongue, Pink Butterfly and Green-winged Orchids. Roman Orchid is found mainly underneath the pine trees. Close to the shore, you reach a small area with dunes, where there are Tree Medicks. Search the area for European Glass Lizard and Three-lined Lizard.

Return to the car and continue along the route, ignoring side tracks to the sea.

3 There are more pools, also with a rich flora, along this stretch. Ruddy Shelduck breeds in the area and is often seen near the pools. Look in the vegetation for Tree Frog. The secretive Eastern Spadefoot spawns in the pools – its tadpoles can be seen in the water, but the adults usually have dug themselves deep into the ground.

The track to Palios is a reliable area to see Ruddy Shelducks. Sometimes you encounter them at close range.

After another 2.4 km beyond point 2, take the turn to the right to the ancient tombs. Take the first track to the right and after 330 m, park near a house.

4 You've now reached the historic port of Palios, used by Christian pilgrims arriving on boats from Asia Minor, to visit the Taxiarchis monastery in Mandamados. To protect the port, a large castle was built. The archaeological significance of the site is also clear from the ancient Hellenistic tombs, dating from the 2nd century BC, carved into the rocks.

There are two tracks to explore. The one to the left (130 m) leads to the ancient tombs and then to the sea, while the one that goes straight on (270 metres), passes by the ancient castle and then continues to the sea.

5 The track left to the sea shore offers good bird-watching, including the wonderful Rufous Bush Robin (from early May onwards). Other species

PRACTICAL PART

ROUTE 9: PALIOS

of interest are Cretzschmar's Bunting, Black-eared Wheatear, Sardinian and Orphean Warblers, Crested Lark and Woodchat Shrike. From the beach look for Shag. There are interesting orchids in the scrubland too, such as Bug, Holy, Pink Butterfly and Milky Orchids (the latter two flower early in spring). Beside interesting nature, you can find here ancient tombs carved in the rocks.

6 The track that goes straight on turns into a path along a stone wall along the fundaments of the old castle. While in ancient time the fortifications kept intruders out, today they enclose olive groves, where Masked Shrike breeds. The path ends at a scenic beach with a small lagoon, where Balkan Terrapin and Levant Water Frog occur. Close to the sea look for the Mediterranean Skipper, one of the few butterflies in Europe that is strictly tied to the coast.

Alternatively, you can cross the lagoon on your right side at a wading place with rocks. Walk 150 m along the beach and find a track near a shed that leads to the main track, turn right to make a circular route (3 km; see map).

Eastern Tongue Orchid grows abundantly in the grassy spots around the clay pits. Another location to see drifts of this species is in the olive groves along the road between Skopelos and Tarti (site H).

Route 10: The north slopes of Mount Lepetimnos

FULL DAY, 25 KM
EASY

Excellent route for scrubland birds.
Beautiful scenery and interesting sites for all naturalists.

Habitats scrubland, oak woodland, oriental plane forest, streams, olive groves
Selected species Persian Squirrel, Black-eared Wheatear, Rüppell's, Orphean and Barred Warblers, Great Spotted Cuckoo, Cretzschmar's Bunting, Lesser Grey Shrike, Sombre Tit, Eleonora's Falcon, Dahl's Whip Snake, Dwarf Snake, Kotschy's Gecko, Dainty Bluet, Turkish Goldenring, Eastern Spectre

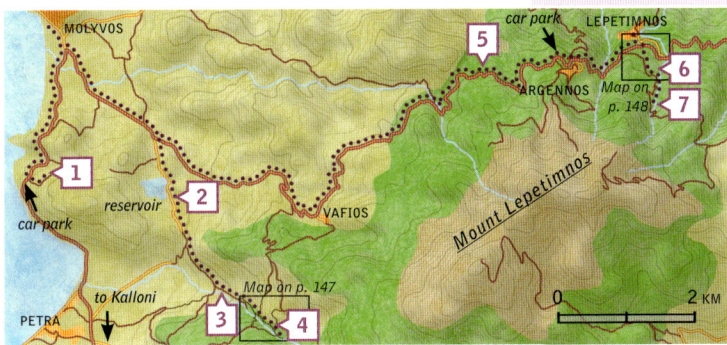

This route brings you along the scenic northern slopes of Mount Lepetimnos, a profound landmark in northern Lesbos, covered in scrubland and lush oak woodland boasting a rich birdlife, with highlights like Rüppell's Warbler and Great Spotted Cuckoo. Various short and scenic strolls enable you to explore the rich insect and reptilian life. The Ligonas valley with its age-old Oriental Plane trees is a secluded spot. Its 18 ancient watermills and, further along, the remains of an abandoned village, add a historic note. All in all it is a very diverse route which can be combined with route 11 to make a long loop, although covering every single stop, would be too much for a single day.

Starting point Molyvos

Getting there Leave town in direction Kalloni and after 2.5 km, park at the car park in a wide bend.

ROUTE 10: THE NORTH SLOPES OF MOUNT LEPETIMNOS

View to the maquis scrubland and Aegean Sea just south of Molyvos (top). Eastern Baton Blue is a frequent butterfly in flowery scrubland (bottom).

1 The scrubland in this area is the best on the island for the rare and sought-after Rüppell's Warbler. Other ornithological attractions are Black-eared Wheatear, Barred, Subalpine and Orphean Warblers, Cretzschmar's and Cirl Buntings plus, on the coastal rocks, Blue Rock Thrush. But it is not just birds that make this an attractive site! Cross the road and walk up the track that leads up the hill to the north. There are plenty of reptiles here, including Glass Lizard and Snake-eyed Lizard. Visitors in May will enjoy Holy Orchid and Long-lipped Tongue Orchid, and many butterflies, of which Eastern Festoon, Persian Meadow Brown, Eastern Baton Blue and Levantine Skipper are just a few highlights.

Return to Molyvos and just before entering town, turn right to Vafios. After 2 km, turn right. After 550 m, park on the right side of road, next to the reservoir.

2 The reservoir (Limno Dexameni) is another birdwatching hotspot that may reveal a much wanted bird: the Great Spotted Cuckoo. Take your time to find it, often it moves between the stream bed and the cliffs on the left side. Other birds of interest include Black-eared Wheatear, Orphean, Subalpine and Sardinian Warblers, which concentrate in the scrubland left of the road. Check the rocky areas for Rock Nuthatch while the wooded streambed on the right is a haunt of Lesser Grey Shrike and Sombre Tit. The steep reservoir sides are hardly attractive, but that doesn't deter the

ROUTE 10: THE NORTH SLOPES OF MOUNT LEPETIMNOS

Squacco Herons and Ruddy Shelducks, which are very visible here. This site too is not only a birders delight. Dainty Bluet and Lesser Emperor occur in the reservoir and rest on the wooden fence along the road. The flowering Oregano draws butterflies like Persian and Oriental Meadow Browns, Hungarian and Oriental Marbled Skippers and Balkan Marbled White, all of which are common. Grassy sites are home to the graceful Grecian Streamertail (a kind of *Neuroptera*, or net-winged insect) and a wealth of grasshoppers and spiders. Expect a score of reptiles of which Three-lined, Glass and Snake-eyed Lizards, Starred Agama and Caspian Whip and Montpellier Snakes are frequent.

Continue on foot along tarmac road, which turns into a track a little ahead, marked with red diamonds.

3 This is a lovely walk through rocky grassland, scrubland and olive groves. It leads into the beautiful Ligonas valley. Persian Squirrel is found in the olive groves and oak woodland. Along the way you pass small pools with Balkan Terrapin and Bedriaga's Marsh Frog. All the afore-mentioned birds may be seen here, in addition to Chukar, which is more often heard than seen.

4 In the valley you find the ruins of 18 watermills that date back to the 19th century. The permanent running water from springs on the slopes of Mount Lepetimnos drove these mills to grind wheat. Follow the signs *Upper Ligona – spring*. At the end of the valley, after a roughly 2.5 km walk, you reach the springs with a wonderful oriental plane forest. Explore the area, the streamside may produce some Dice Snakes and damselflies like Odalisques.
Along the damp path grows Loose-flowered Orchid. Red-rumped Swallows and Crag Martins wheel around the ruins, while Rock Nuthatch is found along the cliffs. Any rocky place offers a good chance to find Snake-eyed Lizard, Worm Snake and Starred Agama. It is possible to make a circular route through the valley (see map).

Retrace your steps and drive to the main road. Turn right, direction *Vafios*.

5 You drive along the oak and scrub covered northern slopes of Mount Lepetimnos. At a bend, just before the exit to Argennos, there is a parking place with a viewpoint. This is a good spot to observe raptor migration, especially in autumn when Eleonora's Falcon, Long-legged Buzzard,

PRACTICAL PART

ROUTE 10: THE NORTH SLOPES OF MOUNT LEPETIMNOS

Short-toed Eagle and Honey Buzzard may drift by. Spring is the better period for passerine migration (including Masked and Woodchat Shrike, Roller, Bea-eater, Spotted Flycatcher and a variety of warblers).

Continue for another 2.2 km and turn left to the village Lepetimnos. Park somewhere along the road in the village and walk back to find the start of a trail right before the first house of the village. It is marked with a yellow hiker symbol and signposted ΧΑΛΙΚΑΣ. Follow the trail as shown on the map.

6 Historically, the ruined and abandoned village of Chalikas, destroyed during an earthquake in 1968, is a curious site. The entire population was moved to Lepetimnos which was constructed to house the villagers.

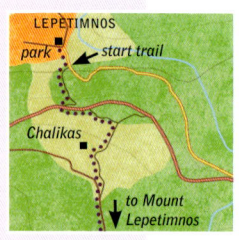

Chalikas is a peculiar place, with many old *kaldarimi*, passages and buildings. Chalikas is a good site to search for snakes (best by turning stones, but also by simply approaching sunny, rocky places carefully and scan them with your binoculars. They may just lie there soaking up the sunshine). Starred Agamas are common and frequently seen on the walls, while Spur-thighed Tortoises rustle along in the bushes. Botanically, the local curiosity is the joint pine *Ephedra nebrodensis*, a rare plant of rocky places with distinctive red berries. Holy and Small-flowered Tongue Orchids are also present. This is a good place for a break. In autumn, enjoy the fresh fruits from the abundant fig and pomegranate trees.

Continue uphill. At the stone tap turn left and continue until you reach a track where you turn left.

7 After 550 m (on the left side, just past the hairpin bend) you reach the chapel of Agia Anna, a scenic place with a stream and some very old, massive Oriental Plane trees. The track and stream running alongside it hosts a great dragonfly fauna, with 'goodies' like Turkish Goldenring, Eastern Spectre and Odalisque. In spring and summer the songs of Golden Oriole and Nightingale complete the paradisiacal atmosphere of the valley.

Continue uphill and you come across even more impressive Oriental Plane trees that may as well function as the end point of the route (although the energetic could continue up the trail which eventually brings you all the way to the top of Mount Lepetimnos).

Retrace to your car and drive back to Molyvos.

Route 11: Skala Sikaminia to Eftalou

4 HOURS, 10 KM
EASY

Stunning coastal scenery.
Excellent for migrating birds.

Habitats scrubland, cliffs, rocky grassland, fields
Selected species Striped Dolphin, Orphean Warbler, Cretzschmar's Bunting, Black-headed Bunting, Rock Nuthatch, Chukar, Short-toed Eagle, Honey Buzzard, Levant Sparrowhawk, Booted Eagle, Eleonora's Falcon, Yelkouan and Cory's Shearwaters, Shag, Sand Boa, Mediterranean Skipper, Levantine Skipper

This route takes you along a track beside the northern coastline of Lesbos with beautiful views over the sea and the Turkish coast. Besides stunning scenery, there are a whole range of migrating birds easily encountered in autumn and spring. All this is supplemented by side shows of butterflies, flowers and reptiles. Note that this route is popular with naturalists (particularly birdwatchers). This is a relatively short route with ample places to stop and explore. It could be combined with route 10 to make an excellent if rather long route.

Starting point Skala Sikaminia

Getting there From Molyvos take the main road to Mandamados and turn left to Skala Sikaminia. As you enter Skala Sikaminia, turn left at the square leading to a track along the coast.

PRACTICAL PART

ROUTE 11: SKALA SIKAMINIA TO EFTALOU

1 Roughly the first 3 km passes through tall and dense maquis with occasional gaps. Such open areas are flowery with butterflies including Cleopatra, Southern White Admiral and Hungarian Skipper.

As you enter an open area of fields, rocks and scrubland, stop near a couple of houses and follow on foot the short loop shown in the map.

2 The maquis birdlife consists of Sardinian, Subalpine and Olivaceous Warblers and Woodchat Shrike, with, in rocky sites, Black-eared Wheatear. The fields and farms are the haunt of Red-rumped Swallow and Spanish Sparrow.

Back on the coastal track, turn left for an interesting geological phenomenon. About 150 m, there is a series of hot springs on the shoreline, roughly where the valley narrows. The springs are invisible, but with your hand you can feel their warmth on the wet stones on the shore.

Return to your car and continue the track which now starts to climb. After 1.6 km, park along the track at a hairpin bend in a valley.

The valleys along the track are excellent places to look for butterflies, with species like Mediterranean Skipper (top) and Hungarian Skipper (centre).

ROUTE 11: SKALA SIKAMINIA TO EFTALOU

3 This valley, where the stream only carries water in winter and early spring, is a 'migrant trap'. During migration, Subalpine and Orphean Warblers and Cretzschmar's Bunting come down here to find shelter, joined by parties of Black-headed Buntings and Bee-eaters. Keep an eye out for Rock Nuthatch and Chukar, which are residents. Besides birds, butterflies are abundant too. To name a few: Lesser Spotted Fritillary, Scarce Swallowtail, Mediterranean and Levantine Skippers, Persian and Turkish Meadow Brown, and even the locally rare Amanda's Blue. Search the rocks for typical flora of cliff coasts. We found here Curry Plant, Senecio bicolor, and the scarce Fringed Rue, a peculiar plant of the citrus family.

4 The valley signals the start of a series of perpendicular valleys along the track, which are all very good for migrating birds. While the bushes in the valley should be checked for migrating warblers and flycatchers, scan the sky for Long-legged Buzzard, Short-toed Eagle, Honey Buzzard and Peregrine, which may well be kept company by a Levant Sparrowhawk, Booted Eagle or Eleonora's Falcon. Lines of tall trees around the fields in this last stretch may attract Bee-eater, Hoopoe or shrikes (including Masked Shrike). The gullies on your way support the typical Lesbos reptile life, so keep an eye open for Sand Boa and Caspian Whip and Montpellier Snakes. Sightings here are, as anywhere, far from guaranteed, but you stand a realistic chance!

On calm days you might spot dolphins, like this Common Dolphin, leaping out of the water.

5 Take advantage of good views for seawatching along the way. Cory's and Yelkouan Shearwaters are frequent over the sea, while Shag and Audouin's Gull may be present on the coast. Keep an eye out for dolphins, which are sometimes seen here as well.

!
Drive carefully, steep track section

After a steep drop down to the seashore, you pass the picturesque location of the hot water springs of Eftalou, built in the rocks. Although not the best on the island, you can take a revitalizing bath here.

PRACTICAL PART

Route 12: Lafionas

3 HOURS, 5 KM
EASY

Archeological site, splendid views and a rich flora and fauna. Circular route, perfect for a tranquil exploration of scrub and rocky grassland.

Habitats scrubland, pine forest, cliffs, meadows, rocky grassland
Selected species Loose-flowered and Long-lipped Tongue Orchids, Sardinian Warbler, Blue Rock Thrush, Cretzschmar's Bunting, Dahl's Whip Snake, Ottoman Viper, Dwarf Snake, Worm Snake, Southern Swallowtail

This is a short and leisurely walk taking you around the hill *Roudi* with its mixture of pine forest and rocky habitats. A good collection of reptiles lurk beneath the bushes and rocks. There are also some interesting birds. On your way you'll come across a peaceful spot with religious architectural remains of different periods, such as an early Christian church, a 4th century Byzantine monastery and a mosque.

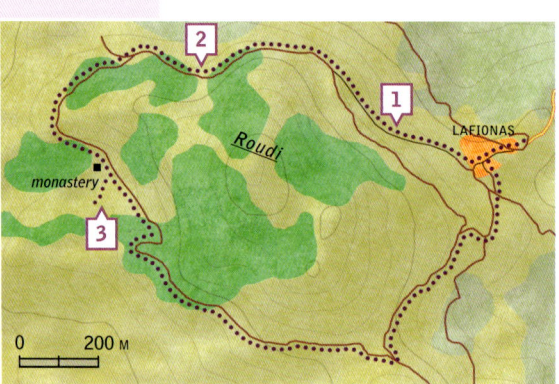

Starting point Lafionas

Getting there Park at the entrance of the village, and walk up the cobbled street. From the square at the entrance of the village, take the lefthand street and subsequently turn left into an alley. Continue straight on – ignoring side streets – and after 130 m, turn left at the tap. Continue uphill and turn right to a concrete road which becomes a *kalderimi*.

1 The first stretch of the trail passes through higher maquis with Kermes Oak shrubs and isolated Valonia Oak trees. At the crossing near the chapel, explore the rocky grassland for Worm Snake, Snake-eyed lizard, Dahl's Whip Snake. Also check the cliffs above you for raptors and Blue Rock Thrush.

CROSSBILL GUIDES • LESBOS

ROUTE 12: LAFIONAS

2 Turn left onto a track which soon leads through a cool Turkish pine forest, with, in the undergrowth, Violet Bird's-nest Orchid. To your right you have a splendid view over the Aegean Sea and, at the shore, the village of Petra. Notice its church on a raised rocky platform, which is the remains of a series of lava chambers. Comprised of harder rock, it persisted while the surrounding rocks eroded away. Soon afterwards the pines give way to an open landscape with scrubland and patches of oak woodland. Keep an eye out for Woochat and Red-backed Shrikes, Middle-spotted Woodpecker, Sardinian and Subalpine Warblers, Black-eared Wheatear and, in the more rocky parts, Cretzschmar's Bunting.

3 Continue for 1 km until you reach the remains of the monastery of the first bishop of Lesbos, Agios Alexandros. In spring, the damp meadow and the patches near oak trees and Oriental Planes are great for wildflowers. Look for Loose-flowered, Long-lipped Tongue and Holy Orchids. Butterflies profit from the abundance of flowers. Hence, this is a good spot for Southern Swallowtail, Amanda's Blue, Eastern Baton Blue, Eastern Dappled White and Knapweed Fritillary.

The handsome Cretzschmar's Bunting is a typical bird of scrubland in the western and northern part of the island. Its good looks and limited distribution makes it a top target for birdwatchers.

The edges of the woodland, especially the parts with stone walls, are likely areas for Ottoman Viper and Dwarf Snake. Keep your eyes open for Starred Agama and Snake-eyed Skink, darting away to seek shelter.

Southern Swallowtail is a rare butterfly on the island that may turn up in the flowery patches around the remains of the monastery.

Continue on the main track through pine forest and at the T-junction, turn left back to Lafionas.

PRACTICAL PART

Route 13: Voulgaris river valley and northwest coast

7 HOURS, 25 KM
EASY

Beautiful river valley with many birds and dragonflies. Unspoilt dune ecosystem with rich flora.

Habitats scrubland, cliffs, dunes, oriental plane forest, river, fields, oak woodland
Selected species Oriental Iris, Sea Stock, Sea Spurge, Monk Seal, Common Dolphin, Bottlenose Dolphin, Audouin's Gull, Blue Rock-thrush, Rock Nuthatch, Rock Sparrow, Masked Shrike, Short-toed Eagle, Turkish Clubtail, Southern Skimmer, Small Skimmer, Dark Spreadwing, Mediterranean Skipper

This route connects various sites within the catchment of the Voulgaris river. Although the distance between them is short, these sites vary greatly from one another. Along this route, you'll enjoy shrub-covered hillsides, cliffs, brooks, riparian marsh, fields and dunes. The coast of Kambos is an excellent example of a Mediterranean dune ecosystem, where you can encounter the flora associated with this habitat. The route ends at the picturesque archaeological site of Ancient Andissa, from where you may see marine mammals.

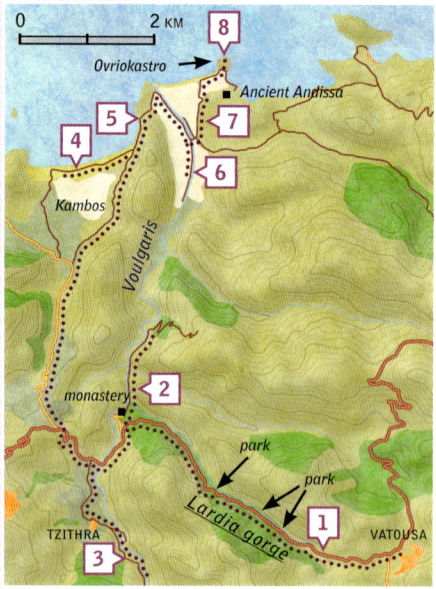

Starting point Vatousa

Getting there Leave the village in the direction Andissa and after 2 km, park at a large car park on the right side of the road, from where cliffs are clearly visible in front of you.

1 This is the first of several spots to park and scan the crags and cliffs. The 2 km long Lardia gorge is a good site for birds of cliffs and rocks, especially in the morning. Look for Blue Rock Thrush, Rock Nuthatch, Crag Martin and Rock Sparrow.

ROUTE 13: VOULGARIS RIVER VALLEY AND NORTHWEST COAST

The scrubland and oak woodland in the valley is home to Subalpine Warbler and Masked Shrike, while Short-toed Eagle, Long-legged Buzzard and Peregrine may pass by in front of the cliffs.

Continue and after 2 km, turn right signposted *Perivoli Monastery*. Park on the shady car park of the monastery.

2 Walk the track down to the river, and follow it downstream along its banks. Apart from being an idyllic stroll, you have a good chance of spotting Masked Shrike in the olive groves. Golden Oriole and Nightingale occur in the riverside trees. The pool near the building opposite the monastery holds many Bedriaga's Marsh Frogs.

Return to the main road, and turn right and 180 m after a bridge, turn left onto a track signposted *Jithra*. Leave your car at a parking spot at the bend just before the village and continue on foot on the left track, leading into the village.

3 Tzithra is a peaceful and idyllic village on the slopes of the beautiful Voulgaris valley. On your way, several tracks to the left lead down to the river. Turn left 200 m beyond the village to reach the river whose banks are clad with Oriental Plane trees. Explore the area which is very good for dragonflies like Turkish Clubtail, Southern and Small Skimmers and Banded and Beautiful Demoiselles. On the cliffs, Blue Rock Thrush

The scenic Voulgaris river valley north of Perivoli Monastery (top). Notice how the river carved the volcanic rock layers. The steep slopes form a sharp contrast with the flat floodplain. We found the rare Turkish Clubtail (bottom), a typical dragonfly of these middle and lower sections of rivers, here.

PRACTICAL PART

ROUTE 13: VOULGARIS RIVER VALLEY AND NORTHWEST COAST

and Rock Nuthatch breed, while raptors soar overhead. It is worth exploring the valley a bit further as it is little visited and may hold some surprises. The track leads all the way south to Chidira (4 km).

Sea Daffodil grows on beaches and in dunes. Unlike what might be expected due to the close proximity of the sea, the salt content of dunes is very low, because the salt carried by wind is easily washed away by rain. The real challenge for plants here is to cope with drought, because sand grains do not retain water.

Return to Tzithra and drive back to the main road. Turn left and after 1 km, go right towards Gavathas. In a wide bend just beyond the exit to a mine, turn right onto a track signposted *Beach Kambos* and *Ancient Andissa*. Continue this track that overlooks Kambos, its fields (with the bright white-yellow flowers of Oriental Iris) and eventually the dunes. Park at the seaside near the gazebo and go down the track to the sea.

4 This is an excellent area of unspoilt dunes, perhaps the best on the island. Take your time to stroll around. Botanists will enjoy the likes of Sea Rocket, Sea Stock, Sea Spurge, Sea Medick, Cottonweed, Dune Galingale and – in summer – Sea Daffodil. The insect life is superb too, with several species of praying mantises and the rare Mediterranean Skipper. Flocks of Audouin's gull roost along the seashore, while Black-headed Bunting, Olivaceous and Sardinian Warblers are found in the shrubby areas. And while you're here, why deny yourself a dip in that paradisical azure Aegean sea?

5 Return to the car and continue the track that rounds a coastal cliff, where Curry Plant and the sand crocus *Romulea linaresii* grow.

CROSSBILL GUIDES • LESBOS

ROUTE 13: VOULGARIS RIVER VALLEY AND NORTHWEST COAST

6 The track leads along the lower reach of Voulgaris river, which is quite wide here. It has a distinct temperate European feel, with willows, Purple Loosestrife and, in the water, Threadleaf Crowfoot. There are many marshy patches and pools with standing water. The birdlife is rich here, with Sand Martin, Ruddy Shelduck, Little Bittern, Purple Heron, Night Heron and Little Egret. Although, as views of the open water are not easy, they may remain hidden. The noisy Cetti's and Great Reed Warblers sing from the vegetation. In the fields in the valley, keep an eye out for Roller, Bee-eater and Red-backed Shrike. The area is also home to Balkan Terrapin and a population of the rare Dark Spreadwing (a damselfly), which prefers densely vegetated coastal wetlands. This is probably just the tip of the iceberg, so explore!

A small bird's nightmare: the very sticky Common Leadwort.

There is a spot where the track crosses the river (you can usually ford the river in spring, in autumn the riverbed is dry). On the other side, take the 2nd turn left which brings you to the sea (the first follows the east bank of the river).

7 On both sides of the track you pass through fields where Oriental Iris grows, while Winged Sea-lavender is common close to the sea. At the beach, you pass a taverna.

8 The beach ends at a raised headland – in classical times a small island – with a trail signposted *Ovriokastro*. Follow the trail (rough underfoot!) to the remains of this medieval Genovese castle. The scattered boulders are the only testimony of the citadel, which was built upon the much older city of Ancient Andissa, one of the seven city states of Lesbos which enjoyed their golden age between the 8th and 2nd centuries BC. The only remaining element of this oldest period is the breakwater of the ancient port which lies, just below the water, on the east side of the headland. In summer and autumn notice the abundant pink flowered Common Leadwort, a rarity. Its very sticky fruits and flowers pose a threat to small birds, as they glue together their feathers.

Scramble your way up the headland and enjoy the beautiful views (especially at sunset). Keep an eye out over the sea for dolphins and the very rare Monk Seal. The area holds a few underwater caves where it is known to seek refuge.

PRACTICAL PART

ROUTE 14: LIOTA

Route 14: Liota

6 HOURS, 18KM
EASY

Two lovely short walks through well developed old oak woodland and scrubland.
Best orchid sites in western Lesbos.

Habitats scrubland, oak woodland, olive groves, fields
Selected species Lesbos Orchid*, Lady Orchid, Monkey Orchid, Bull-headed Orchid, Horned Orchid, Rainbow Orchid, Lesbos Fritillary*, Olive-tree Warbler, Cretzschmar's Bunting, Black-eared Wheatear, Cat Snake, Ottoman Viper, Snake-eyed Lizard, Snake-eyed Skink, European Glass Lizard

Tucked away in the hills of the northwest, the calcareous hills around Liota offer an excellent opportunity for a long walk on which orchids and reptiles can be found with relative ease. The area comprises some stands of old oak woodland which comes close to the Arcadian vegetation of ancient Greece, and has become rare elsewhere on the island. Among the many attractive wildflowers on the walk, one species in particular stands out: the near endemic Lesbos Orchid* (*Ophrys lesbis*), which grows here in an unique geological setting: the area is an island of limestones amidst the volcanic rock of west Lesbos.

Starting point Liota

Getting there From the main Molyvos–Sigri road, take the exit to Gavathas. After 4 km turn left and drive up to Liota. At the entrance of the village, turn right and park at the taverna with a beautiful old plane tree. Walk back to the junction and follow the tarmac road signposted *Lapsarna Beach*. After 700 m, turn left onto a track.

CROSSBILL GUIDES • LESBOS

ROUTE 14: LIOTA

1 At the entrance of the village, look for Bee-eater which breeds in the area. You walk through oak woodland and scrub, where Olivaceous Warbler and Sombre Tit occur, perhaps even joined by the rare Olive-tree Warbler. In the open rocky parts, Cretzschmar's Bunting and Black-eared Wheatear are found.
Ignore the fenced-off area and turn to the left. At the bend you'll encounter the first Monkey Orchids along the track (rare on Lesbos!).

2 Some 200 m further, you reach a steep river valley with oak woodland and olive trees. This place is a delight for botanists. Explore the sidetracks leading down the slope, where an abundance of small-flowered Horned Orchids draws attention. Several different species occur here – just how many depends on which orchid book you use. The size of the 'horns' on the side of the lip is the easiest differentiator – Horned Orchid sports two impressive horns, whereas the Small Horned Orchid has to make do with rather smaller equipment. A stroll through the olive grove will also reveal Rainbow, Bull-headed, Monkey and Pyramidal Orchids, while Narrow-leaved Helleborine is found in the oak woodland closer to the stream. The calcareous rocks supports here a rich flora in general. Besides orchids, Yellow-wort, Lesbos Fritillary* (*Fritillaria theophrasti*), Peacock Anemone, Drooping Star-of-Bethlehem and a score of other wildflowers can be found.

Monkey Orchid is generally rare on the island, but not in the area of Liota. It flowers in April.

Continue on the main track down to Liota. From Liota, drive back to the main Molyvos-Sigri road and turn right. On your way notice the dreadful marble mine, eating its way into orchid habitat.
Just beyond Andissa, after a wide bend, turn right onto a tarmac road signposted *Lapsarna Beach*. It soon becomes a track. After 700 m, park along the road just past a bend and a side track, follow the track on foot.

PRACTICAL PART

ROUTE 14: LIOTA

3 Spring visitors will have little trouble finding Monkey Orchid on the righthand side of the track, in the first section of the trail. A little further down on the first bend you may find the stunning Lesbos Orchid* (*Ophrys lesbis*). Its world population is restricted to limestone pockets in western Lesbos, a few places on Samos and a small area on the Turkish mainland. To see it, take into account that it flowers early, finishing before mid April.

4 The track leads through olive groves and fields, where you may track down Sombre Tit, Hoopoe, Middle-spotted Woodpecker and Nightingale. Along the flowery tracksides and in the streambed butterflies are plentiful, including Scarce Swallowtail, Great Banded Grayling, Lang's Short-tailed Blue and Spotted and Aegean Fritillaries. In the scrubland we found both Ottoman Viper and the elusive Cat Snake.

Return to the main track to Lapsarna and turn right. After 1 km, turn right onto a side track.

5 You cross an open woodland with Valonia, Turkey, Downy and Gall Oaks (a good spot to test your oak identifying skills), with a rich maquis flora. Thyme-leaved Rockrose, Three-lobed Sage, Giant Fennel, Turpentine Tree and Cretan Cistus together make for a colourful and well-scented bouquet. Look for the peculiar Pink Hypocist, a parasitic plant on Cretan Cistus, always growing underneath its host. Along this track we rediscovered Lady Orchid after an absence of almost 20 years! This is good habitat for Snake-eyed and Three-lined Lizards, Snake-eyed Skink and European Glass Lizard.

On the steep slopes of stream valleys between Andissa and Liota you find patches of almost natural stands of oak woodlands.

6 Ignore the side track to the right. After 1200 m from the main track, on a sharp bend, you'll find a patch of dense oak woodland which is again excellent for orchids. Pyramidal, Horned, Three-toothed, Monkey and Violet Bird's-nest Orchids all occur, as does Bee Orchid which is widely distributed in mainland Greece, but very rare on Lesbos. Another scarce species on the island that you might find here is White Helleborine.

Route 15: Faneromeni

4 HOURS, 4 KM
EASY

Excellent for migrating birds, both in spring and autumn.
Pleasant walk through dunes, fields and groves.

Habitats scrubland, cliffs, dunes, river, fields, oak woodland
Selected species Oriental Iris, Tree Medick, Cory's and Yelkouan Shearwaters, Squacco Heron, Lesser Kestrel, Eleonora's Falcon, Red-footed Falcon, Levant Sparrowhawk, Rufous Bush Robin, Masked Shrike, Epaulet Skimmer

This short route covers the coastal plain north of Sigri and offers a delightful walk, jam-packed with birdlife during migration. This site stands out because of its many small fields, dune slacks and bushes which collectively form a magnet for migrant birds that follow the coast. En route, you'll encounter some attractive wildflowers and interesting dragonflies as well. The following route describes the most logical loop you can make, but there are various sidetracks which beg for further exploration. You may visit this area as an intermezzo on route 16.

Starting point Sigri

Getting there Go to the seaside road and follow it in a northern direction. The road soon turns into a track which you continue for 2.7 km (already great for birdwaching) before turning left, signposted to Faneromeni. Take the first turn to the right which leads you to the beach. Park at the bar (careful not to get stuck in the sand).

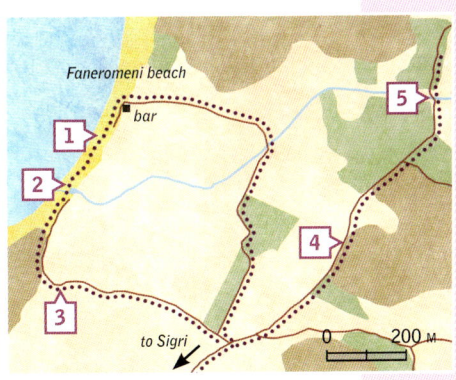

1 Walk to the left (south) along the quiet beach. Scan the sea for Cory's and Yelkouan Shearwaters and Shag and if you're lucky you may catch a glimpse of a dolphin. En route, pay attention to the dune flora, which contains Sea Spurge, Sea Medick, Tree Medick, Yellow Horned-poppy and the rare Cottonweed.

ROUTE 15: FANEROMENI

2 The lower reach of the river holds water most of the year. Here you may find Little Ringed Plover, Little Stint, various species of herons and Ruddy Shelduck. On good migration days, look for Red-footed and Eleonora's Falcons and Lesser Kestrel. Tree Frog and Balkan Terrapin occur along the river. Red-rumped Swallows can often be observed near the conspicuous white rock on the beach, collecting mud for nest making.

3 Ford the stream and continue on the track leading inland to the left. The fields on the right harbour huge beds of the beautiful Oriental Iris, a typical plant of damp meadows near the coast. Keep an eye out for wagtails, shrikes, Whinchats and passing flocks of Bee-eater.

4 At the main track, turn left. The olive groves and fields are one giant migrant trap. Any kind of oddity can come up here during migration, but frequent birds include Masked and Red-backed Shrikes, Olivaceous Warbler, flycatchers, Roller, Golden Oriole, Turtle Dove, Hoopoe and, later in season, Rufous Bush Robin. Besides the wide variety of birds, this site is outstanding for getting good views of the birds. The area is also very good for raptors with the aforementioned falcons plus Levant Sparrowhawk, Montagu's Harrier and Short-toed Eagle.

Red-rumped Swallow (top) and Roller (bottom) are two of the many birds that can be encountered on the coastal plain of Faneromeni.

5 Continue straight on until you reach the riverbed again. Explore the banks on either side. Dragonflies here include Epaulet Skimmer, Broad Scarlet and Eastern Willow Spreadwing. Green Toad is commonly found underneath rocks, while Tree Frogs are well hidden in the vegetation. Keep here an eye out for Squacco and Night Herons, Little Bittern and Sedge and Great Reed Warblers.

Crossing the riverbed you can continue uphill where the fields and groves hold the same migrating species as noted under point 4.

Retrace your steps and walk back to the beach of Faneromeni.

Route 16: Between Eresos and Sigri – the volcanic west

FULL DAY, 60 KM
EASY

Diverse circular route through the spectacular volcanic landscape. A highlight for birdwatching, with all the special species of Lesbos. Rich reptile and amphibian life.

Habitats phrygana scrub, bare rocks, cliffs, oriental plane forest, streams, rivers, wetlands
Selected species Rock Nuthatch, Rock Sparrow, Chukar, Sombre Tit, Long-legged Buzzard, Lesser Kestrel, Eleonora's Falcon, Cinereous Bunting, Isabelline Wheatear, Rufous Bush Robin, Roller, Ruddy Shelduck, Ottoman Viper, Cat Snake, European Pond Terrapin, Eastern Spadefoot, Turkish Clubtail

This long route is one of the highlights of Lesbos. It is the route to take to experience the barren volcanic landscape of western Lesbos. Most visitors will remember this as a top-notch birdwatching route, particularly because of many migrants during passage periods, and breeding birds like Cinereous Bunting and Isabelline Wheatear. But it is equally worth exploring just for the geology or for reptiles and insects. This route combines the well-known highlights of this region with some 'insider tips' on sites rarely visited by naturalists. The route is rather long and jam-packed with good sites, so consider doing it twice, focussing on different sites each day.

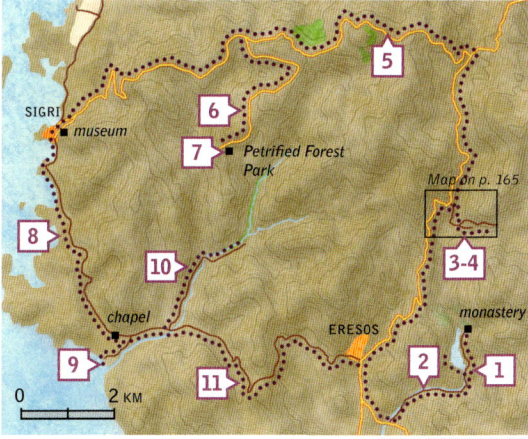

Starting point Eresos

Getting there Head south and turn left along the main road to Mesotopos. After 900 m turn left onto a track to Pithariou monastery, just past a bridge.

PRACTICAL PART

ROUTE 16: BETWEEN ERESOS AND SIGRI – THE VOLCANIC WEST

The reservoir of Pithariou monastery, completed in 2002, is the largest freshwater body of the island. Several bat species, like this Blasius's Horseshoe Bat, live in the monastery.

1 The first stretch along the river is good for migrating wagtails, flycatchers, warblers, waders and herons. After 2 km, park just past the small bridge on the right side of the track and explore the area. Scan the cliffs for Blue Rock Thrush, Rock Sparrow, Rock Nuthatch, Crag Martin and Chukar. This part of the valley is wider and excellent for seeing Long-legged Buzzard, Short-toed Eagle and Peregrine. They sometimes soar right over your head! The scrub holds Black-eared Wheatear, Woodchat Shrike and Cretschzmar's Bunting. Golden Oriole is often found in the riverside vegetation. The area is also very good for reptiles. Check the area around the old buildings and rocks on your right side for Starred Agama, Kotschy's Gecko and Montpellier and Caspian Whip Snakes. The river is the haunt of Dice and Grass Snakes and Balkan Terrapin.

2 Continue the track on foot until you reach the reservoir. Go left over the dam towards the cliffs. In autumn, when the water level is lower, Greater Flamingos are occasionally spotted along the muddy edges of the reservoir, together with egrets, herons and waders. Red-rumped Swallows can be seen near the water. The hills on the east side of the lake consist locally of calcareous rocks, uncommon in the western part of the island. For this reason, look near the track for limestone plants like the rare catchfly *Silene urvillei* and orchids.

Return to the track and walk up to the centuries old Pithariou monastery which is tucked away in the hills of the valley. Along the way, look for the

ROUTE 16: BETWEEN ERESOS AND SIGRI – THE VOLCANIC WEST

aforementioned species. The monastery has a stone collection in a cellar, where summer roosts of Greater Horseshoe and Blasius's Horseshoe Bats are found. The animals are often hanging upside down from the ceiling.

Retrace your steps and drive back to Eresos and continue along to the main road towards Andissa. After 5.5 km from Eresos (set your kilometre counter in the village) there is a bend to the left from where a line of windmills is clearly visible on top of a hill in front of you. At this bend, look for a gate with a concrete pole on your right. This marks the start of a rough track that descends to the valley. Careful, as this site is easy to miss. Park by the side of the road just after the gate and follow the track on foot.

!
Drive down carefully, steep descent

3 The track leads down into the valley where fruit trees and abandoned fields are testimony to the old settlement that existed here about 50 years ago. The valley is a good place to look for Ottoman Viper and Dahl's Whip and Cat Snakes. Birds include Masked Shrike and Hoopoe. Bee-eater breeds here and birds often rest on the overhead wires. Migrating birds like Red-backed Shrike, Grey Wagtail and Black Stork follow the valley in their journey north.

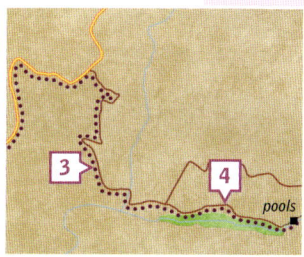

4 After you pass a bridge and the sheep shed, the track bends to the left. On the bend, follow a side trail to the right that leads down to the dense riverine forest. Especially in autumn, this bright green oasis of plane forest couldn't be in greater contrast to the dry rocky landscape around. Unusual for rivers on Lesbos, it carries water throughout the year. As the valley narrows to form a ravine, follow the small trail down to the river (look carefully, as it is easy to miss). Between the rocks there are some pools, look in spring for Balkan Terrapin and tadpoles of Eastern Spadefoot. The adult toads are often buried deep in the

Lush oriental plane forest along the river on site 4.

PRACTICAL PART

ROUTE 16: BETWEEN ERESOS AND SIGRI – THE VOLCANIC WEST

sand of dry patches in the riverbed, hence very difficult to see. The year-round presence of water makes this location superb for dragonflies as well, with Odalisque, Eastern Spectre and Small Pincertail all present. The river also looks promising for Turkish Clubtail.

Return to the car and continue on the main road. After 4 km, turn left to Sigri.

5 En route, you pass an impressive hill with the Ipsilou monastery on top, perfect for a short stop by taking the uphill road on the left (one-way roads!). The Ipsilou monastry is another birdwatching hotspot that we've described extensively in route 17.

The landscape inside the Petrified Forest Park. On your way to the park, keep an eye out for Isabelline Wheatear (top).

After the monastery continue to Sigri. The whole of this stretch is excellent for Cretschzmar's Bunting, Black-eared and Isabelline Wheatears. Turn left onto a tarmac road with signs to the Petrified Forest Park (At the time of writing the road to Sigri was being upgraded so the route may change in the near future).

6 The park is the main excavation site of the much larger pertified forest, which is the geological highlight of Lesbos. But before dashing to the site, scrutinise the phrygana-scrub covered hills and rocky protrusions along the narrow road. This area is rich in birds, with highlights including Isabelline Wheatear, Cretschzmar's Bunting, Cinereous Bunting, Little

ROUTE 16: BETWEEN ERESOS AND SIGRI – THE VOLCANIC WEST

Owl and Rock Sparrow. The latter is best tracked down by its odd, whining call. The small pools along the road harbour Eastern Spadefoot.

7 Inside the park you can follow several signposted trails between impressive petrified trunks (open 9:00-17:00, except January and February). In addition to species noted in point 4, Rufous Bush Robin can be found here, taking advantage of the scattered shrubs. In early April the rare Lesbos Orchid* (*Ophrys lesbis*) grows along the trails. The elusive Cat Snake is found here too.

Return to the main road and turn left. The road winds down to Sigri, where you can connect with route 15. Just before the village, turn left onto a tarmac road with signs to the Petrified Forest Museum which is excellent and well worth a visit (see page 18). Notice the petrified trunks near the museum. The road arrives at the coast, where you turn left at the T-junction. Further ahead, the road changes into a track.

8 The whole stretch back to Eresos is, besides being a year round spectacular scenic attraction, one of the best birding routes of Lesbos. The remote, bone dry landscape is the domain of rock-dwelling birds like Chukar, Rock Nuthatch, Blue Rock Thrush and Cretzschmar's and Cinerous Buntings. Along the way challenge your identification skills by checking the falcons for Lesser Kestrel, Common Kestrel, Hobby, Peregrine, Eleonora's and Red-footed Falcons all of which are regularly present. Promising areas to look for birds are the dry stream beds with small shrubs. Sardinian Warbler, Black-eared Wheatear and various shrikes are among the commonly seen species, with breeding Rufous Bush Robin arriving usually early May. The gullies are also excellent spots to look for reptiles (including Snake-eyed Lizard and Cat and Montpellier Snakes).

9 Park at a chapel (about 5.5 km beyond Sigri). Check the fields for incoming migrants like Sardinian Warbler, Lesser Grey Shrike and Black-headed Bunting. Continue on foot and after 400 m turn right onto a track along the river. Look here for Ruddy Shelduck, herons and egrets. The site supports an interesting damselfly fauna, which includes Dark and Eastern Willow Spreadwings. The track ends at the tranquil Tsichliondas beach, where you can enjoy the peaceful atmosphere. Although the dunes are overgrazed, Sea Daffodil is still present, flowering beautifully in autumn. Inspect the rocks on the left side of the beach. The ancient layers of

ROUTE 16: BETWEEN ERESOS AND SIGRI – THE VOLCANIC WEST

The dry and barren landscape along the track between Sigri and Eresos (top). Here Lesser Kestrel (bottom) is most often seen.

volcanic ash, responsible for the petrification of ancient trees, are clearly visible here (see page 17).

Return and continue on the track by car. Park just before the bridge (1.3 km from the chapel) and walk down the track to the left and upstream along the river.

10 This valley is excellent for migrating birds in spring and autumn. Basically anything can appear, but likely candidates are Roller, Bee-eater, buntings, chats, warblers, flycatchers and raptors like Eleonora's Falcon and Short-toed Eagle. Local breeding birds are Sombre Tit (present year-round) and Rufous Bush Robin (late spring and summer) After 2.8 km, the oriental plane forest along the river is a good spot for Golden Oriole and Nightingale, while in the pools in the riverbed, both European Pond and Balkan Terrapins occur. Reptiles in stony grasslands include Cat Snake, Sand Boa, Snake-eyed Lizard and European Glass Lizard.

Return to the car and continue on the track towards Eresos.

11 This final section may hold similar species as described at point 8.

CROSSBILL GUIDES • LESBOS

Route 17: Ipsilou Monastery

2 HOURS, 2 KM
EASY

Short and easy route, offering superb birdwatching. Top site for Cinereous Bunting, reptiles and insects.

Habitats scrubland, bare rocks, cliffs, oak woodland
Selected species Persian Squirrel, Cinereous Bunting, Cretzschmar's Bunting, Isabelline Wheatear, Black-eared Wheatear, Rock Nuthatch, Alpine Swift, Rock Sparrow, Hoopoe, Little Owl, Starred Agama, Snake-eyed Skink, Spur-thighed Tortoise, Worm Snake, False Apollo, Eastern Grayling, Aegean Grayling

Apart from impressive scenery, this compact route provides some of the best and easiest birdwatching on the island, with highlights including Cinereous Bunting and Isabelline Wheatear. Besides birds, there are a number of interesting reptiles and butterflies.

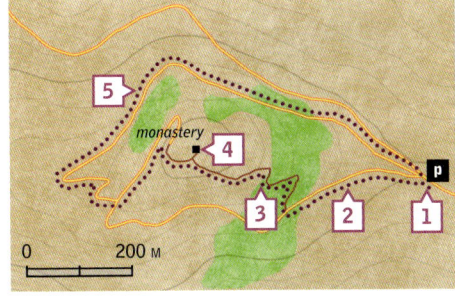

p = car park

A short, steep walk brings you to the picturesque monastery, splendidly perched on top of a lava dome, which at 600 m, risies above the surrounding landscape.

Starting point Car park on the right side of the main road below Ipsilou monastery, half way between Andissa and Sigri.

1 Before leaving the car park, scan the barren area towards the north-northeast for Isabelline and Black-eared Wheatears, Hoopoe, Sombre Tit, Subalpine Warbler and Rock Nuthatch.

2 Of the two tarmac roads up to the monastery, take the lefthand one. Near the edge of the oak woodland, look for Cinereous Bunting. It is often singing from a perch, either a shrub, tree or pointed rock.

PRACTICAL PART

ROUTE 17: IPSILOU MONASTERY

A visit to the beautiful monastery is recommended (bottom). Little Owl breeds in the area of the monastery.

The tall vegetation in the otherwise barren and windswept area makes this hill an excellent migrant trap. All kinds of flycatchers, warblers and other passerines may be found here, so prepare to be stuck here for a while! In spring, keep an eye out for approaching raptors from the south. Levant Sparrowhawk might be among them.

After 300 m there is stone wall on your right. Here a steep *kaldarimi* leads uphill. Follow it.

3 The open woodland offers a good hiding place for Little Owl. Cinereous Bunting can be spotted at close range here, singing from a tree. In the area just below the monastery keep an eye out for Rock Sparrow, Blue Rock Thrush, Cretzschmar's and Cirl Buntings, all of which breed in the area. Not everything that moves has wings and feathers, though. Persian Squirrel is commonly found jumping around the trees and between the rocks there is a remarkable reptile fauna, featuring Starred Agama and Snake-eyed Lizard. In the leaf litter along the trail, Snake-eyed Skink, Glass Lizard and Spur-thighed Tortoise further represent the reptile fauna. You might even

ROUTE 17: IPSILOU MONASTERY

spot Worm Snake between the stones. In early April, the stunning False Apollo is present. The grassy patches and open scrubland are excellent for butterflies. Look for Eastern and Aegean Graylings, two species with an oriental distribution range that boost Lesbos' otherwise rather limited butterfly fauna.

4 Swing around the building and enter the monastery through the main gate. Check the cavities high in the walls for Little Owls, which often rest here. The foundation of the monastery goes back to Byzantine years, before 800 AD. The current buildings, however, were constructed at the beginning of the 19th century. Take the time to visit the monastery. It harbours an interesting museum with ancient Christian manuscripts, books and ornaments. If the museum is closed, just ask one of the monks to open it for you.

Climb the stairs for beautiful views over the volcanic landscape from the top of the monastery. The vista is breathtaking, especially in the afternoon. It is also an excellent spot to witness the migration of broad-winged birds like storks and raptors. Some days, Alpine Swifts fly by at close range.

5 Descend along the tarmac road on the north side of the dome. This road is just as good for birds as the ascent, with roughly the same species.

!
Military area
careful with optics

Cinereous Bunting is one of the greatest avian attractions of Lesbos, holding the largest known breeding population in the world. The monastery of Ipsilou is the most reliable spot to see it.

PRACTICAL PART

Additional Sites

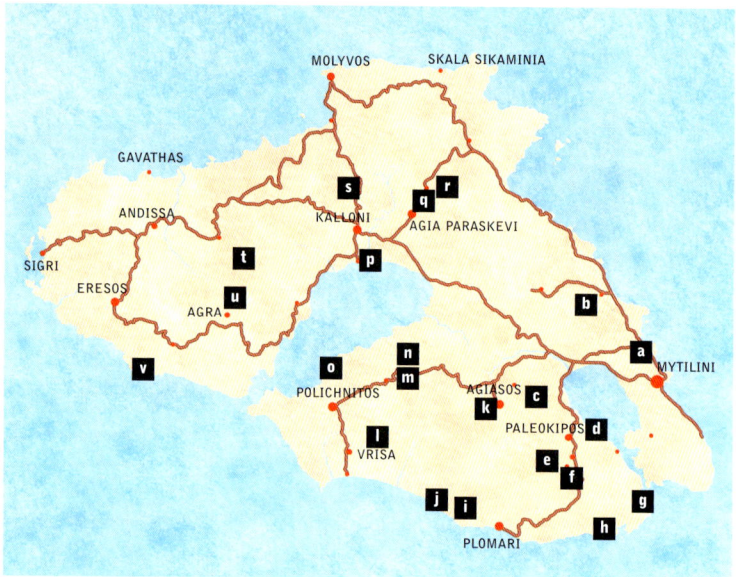

A – Mines of Moria

  Yes they exist! The mines of Moria are not simply fiction that sprung from Tolkien's Lord of the Rings. The Lesbos' variety is much more modest than that of Middle Earth – a little known marble quarry near the village of Moria. Nevertheless, during Hellenic and Roman times (400 BC – 300 AD) it was one of the most important marble mines in the East Aegean. Moria marble features in famous statues and buildings in France, Rome, Pompeii and ancient Greek cities of Ephesus and Pergamon. Today, unfinished pillars and capitals (topmost parts of a pillar) lie scattered in several huge pits, almost as if ancient carvers are only having a lunch break. Sadly, in places its historical grandeur is undermined by litter.

The mines and surrounding scrubland are good for finding lizards and snakes. For this the rubbish is quite helpful: as snakes and certain types of lizards prefer to hide underneath flat surfaces, lifting some of the plastic and cardboard gives you a good chance of finding them.

To get there, take the exit to Moria 2 km from Mytilini. 550 m from the exit, turn left onto a track opposite a white house with a fence.

ADDITIONAL SITES

After 450 m the mines are on your right. Just south of the village Moria, you find the best preserved and partly renovated remains of the Roman Aqueduct with impressive arches (see route 2 and history section).

B – The Agios Filippos cave

A short walk takes you to the Agios Filippos cave near Loutropoli Thermis. The cave has a shrine inside. Until late April, the walk up to the cave is good to find Dull Bee, Naked Man, Man, Four-spotted, Horned, Rainbow, Mirror and Horseshoe Orchids.
The access track lies opposite a football pitch 700 m beyond Loutropoli Thermis towards Pigi. Follow the track by car and park along the first track to the right. Continue this track on foot and find, after 1.3 km, a trail to the left signposted ΑΓ. ΦΙΛΙΠΠΟΣ and ΣΠΗΛΑΙΟ. This brings you to the cave. Along this trail most orchids are found.

In the ancient marble quarry of Moria you can see fishbone patterns carved in the rocks (middle) and unfinished pillars (bottom), as if the ancient workers just left for a break.

C – Olive groves around Mychou

In spring, the area west of Mychou holds large numbers of orchids and other wildflowers. During a pleasant walk through olive groves and wooded hills you can find Naked Man, Umbilical,

ADDITIONAL SITES

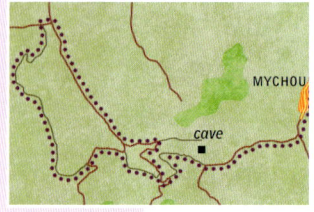

Homer's, Horseshoe, Bergoni's Tongue and Long-lipped Tongue Orchids, Yellow-wort, Italian Gladiolus and Eastern Bugle. With Masked Shrike, Middle-spotted Woodpecker and Olivaceous Warbler, it is reasonably attractive for birders too. There is a 9 km walking route in the area. Along the way you pass the 95 m long Fousa cave, which you can explore at your own risk (bring a torch!). Artifacts dating back to the 5th century BC have been found here.

To get here from the main Mytilini – Kalloni road, take the road to Plomari. After 3 km, just past a wide bend, turn right signposted ΚΑΤΩ ΤΡΙΤΟΣ and ΜΥΧΟΥ. Park in Mychou and continue on foot via the main road and take the first concrete road to the right into a narrow valley with Plane trees. From here follow the route on the map.

D – Coastal meadows along the Gulf of Gera

In May, the thousands of Loose-flowered Orchids found along the Gulf of Gera, are a spectacular sight. The stunning pink drifts in the meadows are hard to miss, even extending into people's gardens. Also Marsh and Elegant Marsh Orchids and a white variety of Loose-flowered Orchid can be found, albeit in lower numbers.

In the reedbeds, Tree Frog is abundant. At an arm's length from the shore, beneath the water surface there are sea urchins, sea anemones and sea-cucumbers.

For the best stretch, take the main road to Plomari along the shore. After 2.7 km, as the road bends inland, turn left to Pigadakia and follow the road along the shore until you reach the main road again.

The spectacular drift of Loose-flowered Orchid along the Gulf near Pigadakia is an unforgettable sight.

E – Agriomelissa

Just above Skopelos there is a great patch of mature pine forest. In spring, it sports huge stands of Balkan Peony, together with Narrow-leaved Helleborine and Violet Bird's-nest Orchid, while in autumn a pink wash of Ivy-leaved

ADDITIONAL SITES

Cyclamen and the autumn crocuses *Colchicum bivonae* and *Colchicum variegatum* covers the forest floor. The track up to the forest winds through olive groves with many orchids. We found 15 species here on a casual evening walk, including Three-toothed, Naked Man, Four-spotted, Anatolian, Horned, Homer's and Bee Orchids. The latter is extremely rare on Lesbos, we were the first to rediscover it on the island after 20 years. Further along the route, near the small village of Karionas, you can add Reinhold's and Sawfly Orchids to the list.

It is possible to take a 9.5 km circular walk, departing from the guesthouse Xenonas. To get there, take the main road from Perama to Skopelos. Go straight at the junction with a stop sign and take the first turn right. After 600 m, turn right again at the junction leading uphill. At the next junction make a sharp left turn to arrive at the guest house. From here walk back to the junction and turn left onto a concrete track rounding a sports field (signposted *Karionas*). Take the first turn left to a track and follow it uphill. Much further on a junction, turn right signposted Αγριομέλισσα. In the forest, keep on the main track and after some bends take the second turn left at the junction. Keep turning left at the junctions to Karionas, then turn left and after 700 m right, signposted *Skopelos*.

F – The crooked Plane Tree of the Kanatsi watermill

  Oriental Plane trees have a reputation for growing up to formidable natural monuments and the one of the Kanatsi watermill is testimony to this. This spectacular botanical oddity grows inside the remnants of an old mill. Apparently the tree germinated in the disused water channel, as its roots follow the channel over the entire length of the construction before sprouting a mature, fully grown canopy, standing like a crown on the main structure. A bizarre sight worthy of any list of the world's weirdest trees! To get there, take the main road from Pappados to Plomari. After 600 m out of Pappados, turn left onto a track with an information panel about the mill and follow the signposts.

Oriental Plane tree grows inside the walls of the Kanatsi watermill.

PRACTICAL PART

G – Avlonas and Mount Oros

The narrow channel that separates the Gulf of Gera from the sea is a beautiful, but rarely visited, area with secluded bays. Rising steeply from the sea on the south coast, Mount Oros is a conspicuous marble hill (a good example of a geologically active fault) with scrub, olive groves and bare rocks. The track over to the headland from Perama makes for a wonderful excursion. It has something to offer to all, but particularly to orchid lovers.

In suitable wet meadows along the road south of Perama Loose-flowered and Heart-flowered Tongue Orchids grow. Drive further beyond Avlonas where the tarmac road turns into a dirt track and explore the olive groves on your way. Umbilical, Bull-headed and Sawfly Orchids and many more are found here in April. Continue on the main track to Katsinia Bay and beyond a few houses, find a track leading uphill to the right, blocked by a barrier. Park here and follow this track on foot. Early in spring, this is a good area to find orchids including Pink Butterfly, Rainbow and Horned Orchids. On your way keep an eye out for Ottoman Viper, Caspian Whip Snake and Glass and Snake-eyed Lizards. Check the scrubland for Sardinian, Orphean and Subalpine Warbler. Alternatively, the whole stretch can also be tackled on foot, by parking your car along the track south of Avlonas. This site is easily combined with a good meal at the excellent taverna in Avlonas, just where the tarmac ends (see page 197).

H – Tarti

Tucked away in the south of Lesbos lies the beautiful sandy beach of Tarti and nearby bays. Besides being a wonderful place to relax and swim in the clear turquoise water, it is a very good spot for snorkelling. Especially the rocks on the west end of the beach are perfect for finding sea urchins, sea-cucumbers and colourful fish. Approximately 120 m further along these rocks there is a marble pillar in the water, a reminder of the ancient mines of the area. Onshore, there are a number of mines still visible, recognisable by the fishbone patterns carved in the rocks – scarring from the tools that were used. A good example is to be found in the rocks across from the excellent fish taverna *Sebastian*, on the east side of the beach. The tracks to the east and west of the beach are worth exploring for wildflowers and snakes. We found Ottoman Viper and Sand Boa in this area.

ADDITIONAL SITES

To get to Tarti Beach, take the road that branches off from the Pappados-Plomari road, 1200 m beyond Pappados. Make a short orchid hunting stop in the olive groves 6 km before Tarti.

I – Paleochori

  This beautiful circular route of 6 km leads through olive groves and passes a lush river valley. In spring, you will find many orchids and other wildflowers, together with birds like Middle-spotted Woodpecker and Olivaceous Warbler. The odd and rare False Hemp, which is an Asian species, grows on the riverbanks and flowers May-July (see page 60). *Arum concinnatum* can be found here too.

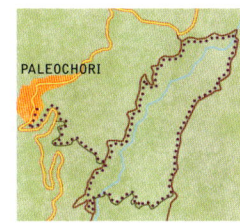

From Paleochori, walk along the tarmac road towards Plomari and at the first hairpin bend turn left onto a *kaldarimi*, signposted ΜΕΛΙΝΤΑ and marked with a red diamond. Follow the circuit shown on the map (in the valley follow the sign ΚΟΥΡΝΕΛΑ). This site is easily combined with the next one.

J – Panagia Krifti

  Panagia Krifti is a hidden chapel beautifully located on the impressive rocky south coast. A scenic track leads to good bird habitat with cliffs where you can spot Red-rumped Swallow, Crag Martin, Subalpine Warbler, Sardinian Warbler, Blue Rock Thrush and Black-eared Wheatear. The bay itself is perfect for a swim. Below the cliffs on the west side lies a natural hot spring (distinguished by a small artificial pool).

To get to the site, leave Plomari in the direction of Paleochori. Beyond Melinda, the road climbs in a series of sharp bends. At the last hairpin, turn left onto a wide coastal track. Walk or drive (careful, rough track!) for 3 km to the end of the track. Follow the narrow track further down (on foot!), which turns into a steep path with steps leading down to the chapel. This site is easily combined with the previous one.

K – Hiking routes between Agiasos and Mount Olymbos

    The Olymbos massif offers excellent hiking. One particularly attractive walk leads from Agiasos to the summit of Mount Olymbos – a route with various branches that each offer different views

ADDITIONAL SITES

but all eventually lead up to Olymbos. All the way you pass through chestnut forests with lots of Lesbos Fritillary* (*Fritillaria theophrasti*), Narrow-leaved Helleborine and Provence, Three-toothed and Green-winged Orchids. Beautiful old fruit orchards are the haunt of Large Tortoiseshell and Nettle-tree Butterfly, while flowery forest edges attract Amanda's Blue and Southern White Admiral. With some luck you might encounter Dwarf and Leopard Snakes.

The upper slopes of Mount Olymbos support a unique woodland with Hawthorn, Blackthorn and Cretan Maple cloaked in grayish-green beard lichens which hang from the branches. Thanks to the clean air and local moist conditions the lichens reach impressive sizes.

The routes start at the car park at the bottom of the valley (see point 9 on route 4) and follows mainly ancient *kalderimi*, which are marked by red diamonds (not always clear). The last stretch to the summit is described in route 4.

P = car park

L – Mount Koutra

Close to Vrisa lies Mount Koutra, where in April large drifts of Wrinkle-leaved Tulip* (*Tulipa undulatifolia*) brighten the pine forest. This slope is the only known location of this species on Lesbos and grows together with Italian Gladiolus and various orchids (including Roman and Pink Butterfly). En route you will pass some old quarries. These are excellent sites to look for dragonflies, like Robust Spreadwing, Dainty Bluet and Red-veined Darter. Raven occurs here in good numbers. From Polichnitos take the main road south to Vatera. After 800 m, on top of a hill, turn left onto a track opposite a group of low pine trees with white painted barks. Ignore the right turn signposted VATEPA and after 1.3 km go right at the T-junction. At the chapel turn left and continue until you see a dry quarry on your right. Park and continue uphill on foot for about 2 km to find the tulips. The two quarries are located next to the track.

M – Mikri Limni

Surrounded by pine forests, Mikri Limni is one of the few natural lakes on Lesbos. It is choked with rushes and almost completely dry in summer. Nevertheless, it is an excellent site for dragonflies, including Vagrant and Lesser Emperors, Small Skimmer, Small Spreadwing and Hairy and Green-eyed Hawkers. The latter two species are rare on the island. The area is interesting for plants as well, with various orchids and several rather uncommon wildflowers

of aquatic habitats like Gratiole, Lesser Water-plantain and Adder's-tongue Spearwort. Krüper´s Nuthatch and Short-toed Treecreeper occur in the pines.
Mikri Limni lies close to the main junction of roads east of Vasilika. At the junction, take the track opposite of the turn to Kalloni. After 150 m there is a parking place, from where you can take a circular walk around the lake. This site is easily combined with the next one.

N – Pessa waterfalls

The Pessa waterfall and springs (dry in summer) form a lush site, easily reached by a leisurely walk. This is a good walk to find dragonflies of wooded streams like Eastern Spectre, Odalisque, Keeled Skimmer and Beautiful and Banded Demoiselles and Turkish Goldenring. Along the trail there are Pink Butterfly, Provence and Milky Orchids and Autumn Lady's-tresses - the latter flowering in October.
To get there, turn left onto a track, 4 km south of Achladeri (end point of route 10), indicated by a green sign and an information stand. Continue for 700 m to the car park from where a trail takes you down to the waterfall. This site is easy to combine with the previous one.

O – Polichnitos saltpans

The Polichnitos saltpans are situated on the east side of the Gulf of Gera. Although smaller and lesser known than the ones near Kalloni, they still offer exciting birdwatching. Autumn is the best period to visit the saltpans, although in spring there are good numbers of birds too. The bird list is long and includes 'goodies' such as Greater Flamingo, Spoonbill, Ruddy Shelduck, Black Stork, Mediterranean and Slender-billed Gulls, Kentish Plover, Temminck's Stint, Stone Curlew, Marsh, Broad-billed and Curlew Sandpipers. At sea, look for Shag and the rare Gull-billed Tern – the latter is only present in spring. The fields and the ridge east of the saltpans are the haunt of migratory raptors like Red-footed and Eleonora's Falcons, Short-toed Eagle and Montagu's Harrier. Check the wires for Black-headed and

Little Stints are common in the saltpans of Polychnitos and Kalloni.

ADDITIONAL SITES

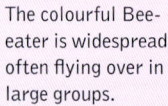

The colourful Bee-eater is widespread, often flying over in large groups.

Corn Buntings, Woodchat and Red-backed Shrike, Bee-eater and Roller. The area can be explored by car along the track running along the eastern side of the saltpans or by a 5 km walk around them. The sought-after Olive-tree Warbler and Masked Shrike breed in the olive groves along the main track just east of the hamlet of Skamnioudi, about 3 km northeast from the saltpans.

The saltpans are easy to find and lie just north of Skala Polichnitou. Coming from the north consider taking the scenic, but long, coastal track (about 10 km from Achladeri connecting with route 10). It crosses an area where Anise is cultivated for the famous ouzo which has its origin in the Plomari region of Lesbos. Park either at the north or south end of the saltpans.

P – Tsiknias river

The Tsiknias river is an excellent (and for this reason very popular) birding area, 1 km east of Kalloni on the main road to Mytilini. Tracks run along both sides of the river from the main road to the river mouth at the Gulf of Kalloni. Particularly during passage, the river supports Black Storks and many egrets, herons and waders, while the riverside vegetation can be dripping with warblers and flycatchers. This is the most reliable site for Rosy Starling, which prefers the Mulberry trees along the banks, more often in late May. The river mouth is best viewed from the western track. This is a very good area in general, but in particular for, Stone Curlew, Collared Pratincole (rare), Slender-billed and Mediterranean Gulls.

ADDITIONAL SITES

Q – Valley between Napi and Mandamados

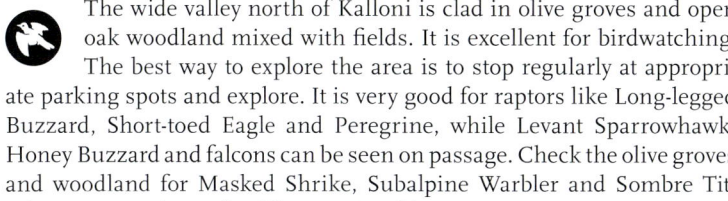

The wide valley north of Kalloni is clad in olive groves and open oak woodland mixed with fields. It is excellent for birdwatching. The best way to explore the area is to stop regularly at appropriate parking spots and explore. It is very good for raptors like Long-legged Buzzard, Short-toed Eagle and Peregrine, while Levant Sparrowhawk, Honey Buzzard and falcons can be seen on passage. Check the olive groves and woodland for Masked Shrike, Subalpine Warbler and Sombre Tit. It is a renowned area for Olive-tree Warbler too.

A good area to search is the track 800 m south of Napi (signposted Πλάκεσ Τζίγκουνα). Explore it on foot. North of Napi you find several small parking spots along the road from where you have clear views over the valley, for example around the solar panels, in a sharp left curving bend. The area is popular with birders and can be busy at times.

R – Platania

Along the ridge of the aforementioned valley, opposite the main road, runs a track which is known by birders as *Platania*. The main attraction here is Olive-tree Warbler, which can be spotted from the track. Other species include Rock Nuthatch, Black-eared Wheatear, Subalpine Warbler, Cretzschmar's Bunting and Masked Shrike which, together with a score of migrating raptors, makes it an excellent birding site in an attractive setting.

The track is about 3 km and starts from the tarmac road 3 km from Mandamados in the direction of Napi, and is situated in a wide bend. We do not recommend driving this track without a 4x4. The best option is to park along the track opposite (and to the left when coming from the south) and exploring the track to Platania on foot for about 3 km.

S – Klapados waterfall

Klapados is an abandoned Ottoman village situated north of Kalloni. There is a beautiful waterfall nearby, with a pond and a damp valley with some old, moss-covered plane trees. The pond holds Balkan Terrapin and Levant Water Frog, and we found Snake-eyed Skink and Worm Snake in the valley. The stream supports damselflies like Odalisque and Beautiful Demoiselle, and Small Spreadwing in the pond of the waterfall. Loose-flowered Orchid grows along the stream – this species is rare inland. Bonelli's Warbler is found in the woods.

PRACTICAL PART

ADDITIONAL SITES

Autumn Lady's-tresses (an orchid) grows here in October.
To get to the site, take the main road from Kalloni to Petra. After 5.5 km turn left onto a track signposted *Klapados – Lafiona*. Continue until, after 2 km, you reach an open area with picnic tables. Park and follow the trail down to the waterfall.
The remains of the village are 1.3 km to the north along the main track. This is the place where in 1912 the last battle against the Ottomans took place for the liberation of Lesbos. The few ruins of houses and a hamam are the only evidence of the original village. *Tulipa orphanidea* grows along the track and keep an eye out for snakes – you might come across Ottoman Viper and Caspian Whip Snake.

T – Parakila Forest and Pterounda

The massive flowering of thousands of Pontic Azalea form the main attraction of Parakila Forest. The area consists of extensive Turkish pine forests. A walk takes you through the forest to the summit of Profitis Ilias, where you also can find remnants of Black Pine forests, which are very rare on Lesbos (see page 33). The grassy spots around the summit area are rich in wildflowers, including Pink Butterfly Orchid, Crown Anemone and beautiful drifts of Pink Hawk's-beard. Underneath the trees and shrubs look for Balkan Peony, and Lesbos Fritillary* (*Fritillaria theophrasti*), Narrow-leaved Helleborine and Drooping Star-of-Bethlehem.

The long trail of 9.5 km through the silent forest is a bit boring, but the relaxed atmosphere together with the regular valleys jam-packed with Pontic Azaleas, makes it more than worthwhile. On your way, keep an eye out for Roman and Violet Bird's-nest Orchids.

The route starts in Pterounda, situated in the centre of one of the major ancient volcanos of Lesbos (see page 18). Its existence is best testified to by the houses themselves, of which the stones are carved from local volcanic rocks. A closer look at the stones in the walls reveals an assemblage of multi-coloured rocks of varying

The houses of Pterounda are built with local volcanic rocks.

ADDITIONAL SITES

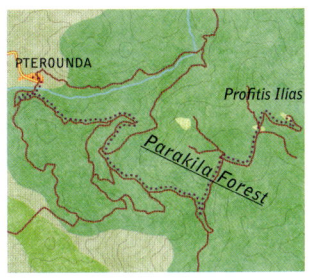

size, intersected by small air gaps and volcanic glass – all geological features of rock found close to the eruption site. In contrast, rocks found in areas much further from the caldera have a distinctly even structure.

On the access road to Pterounda, look for Long-legged Buzzard, Short-toed Eagle, Isabelline and Black-eared Wheatears, Rock Nuthatch, Blue Rock Thrush, Cretzschmar's Bunting and Subalpine Warbler.

In Pterounda, park at the village car park and continue on foot.

White-flowered Rue* (*Haplophyllum megalanthum*) is a very special wildflower on Lesbos. In fact, it is the only rue with white flowers.

U – Crater of Agra

Agra has two places of interest. Botanist will want to visit the area north of Agra as it is here that you can find (mid-May to July) the very rare White-flowered Rue* (*Haplophyllum megalanthum*; see page 60). It grows along the track that eventually leads to a scenic area with rough pastures and oriental plane forest 4.5 km from Agra, where you can find the tulip *Tulipa orphanidae*, Balkan Peony and Lesbos Fritillary* (*Fritillaria theophrasti*) (see map). Eventually the track connects with another that leads to the summit *Profitis Ilias* (see site T). Along the scenic route north to Chidira, Pontic Azalea grows along streambeds.

To get here, take the eastern exit to Agra on the main road Kalloni – Mosopotos (this stretch has been constructed recently). Just after entering the village, turn right, just before a pink-walled café, then turn immediately right again. Continue uphill where the road turns into a track and take the second track to the right. If it is in bad condition, park

!
Road in bad condition after rain

PRACTICAL PART

ADDITIONAL SITES

Certainly don't miss out the spectacular display of Pontic Azalea late April, as here along the track between Agra and Chidira.

and continue on foot. Continue straight on the main track for the route to Chidira.

The second place of interest is for birdwatchers. Cretzschmar's and Cinereous Buntings, Rock Nuthatch, Blue Rock Thrush and various raptors occur south of the village. In Agra, park just before the two towers on the right side of the road and explore the area.

Both the wildflower and the bird site are, in fact, situated on a crater rim, from where you have excellent views to two of the three main volcanic centres on Lesbos (see page 18).

V – Chrousos

On the southwest coast lies the hamlet of Chrousos, an isolated area with dry volcanic rocks, irrigated fields, a river valley and a sandy beach. This variety of habitats promises a rich wildlife, which is best explored on a 2.5 km circular walking route (see map).

The hills on the west side of the valley are covered in *phrygana* scrub, where Isabelline and Black-eared Wheatears, Rufous Bush Robin, Cretzschmar's Bunting and Rock Nuthatch breed. The area is very good for (migrating) raptors like Eleonora's Falcon, Lesser Kestrel, Long-legged Buzzard and Short-toed Eagle.

From the main track, the dry hillside can be explored by a trail leading

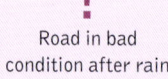
Road in bad condition after rain

ADDITIONAL SITES

to the remains of an ancient watchtower dating around 800-600 BC. On the walk, keep an eye out for Snake-eyed Lizard, Starred Agama and Montpellier and Dahl's Whip Snakes. In a pile of stones we found a Greater Horseshoe Bat. The irrigated fields in the valley are excellent for migrant birds like Bee-eater, Black-headed Bunting and shrikes – especially in autumn when the bone dry landscape offers little food and shelter. The loose soil in the fields provides perfect habitat for the Lesser Mole Rat to dig its burrow.

At the beach, scan the sea for Cory's and Yelkouan Shearwaters and Shag, while Little Ringed Plover, Green Sandpiper, Little Stint and herons dwell near the river mouth. It holds water most of the year and is home to Balkan Terrapin and Grass and Dice Snake. Tree Frog occurs in the dense vegetation along the river, together with typical birds of this habitat like Nightingale, Golden Oriole and Cetti's and Great Reed Warblers. The rocks on the eastern end of the beach show clearly the different layers of volcanic ash and pyroclastic material, which played an important role in the petrification process of ancient trees (see geology section). On this part of the beach you can find, in summer, Sea Daffodil.

From the village of Mesotopos, head to the shore to Tavari and turn right. After 400 m turn right at the small roundabout, signposted Χρούσος. Soon the road becomes a track. After 1.3 km turn left at the junction. Park just after the bridge before Chrousos or continue straight on the main track to the sea shore.

During walks in rocky habitat and along streambeds, especially after rainfall, you might come across the secretive Worm Snake.

TOURIST INFORMATION & OBSERVATION TIPS

Travel and accommodation

Travelling to Lesbos
Most visitors to the island will arrive by air. Between late April and the beginning of October you can take a direct flight from several European cities (e.g. Amsterdam, Düsseldorf, Köln, Birmingham, Manchester and most London airports). For the cheapest prices, book directly with the airlines or book a package holiday. If your main interest are orchids you'll need to fly out earlier. The best option is to take a scheduled flight to either Athens or Thessaloniki and continue on a domestic flight to Lesbos (for example Aegean Airways), or take the daily night ferry from Athens to the island (departure usually 20:00; with stopover in Chios).

Note that you'll need to set aside some time to get from the airport to the docks. In Athens, this is 1.5 hours minimum. At the airport, take the suburban train to Nerantziotissa station and change here onto Metro line 1, towards Pireas (the harbour). At Pireas, cross the main street from the station and take the free bus to the boats to Lesbos alighting at the last stop in the docks. You can purchase the tickets directly from a booth here, or in advance via **www.petas.gr** or **www.euroferries.com**, or have Sappho Travel do it for you (see page 188). Be aware that during Orthodox Easter the ferries might be fully booked. Outside this period there are usually vacancies.

Travelling on Lesbos
Travelling by car is by far the easiest way to go around the island. To explore the routes and sites in this guidebook a car is virtually indispensable. The roads are in a good condition and it is easy to travel between different parts of the island. The winding roads mean travel is slow, but since the island is not so big (it takes about 2 hours to drive from Mytilini in the east to Sigri in the west) and there is plenty to see en route, this gentle progress only adds to the charm of the island. The quiet roads have plenty of opportunities for the naturalist to pull off to explore interesting spots.

Car rental
All the large car rental companies are available on Lesbos. Their offices are situated in Mytilini, Molyvos and at the airport. A few are also found in Eresos. Depending on your needs you can rent ordinary cars, vans or 4x4 vehicles. Some package holidays include a rental car, but it is also easy to book one in advance at different companies. Contact them by email for pricing and availability. The prices depend on season and duration of rental. In all cases cars are picked up and delivered back to the airport or the harbour.

Bicycle rent
Bicycles offer a fun way to explore the area. They can be rented in Plomari, Skala Kalloni, Molyvos and Mytilini. Be aware that the hilly terrain and summer heat limits the distance you can cover. The coastal area of Kalloni and flat river valleys (for example Potamia river; see route 8) are often visited by cyclists.

Public transport
Buses service towns and (bigger) villages around the whole island, but most of them run only a few times a day. Travelling by bus is inexpensive, great fun and adventurous, but also time consuming. When getting on the bus tell the driver your destination so you can be notified of your arrival. Consult **www.ktel-lesvou.gr**.

Accommodation
There is a wide range of accommodation available on the island, including studios, apartments, and houses. Most cheap package deals (flight and hotel) take you to the Molyvos area. Unfortunately, you often end up in uninspiring hotels. You'll find better, more suitable accommodation when you book through more nature and small-scale oriented companies. In the Netherlands, *Lopen op Lesbos* (**www.lopenoplesbos.nl**) and *SNP* (**www.snp.nl**) offer to arrange accommodation. Lopen op Lesbos also offers package holidays (without flight) for birdwatching, finding orchids and enjoying local food, including a rental car and a wide variety of good accommodations. Most UK based wildlife holiday companies offer guided tours of Lesbos, but some also provide non-guided holidays for those who want to 'do their own thing' (for example *Hibiscus Travel* - **www.lesbos-ecotourism.co.uk**). Local companies like *Sappho Travel* situated in Skala Eresou (**www.lesvos.co.uk**) also offer to arrange accommodation, car hire and even ferry tickets in advance. Of course you can also plan your own stay with **www.airbnb.com** where a wide variety of accommodations can be booked throughout the island.

When to go
Lesbos is of interest at any time between mid-March and mid-October. Each period has its own attractions. Orchids start to flower in March, while the highest diversity is found in early to mid-April. Some sough-after species like Komper's Orchid and lizard orchids usually flower from early May. The massive bloom of wildflowers in olive groves and scrubland is between mid-April and mid-May.

Spring bird migration is roughly in line with the flowering period of the spring species: the first migrants appear in early March, with the peak of migration taking place in mid to end April. This is also an excellent period for hiking, as the landscape is alive and green. In May more butterflies, dragonflies and reptiles appear, which can be found throughout the summer. Mid-May is still an excellent period for birdwatching, particularly for late arrivals like Rufous Bush Robin.

Between mid-July and mid-August the island is in a state of summer slumber. The hills are yellow and dry, most plants have finished flowering and it is generally too hot for tracking down wildlife. All in all, mid-summer is not the best time for the naturalist to visit Lesbos, but if you limit your explorations to early morning and late afternoon there are still reptiles, butterflies and summer birds to find. During the day, relax your pace and enjoy the island's tranquil atmosphere.

September and October bring a modest autumn flora, mostly flowering after the first rains. The beautiful autumn colours of oak woodlands and chestnut forests in October make for scenic walks, especially around Agiasos, Mount Lepetimnos and Filia.

The period of autumn migration (late August-September) is another time for birdwatchers. Although spring migration of most species is more pronounced on Lesbos than autumn migration, there still is a marvellous amount to see. The tranquillity of the island and overall stable weather (more reliable than in spring) are attractive features of an autumn trip. Be aware that far fewer birdwatchers will be around so finding out 'what's about' is harder. Autumn is a good period for raptor watching, while wetlands hold plenty of egrets and herons and the scrub and woods are full with songbirds.

ATM's and petrol stations

ATM's are found in the bigger towns around the island. In the western part they are more thinly distributed. Here you can find cash machines only in Eresos and Skala Eresou.

The same goes for petrol stations – in the western part they are only found in Andissa, Eresos, Agra, Parakila and Skalochori. In general it is best to top up when you can to ensure having sufficient petrol at all times.

Convenient travel and safety issues

Weather

Lesbos has a typical Mediterranean climate, which means that in March and April the weather can be rather unpredictable, with rainy spells and wind. If you plan your trip early in spring don't forget to take a waterproof and a set of warm clothes. Day temperatures of only 12°C are not uncommon at this time of year, while during the night temperatures may plummet below 6°C in upland areas. From May to September solar radiation can be very strong, which can be deceptive in combination with a cool sea breeze. Protect your skin with high factor sun cream and prevent sunstroke by wearing a hat. The summer period is hot and dry. Always take enough water with you to prevent dehydration. From September until mid-October temperature and weather are usually good. This is, weatherwise, the nicest period to be on Lesbos.

Water
Tap water is safe to drink all over the island. For excellent fresh water you can just fill your bottle at one of the many springs which is tastier than tap water and, arguably, better than bottled water plus much more environmentally friendly. Year round water sources are found along roadsides near Ippio, at the bridge over Evergetoulas river along route 2, at Karini (route 2), Agios Dimitrios (route 2), Agii Anargyri (route 3), about 800 m south of Agiasos (route 4) and along the road from Skopelos to Tarti. Water taps can be found in many villages on the main square. In the area of Agiasos and Asomatos they are also found along the hiking trails.

Driving on unpaved roads
More remote areas are only accessible by gravel roads or tracks. Some of them are in good condition and easy to drive in a standard car, while others are not. If you choose to explore areas this way, consider the road conditions constantly (they may vary from year to year due to rainfall). Decide whether you want to continue when facing blockages like potholes and river crossings. As a rule of thumb, avoid steep rocky tracks and don't drive a track you don't trust. Take also into account that any damage on a rental car, sustained off the tarmac is not insured. In any case, renting a 4x4 vehicle is a good option for exploring tracks in the interior of Lesbos. Mind you: even when renting a 4x4, check carefully if insurance covers damages sustained on tracks and unmetaled roads.

At the time of writing, all routes and sites described in this guidebook were easily accessible in a standard car. Only route 16 and sites J, U and V require extra care when driving.

Hiking, rambling and private property
Lesbos is an excellent destination for walking aficionados. The island's landscape is varied, tracks and trails lead you through all kinds of habitats and there is plenty of exciting flora and fauna on the way. In the villages on your itinerary, you can enjoy traditional meals (see page 195) and engage with friendly local people.

Like other regions in Greece, there is little fenced off land on Lesbos and you are usually free to explore almost any terrain. However, where land is clearly fenced off (for example some chestnut plantations around Agiasos) you are expected to respect this by not entering the enclosed area. On unfenced land, when people ask you to leave, it is probably the owner, so go back to the main track. Sometimes, the track itself is blocked by a movable fence. In this case you are allowed to enter. The fence serves to keep livestock inside. In such cases, leave fences as you found them (so close them behind you when they were closed!).

In areas around Agiasos, Molyvos and Plomari many trails are marked with signs, either red diamonds or red dots. These are generally well-maintained, but outside these areas this cannot be guaranteed. Unfortunately, there are still few detailed

hiking maps available for the island (see below). If you do decide to set out to explore remote dirt tracks in the interior of the island (which is fun to do!), we advise to use a GPS device or smartphone with GPS with maps (see below).
Although not frequently encountered, off-road motorcycling takes place on the *kalderimi*, especially around Agiasos, Asomatos and on Amali pennisula. This is illegal, hugely annoying and very damaging to the centuries old paths. It is obviously also a major disturbance of wildlife. Illegal off-road motorcycling, particularly at the weekend, is a recent phenomenon largely practised by town folk from Mytilini. When you hear a motorcycle coming, step aside quickly for your safety.

Dangerous animals
The Ottoman Viper occurs widely on Lesbos. It is Europe's most poisonous snake. Fortunately, these snakes stay well away from people and you can consider yourself lucky to see one sliding away! Do take care, though, when leaving trails and entering dense brushwood.
Beehives are found scattered over the island, mostly in olive groves and scrubland. They are harmless if you don't come too close, but you need to stay well away when beekeepers with protective suits are around. Triggered by an alarm pheromone, bees can become very aggressive, which may happen when handled or when honey is harvested. At such times, they can be dangerous.

Military compounds and objects
There are several military compounds spread over the island. Some are located close to the sites described (see routes 5, 6, 17). Be aware that taking photos of military objects is not allowed and the authorities can be very sensitive about this issue.

Responsible tourism and behaviour
'Take nothing but your photo, leave nothing behind but your footprint', is the well-known phrase that summarises the idea of responsible tourism. It goes without saying that, as a visitor to the countryside, you have the responsibility to leave your surroundings and everything in it undisturbed.
If you book a package holiday, try to find one offering small scale accommodation and avoid larger resorts which have recently been developed. In this way, you are sure to support the local community and it is likely you have a more enjoyable stay too. Even better, book your flight separately and arrange your stay locally or online.
Buying local products is a good way to support traditional land use, the local economy and even conservation. The food and products of Lesbos are excellent and generally involve olive oil, olives, honey, vegetables and meat. These products are found in small shops in towns or just along the roadside, for example by Women's Cooperatives. These are initiatives by women in rural areas to preserve the culinary traditions and crafts passed on from generation to generation. These cooperatives gradually

developed into small-scale businesses due to the superb quality of their handmade products. Try their variety of products, like traditional sweets, pastas, jams and syrups. These initiatives usually take the form of a shop combined with a workshop. You can recognise them by the goods on display and some sort of sign (usually white and the words ΑΓΡΟΤΟΥΡΙΣΤΙΚΟΣ ΣΥΝΕΤΑΙΡΙΣΜΟΣ ΓΥΝΑΙΚΩΝ. You can find them for example in Mesotopos (along the main road to Eresos on the north side of town), Parakila (north side of town), Petra (on the main square), Agra (follow the directions to site U, but continue straight at the pink café for 100 m; on the left side), Agia Paraskevi (coming from Kalloni, in town 550 m after the exit on the left) and Polichnitos (near Alpha bank in the centre). They are all open during normal shopping times (09:00 - 13:00 and 17:00 - 20:30).

A large number of birdwatchers and photographers will be around in spring. They often gather around the popular spots, like Kalloni saltpans (route 7), Metochi lake (route 8), Faneromeni (route 15) and along to road between Sigri and Eresos (route 16). This may put an unintentional strain on the birds, environment, local people and fellow naturalists. To keep your impact as low as possible, keep in mind the following:
- Don't trample upon sensitive vegetation, like marshes and orchid-rich grasslands. If you are in a group, please warn others not to do so.
- Keep sufficient distance between you and the birds to avoid disturbance, especially at nest sites. Be particularly careful when rare breeding birds are involved (e.g. Krüper's Nuthatch, Rüppell's Warbler, Cinereous Bunting and all marsh birds).
- Never use 'playback' tapes to attract birds (with so many birders around, often after the same species, this can cause undue disturbance).
- Don't enter fenced off private property.
- Don't block roads, nor park on tracks in dry river beds.
- Respect other naturalists' interests (some sites are so popular that birdwatchers, photographers and hikers get on each other's nerves).

Additional information

Recommended reading

Wildflowers The best starting point is the *Wild Flowers of the Mediterranean* by Blamey et al. (2004, A&C Black, ISBN 0-7136-7015-0) which gives an overview of the most commonly encountered species. For more detailed information we recommend *Flowers of Greece and the Balkans* by Polunin (2005, Oxford University Press, ISBN 0-19-281998-4), and the excellent (but expensive) *Flowers of Greece* by Lafranchis and Sfikas (2 volume set, 2009, Diatheo, ISBN 978-2-95216-204-3). Nearly all species of Lesbos (except orchids) are covered in *Φυτά της Ελλάδας – Η έρευνα στη Λέσβο* (Flowers of Greece – the research on Lesbos) by Axiotis (2012,

Entelecheia, ISBN 978-960-7886-18-7). Unfortunately only in Greek, but the photos in combination with scientific names are a very good guideline. It is available in bookshops in Mytilini. For the identification of orchids, the book *Ophrys – the Bee Orchids of Europe* by Pedersen & Faurholdt (2007, Kew Publishing, ISBN 978-1-84246-152-5) is very useful (emphasizes on lumping the species). Or try *The Bee Orchids of Greece ß The genus Ophrys* by Antonopoulos, in contrast to the previous book, the author treats many types as separate species. A complete reference guide to all orchids is *Orchids of Greece* by Petrou (2011, Hellenic Society for the Protection of Nature, ISBN 960-7895-95-9). A good overview of the orchids on the island are described in *Ορχιδέες αγριολούλουδα της Λέσβου* by Karatza (2012, Entelecheia, ISBN 978-960-7886-4-0), but the distribution information is rather outdated. An excellent blog with lots of information about the orchids of Lesbos is **www.janvanlent.com/blog**. A useful website with many pictures of Greek orchids is **www.greekorchids.gr**.

- **Birds** Apart from your field guide to European birds, we recommend two site guides: *A Birdwatching Guide to Lesvos* by Steve Dudley (2010, Arlequin Press, ISBN 978-1905268-061) and (for Dutch readers) *Vogels kijken op Lesbos* by Luc Hoogenstein (2014, KNNV, ISBN 978-90-5011-455-4). Although there is some overlap with the Crossbill Guide, both cover other sites as well.
- **Reptiles and amphibians** The best, but expensive, 'herps' book for Lesbos (and whole Greece) is *The Amphibians and Reptiles of Greece* by Valakos et al. (2008, Chimaira, ISBN 978-3-89973-461-4). The standard general guide *Reptiles and Amphibians of Britain and Europe* by Arnold and Ovenden (2002 Collins ISBN: 0002199645) is now rather dated, but the forthcoming *Reptiles and Amphibians of Britain and Europe* by Beukema et al (2016 Helm Field Guides) should prove very useful.
- **Insects** The *Collins Butterfly Guide: The Most Complete Field Guide to the Butterflies of Britain and Europe* by Tolman (2009, ISBN 978-0-00-727977-7; also available in Dutch) and *Butterflies of Europe* by Lafranchis (2004, Diatheo, ISBN 978-2-95-216200-5; also available in Dutch, French and Polish) are both excellent guides that help you name the butterflies of Lesbos. *The Field Guide to the Dragonflies of Britain and Europe* by Dijkstra (2006, British Wildlife Publishing, ISBN 0-953-1399-5-6; also in Dutch) contains superb illustrations which is an indispensable tool identifying all the dragonflies and damselflies of Lesbos.
- **Hiking** There are several good walking guides on Lesbos available. For example *On Foot – Circular Walks on Lesvos* (2012, Olive Press, ISBN 0-953-9214-76) and *On Foot in North Lesvos* (2010, Olive Press, ISBN 0-953-9214-33) both by Van der Zee et al. (also in Dutch), and *Lesvos Walks and Car Tours* by Anderson et al. (2013, Sunflower, ISBN 978-1856914390). *The Lesvos Hiking guide* by Tsouris (2013, Geopsis, ISBN 978-960-934041-0; bilingual English/Greek) includes detailed maps and (long distance) routes.

Geology The museum of Lesvos Petrified Forest publishes several English guides about volcanism and the petrified forest park. They can only be purchased in bookshops on the island and the Petrified Forest museum in Sigri.

General The pocket sized *A girl's guide to Lesbos* by Hadjidimitriou (2012, T. Hadjidimitriou, ISBN 978-960-90330-3-9) is very useful for every visitors (including men!). It is full with information about the different regions on Lesbos, culture, museums and gastronomy.

Guided tours

There are a number of companies that offer guided tours, either as day trip or a fully organised holiday. They will help you to find birds and orchids, or tell you about history, land use, geology or let you taste the delights of the local cuisine. Some of them are listed below.

Pandora travel a local company offering all kinds of excursions and activities to discover the island, like hiking, mountain biking, jeep safaris, photography and much more. **www.pandoralesvos.com**

Lesvos birding a British company, run by the author of *A Birdwatching Guide to Lesvos*, offers birding day trips with orchids, insects and reptiles as a secondary goal. **lesvosbirding.com/day-trips**

Jan van Lent a Dutch photographer, living on the island, organises orchid excursions to find sought-after species. Email: vanlentlesvos@gmail.com

Hellenic Whole Foods a Dutch company run by Alex Tabak, author of this Crossbill Guide. Hellenic Whole Foods organises day trips or week holidays (both in Dutch and English) with a focus on local gastronomy, history and culture combined with wildlife, orchids and geology. **www.hellenicwholefoods.com**.

Maps

The best maps covering the whole island are the 1:80.000 Road Editions *Lesvos* (nr. 212) and the 1:50.000 Freytag & Berndt *Lesbos*. There are two excellent hiking maps with routes available of the areas *Mytilini* and *Aghiasos* (Geopsis, 1:12.000), and a detailed map of the area *Kalloni* (Geopsis, 1:33.000). Digital versions of these maps can be ordered online through **www.geopsis.com**.

When you use a GPS device you can download free maps from **www.openmtbmap.org**. Install for your tablet or smartphone for example the app *Offline Maps* (elderorb) which can be used without being connected to the internet.

Greek cuisine and local dishes

The tradition of Greek cuisine embraces the Epicurean ideal of living to eat rather than eating to live. Tasting traditional and local food is therefore an adventure. Greek food is characterized by rich and fresh tastes, with seasonal products straight from the land and plenty of excellent olive oil. Dishes are often seasoned with oregano, dill and laurel. Fresh lemon juice is one of the most defining flavours. It is used with nearly all dishes. There are many different types of food, like *ladera* (lush vegetarian dishes often containing eggplant, tomato, garlic and onion), various meat dishes (lamb, pork and rabbit), seafood and both cooked (like beans, beetroot and wild vegetables) and fresh salads (like tomato, cabbage and cos lettuce). In contrast to common belief, there are many vegetarian dishes in Greek cuisine. In short, there is so much more to discover than the well-known souvlaki, gyros and mousakas.

There is not one traditional Greek kitchen, but every region within the country has one of its own. On Lesbos the local flavour is influenced by the fertile land, the free roaming sheep and the surrounding Aegean sea.

Usually the best way to experience local food is by eating outside the main tourist areas. In traditional tavernas it is customary to order all kinds of small dishes and share them amongst your companions. The final seasoning of any dish is regarded a personal taste, therefore olive oil and lemon is provided to apply at your own discretion. Dining times are usually 13:00-15:00 and in the evening after 19:30.

Eat fish and seafood only where it is fresh, that means only in tavernas close to the sea. It is the custom for guests to go to the kitchen and check the fish first hand. As a rule of thumb: fresh fish doesn't smell, the gills should be red on the inside, the eyes of the fish clear and its skin tight. In tavernas you pay for fresh fish by the weight rather than by the plate, so ask for the price beforehand.

By eating in small or traditional tavernas, you support the continuation of small-scale farming and the wildlife that comes with it. Local and traditional food is a delight both on your plate and for your palate, but it also sustains unforgettable experiences in the field too. Listed below are some great and sometimes adventurous traditional (side) dishes.

Ladotýri (Λαδοτύρι) Traditional sheep cheese from Lesbos, matured in olive oil. Served fried or grilled with lemon.

Giouzlemés (Γκιουζλεμές) Fried pastry with feta cheese filling (a traditional Lesbos dish).

Kakaviá (Κακαβιά) Traditional fisherman's soup with different kinds of fish (depending on what was caught that day) and vegetables. For a genuine eating experience you should first eat the fish and vegetables and you finish by drinking the soup from a glass. The best *Kakaviá* (in our opinion) is at the fish taverna *To Limani* in Skala Polychnitou. It is essential to call beforehand due to the long preparation time: 0030 6984328891. The owner doesn't speak English well, but you can arrange it through your accommodation. It's worth it!

Háchles Yemistés (Χάχλες γεμιστές) Coarsely grained wheat, cooked with fermented sheep milk and filled with tomato and feta. Served at *To Stavri* in Agiasos (see below), sometimes elsewhere.

Sougánia (Σουγάνια) Onion filled with rice and minced meat, spiced with cumin and parsley and covered with lemon-egg sauce.

Stifádo (Στιφάδο) Stew of rabbit (or beef) with shallots, cooked in a rich tomato sauce, seasoned with laurel and cinnamon.

Sardines of Kalloni (Παπαλίνα) These are considered the best in Greece. They are traditionally cured for five hours in coarse sea salt. Best eaten with ouzo in Skala Kalloni.

Oúzomezédes (Ουζομεζέδες) Drinking ouzo is a social custom, best enjoyed in combination with food. Ouzomezédes are a variation of small tasty side dishes to accompany ouzo. They have a particular taste that combines well with the spirit and consists usually of fish, seafood and pickles.

Youvarlákia (Γιουβαρλάκια) Meatballs mixed with rice and a sour and creamy sauce.

Fáva (Φάβα) soft cooked split peas topped with chopped onion, oregano and olive oil.

Choriátiki (Χωριάτικη) Greek salad with tomatoes, cucumber, green pepper, onion, oregano and feta.

Chórta (Χόρτα) Cooked wild vegetables, served with olive oil and lemon juice.

Briám (Μπριάμ) Rich oven-baked dish with eggplant, potato, courgette, tomato, garlic and onion.

Yemistá (Γεμιστά) Tomatoes and peppers filled with rice and mint, baked in the oven.

Fasolakia (Φασολάκια) String beans in red sauce with olive oil.

Bámies (Μπάμιες) Okra with tomato and olive oil. Traditionally served with meat like veal or as vegetarian side dish.

Kolokýthia yemistá (Κολοκύθια γεμιστά) Stuffed courgette with rice and minced meat in an egg-lemon juice sauce, seasoned with dill.

Aginós (Αχινός) Fresh Sea Urchins served in their shell, with lemon juice. Best eaten at *Australia* in Sigri (see below).

Foúska (Φούσκα) Fresh Sea Cucumber with olive oil and lemon. Best eaten at *Australia* in Sigri (see below).

Recommended restaurants

There are too many good tavernas on Lesbos to mention them all. Listed here is a number of our personal favourites, not only for food, but also because of their scenic location or position close to interesting sites and routes described in this book. If no directions are given in list below, the taverna is easily found.

1 **Avlonas in Avlonas** Set in a spacious and lush garden, with views over the mouth of the Gulf of Gera. Delicious, traditionally made dishes, but also 'newer' ones like grilled oyster mushroom (locally cultivated). In early spring only open in the weekends (0030-2251051950). English and German spoken (near site G).

2 **Ntam in Perama** Situated between Perama's old industrial heritage buildings (see history section), halfway between the mainroad and the port. It's an unpretentious, small venue but known for the best gyros on the island made from local meat. Tip: go early in the evening before it's all eaten! (near sites D, E, F and G).

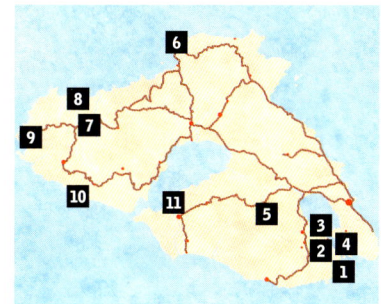

3 **Despotis in Perama** A superb fish taverna peacefully set along the shore of the Gulf of Gera, 300 m south of the village (first house on the left). The owners have their own fishing boat to bring in a fresh catch every day (near sites D, E, F and G).

4 **The tavernas at Koudouroundia** Koudouroundia has two tavernas, both of which offer good food, and views over the Gulf of Gera. The big draw at this location is the combination of a visit with crossing the Gulf of Gera by the small ferry from Perama. It leaves from the harbour of Perama and goes about 10 times a day (small charge; near sites D,E, F and G (by ferry) and starting point of route 1).

5 **To Stavri in Agiasos** Situated in the upper part of town, this taverna is for the locals and has the best 'mountain food'. Tip: ask for the exquisite dishes like *Briám*, *Háchles Yemistés*, *Touloumotýri* (young sheep cheese ripened in a goats skin) or even fried morel (μοχέλες; kind of wild mushroom) with lemon (near routes 2, 3, 4 and site K).

6 **Majoran (or Manzourana) in Molyvos** There are a lot of eateries in touristy Molyvos, but it is not always easy to find good, local food. One of the exceptions is Majoran, situated along the main road on the south side of town. It is more a restaurant than a taverna, but retains an informal ambiance and offers Greek cuisine with a modern twist. Intriguing dishes and abundant tastes (near route 10 and 11).

7 **To Kati Allo in Andissa** Situated on the main square under majestic plane trees, where Scops Owl is often seen from the dinner table. Known for its *fava*, meat dishes and savoury salads (near routes 13 and 14).

8 **Liota in Liota** Situated under a centuries old plane tree, next to a small historic church with frescos. Tasty lamb chops and generally just good food in a tranquil setting (starting point of route 14).

9 **Australia in Sigri** Set beautifully at the coast of Sigri. This taverna offers some of the best seafood and fish, straight from the Aegean sea. Tip: the *Aginós* and *Foúska* (see above). Australia (emphasis on the i) is run by Lesbos natives who have returned from Australia (see history section; near routes 15 and 16).

10 **Chrousos in Chrousos** Situated in a sparsely inhabited area close to a sandy beach. The peaceful location and surrounding flowery garden gives it the air of a ´hide-out´. The owner Stavritsa will serve you fantastic grilled local meat (like lamb chops

from her son's flock of sheep) and tasty cooked dishes. The taverna also has a few apartments (at site V).

11 **To Limani in Skala Polichnitou** Another excellent fish taverna located by a tranquil village harbour, along the Gulf of Kalloni. Famous for its *Kakaviá* (traditional fisherman's soup, see above) and the right spot to try *oúzomezédes* (see above) (near route 5 and sites O, L).

Archeological sites, monuments and museums

1 **Prehistoric Thermi** The site and small museum show the foundations and findings of a settlement in the early to late Bronze Age (3200-1300 BC). The site is located near Pyrgi Thermi, 10 km north of Mytilini, from where it is well signposted. Easy to combine with sites A and B.

2 **Sanctuary of Klopedi** On this site the foundations of an Aeolian temple from the 6th century BC can be seen. The temple was most likely dedicated to the God Apollo. Columns and capitals (topmost parts of columns) are exhibited. The site was a sanctuary even earlier, in the 8th century BC, while the remains of a living quarters date from the 12th century BC. Open daily, except on Mondays, Sundays and on public holidays.
To get there, take the south exit to Agia Paraskevi from the main road Kalloni – Mandamados. After 450 m turn left to a tarmac road signposted Πρινή Κλοπεδή (Klopedi), opposite a blue building. The road becomes a track and after 3 km, turn left and cross a bridge. Immediately turn left onto a track which leads uphill to the site. Combine with route 7 and sites Q and R.

3 **Sanctuary of Mesa** Between the 7th and 2nd century BC this was both the most important place of worship on the island and the centre of deliberation for the different city states. In early Christian times, a shrine and Byzantine church were consecutively built on top of the temple. On the site Aeolian foundations and elements from the earliest temple can be seen. Open daily 8:30-15:00, except on Mondays and on public holidays.
To get there take the exit to *Mesa* from the main road Mytilini to Kalloni, 800 m east of the exit to Achladeri. Easy to combine with route 6 and 7.

4 **Ancient Andissa** One of the ancient city states of Lesbos. See route 13 for more details.

5 **Palios** Remains of a medieval castle and tombs from between 200 and 100 BC) See route 9 for more details.

6 **Ancient Theatre of Mytilini** The theatre was initially built in the 2nd century BC and later reconstructed in the 2nd century AD. In ancient Greece it was one of the largest of its kind, housing more than 10,000 spectators. Over the years the theatre was subject to severe erosion and the stone seats unfortunately washed away. The theatre is situated on a forested hill on the northwestern side of Mytilini.
Coming from town via the main road to Kalloni, turn right after 500 m onto the

road towards Mandamados and Thermi. Then take the first tarmac road to the right, signposted *Ancient Theatre of Mytilene*. After 400 m turn right onto a car park and walk uphill. It can be visited the whole year round.

7 **Kremasti bridge** The remarkable 8.5 m high single arch Kremasti bridge was built between 1355 and 1462, in Genoese times. To get there, follow the main road Kalloni – Mandamados road. Approaching from the south, turn left about 500 m north of Agia Paraskevi onto a track sign posted Kremasti bridge. The bridge is 2.8 km further. Combine with site Q and R.

8 **Roman Aqueduct** There are on Lesbos impressive remains of an aqueduct that was built in the 2nd century AD. It transported water from springs of Mount Olymbos to Mytilini. For more information see route 2 and site A.

9 **Castle of Mytilini** Towering over the city, this is one of the largest medieval castles in the eastern Mediterranean. It is built on the foundations of an older fortress and Acropolis. It is open daily (except Monday) from 8:30-15:00. When accessing Mytilini from the north (from Mandamados), the road makes a sharp bend to the right just before the castle. Park approximately 150 m further along the road. A tarmac road leads uphill to the castle entrance. Easy to combine with route 1.

10 **Castle of Molyvos** This castle is an impressive landmark of the north of Lesbos. It is built in the early Byzantine period and reconstructed later in the Genoese era. It is open daily (except Monday) from 8:30-15:00. From Molyvos take the tarmac road in the direction of Eftalou and follow the signs *Castle*. Alternatively, park in Molyvos and continue uphill through the narrow streets. Easy to combine with routes 10 and 11.

11 **Castle of Sigri** The castle of Sigri is a conspicuous building along the coast, built in the 18th century by the Ottomans to protect the port of Sigri, which was important for trade. The castle is closed to the public. Easy to combine with route 15 and 16.

12 **Ipsilou Monastery** See route 17 for more details.

13 **Monastery of Taxiarches in Mandamados** A monastery where an eerie icon, made from a mixture of dirt and blood, can be seen, decorated with a silver aureole. According to the legend it was made by a monk, who was the only survivor of a pirate raid somewhen between 800 and 1000 AD. He used the blood of his massacred fellow monks. Open daily, usually from 8:00 till dusk. The monastery lies just north of Mandamados, on the main road signposted *Moni Taxiarchon*.

14 **Natural History Museum of the Petrified Forest** Excellent museum in Sigri where petrified trees and the fossilised remains of mammals can be seen. The museum also has a display of fossils from elsewhere in the world and an informative exhibition

about geological evolution and processes. The museum is situated on the main road in the village. Open daily 10:00-17:00 (October-June) or 9:00-18:00 (July-September), but closed on public holidays. Easy to combine with routes 15 and 16.
15 **Petrified Forest Park** See route 16 for more details.
16 **Archaeological museum of Skala Eresou** This is a museum of archaeological finds made on the western side of the island. Situated in the centre of Skala Eresou. Open daily 8:00-15:00. Easy to combine with route 16.
17 **Archaeological museum of Mytilini** This museum exhibits a great collection of archaeological finds from excavations around the island, such as inscriptions, mosaics, capitals and gold artefacts. Open daily 9:00-14:30 and 18:00-22:00 (May-October) or 9:00-14:30 (November-April). The museum lies just behind the main ferry dock. Easy to combine with route 1.
18 **Olive press museum Papados** Informative museum that presents the history of the olive oil production on Lesbos. The exhibition shows production process, olive presses and steam engines. It is located in an historical olive press building. Open Tue-Sun 9:00-16:00 (November-April) or 9:00-19:00 (May-October), except on public holidays. The museum is well signposted in the village of Papados. Easy to combine with sites C, D, E, F and H.
19 **Theophilos Museum** This museum exhibits a large collection of paintings of Theophilos (see page 44). Open daily 10:00-14:00, except weekends and on public holidays. This museum (as well as the Museum of Modern Art) is located in the suburb Akrotiri in Mytilini, and signposted throughout Mytilini.
20 **Thermal baths** There are several thermal baths at the natural hot springs of Lesbos. These are therapeutic, relaxing wellness centres. The water is heated naturally, through geothermal processes. The temperature varies between 42° C and 44° C. Currently the ones in Polichnitos, Eftalou and Kendro (along the northern shore of the Gulf of Gera) are open to the public.

Observation tips

Finding orchids

Orchid hunting is an exciting and highly addictive 'discipline', which requires much dedication. First, naming them is a daunting task as many species' characteristics are rather unstable (for that reason, amongst others, the viability of some 'species' is contested; see page 74), Second, finding them is difficult, if you don't know where to look. So here's some advice.

If you have never searched for orchids before, be aware that most pictures in guidebooks (including this one!) are close-ups that make the flowers appear much larger than they actually are. Some species, like Marsh and Balkan Lizard Orchids with their bold spikes are hard to miss, but the bee orchids (*Ophrys*), which are generally small, are a different matter, despite their brightly coloured and patterned flowers. The plants do vary considerably in size (with spikes of between 10 cms to over 50 cms) but the flowers are invariably small – between 1.5 and 4 cms, depending on the species. This makes them easy to overlook. It frequently happens even to us (and we have been orchid hunting for quite some years) that after finding a beautiful specimen, having turned away to grab our macro lenses, upon turning back the plant seems to have disappeared into thin air. The flower can be that cryptic! The mental image you need to make for yourself is of the whole plant rather than the flower alone. If you scan the vegetation, it is often the thick and rather pale stalk that stands out first and makes it easier to pick out the orchids amidst the more colourful wildflowers.

Most bee orchids (*Ophrys*) flower in early spring – that is between late March and late April. Other species, belonging to groups such as *Serapias* and *Orchis*, flower mainly between May and early June. Beware, though, that it all depends on the temperature and rainfall in winter and early spring. With high temperatures early in season, flowering time might start a week, or even two, earlier.

The most splendid display of orchids on Lesbos, especially of *Ophrys*, tend to be found in old, unploughed olive groves on calcareous soil (mostly in the southeast of the island). Since orchids are not the most resilient plants, disturbed and overgrazed olive groves are not the best places to search for them. These unfavourable conditions are distinguished by the dominance of Summer Asphodel (which is poisonous and benefits from sheep grazing away the competition), so any grove with lots of asphodels is best skipped. In promising olive groves, make sure you search the various corners of the site – orchids often grow together in clumps, with different species growing in different parts of the grove. This being said, the best parts are usually close to tracks and around the trunks that are supported by stone walls.

The chestnut and pine forests in the area of Agiasos are other top notch locations where you'll find a different array of species, such as Komper's and Reinhold's Orchids.

Finding reptiles

Lesbos hosts 22 species of reptiles. Some of them are hard to find, but with some effort and a little luck, a rendez-vous with some of the island's snakes, tortoises, and lizards is more than a distinct possibility.

The lizards and tortoises are most easily seen. They simply cross your path during your walks or are found rumbling in the leaf litter or basking on an old stone wall. The way to enhance your chances is simply to lace up your boots and go hiking, rather than visiting all sites by car.

Terrapins are best found by scanning the banks of rivers and small lagoons near the coast. The same applies to both 'water snakes' (Dice and Grass Snakes). Whenever you approach a bridge or the water's edge, do so slowly and with care, as it is vital that you scan the favoured sites before the animals have sensed you. To make it more specific, tread lightly as snakes are sensitive to ground vibrations by which they detect the approach of danger; that's why the snake-eating Short-toed Eagles are so infinitely more successful in finding snakes than ourselves. The same considerations will increase your chances of spotting terrapins.

Most other snakes are secretive animals. You encounter them most often in the morning when snakes are still warming up in sunny patches. Species like Caspian Whip, Montpellier, Leopard and Worm Snakes can be found basking on the trail ahead of you. At this time of the day, it is rewarding where possible to look ahead along the trail, to scan the open patches or tracks with your binoculars. Again, this is the way to spot them before they have noticed you.

Snakes like to hide underneath flat stones, logs and rubbish like cardboard or plastic. Lifting up such material can be very rewarding for finding snakes. However, do keep in mind that suddenly lifting up the roof of someone's house is a rather invasive way to say hello. You are seriously disturbing whatever lives underneath. Makes sure the disturbance is short, put the stone (log, cardboard, plastic) back exactly as you found it and don't lift stones at all in places that are crowded with people who might follow your example. In general, good areas to find snakes are scrubland and olive groves near (dry) river beds, with some cover of vegetation.

Birdlist Lesbos

Birds that occur only occasionally are omitted from this list.

Ducks Ruddy Shelduck is the only breeding species of duck on Lesbos. It is a frequent and increasing bird (very good are 6, 7 and 9, also 13, 16 and site O and P) Shelduck is a frequent winter visitor (has bred) of salt marshes (6, 7 and site O and P). Garganey is a frequent passage migrant on all types of standing water (2, 6, 7, 8, 16). Shoveler, Mallard, Wigeon, Teal and Pintail all winter in low numbers in coastal wetlands (6, 7 and site P). Red-breasted Merganser is a rare winter visitor off the coast and bay of Kalloni.

Partridges Chukar is a common breeding bird throughout rocky areas, in particular in the centre and western part of the island (9, 10, 11, 16, 17 and sites U and V). Quail is a scarce visitor mainly in spring, but has bred.

Divers and grebes Black-throated Diver and Black-necked Grebe winter in small numbers off-shore (e.g. 1). Great Crested Grebe winters off-shore and in large numbers in both gulfs (1, 2, 5 and site D). Little Grebe breeds in small numbers in Potamia and Metochi (8).

Shearwaters Both Yelkouan (very common) and Cory's or Scopoli's Shearwater (fairly common) are breeding birds of the general region and seen commonly from off-shore vantage points (1, 5, 9, 11, 13, 15 and site V).

Pelicans Great White is a near annual passage migrant, sometimes found in small flocks (6, 7 and site O). Dalmatian Pelican is less common but has increased in recent years, and infrequently recorded in both saltpans in July (7 and site O).

Cormorants Great Cormorant is a common winter bird in the gulfs. Small numbers are at sea during the other months. Shag is a fairly frequent resident breeding bird (5, 9, 15).

Herons, bitterns and egrets Little Bittern, Little Egret and Squacco Heron are common and Night Heron and Purple Heron fairly common passage migrants (mostly spring; 2, 5, 6, 7, 8, 13, 15, 16 and site O, P and V). Grey Heron and Great White Egret are uncommon wintering birds. A few summer.

Storks White Stork is a rare breeding bird, but found in several towns (e.g. Kaloni, Polichnitos, Agia Paraskevi). Large numbers pass through early in the year. Black Stork is a common passage migrant, often seen flying over river valleys (especially good are 5, 6, 16 sites O, P, Q and R). A few birds remain to breed in wooded hills in the vicinity of wetlands.

Ibis, Spoonbill and Flamingo Greater Flamingo is fairly numerous in the salt marshes in winter, with a few specimens spending the summer months (7 and site O). Glossy Ibis passes through in good numbers during spring passage (best 7 and site O). The same goes for Spoonbill, but in lower numbers and mostly seen at Polichnitos (site O), slightly more in autumn than in spring.

Raptors Raptors are most common during autumn migration. They follow the broad north-south valleys and are best seen at Napi (site Q, Platania (site R), Ipsilou (16, 17), Ambeliko valley (5), Pterounda (site T), the north slopes of Mount Lepetimnos (10) and Lafionas (12). The typical raptors that pass through are Honey Buzzard (fairly common), Buzzard (Common), Long-legged Buzzard (fairly common), Short-toed Eagle (fairly common), Sparrowhawk (common), Levant's Sparrowhawk (scarce, best Napi valley), Booted Eagle (rare). Many other species of raptors are recorded on passage occasionally, of which Bonelli's Eagle is seen most often. The coastal lowlands (6, 7) see many Marsh and Montagu's Harriers on passage. Osprey and Pallid Harrier pass through in smaller, but still good, numbers.

In winter, Goshawk, Sparrowhawk, Buzzard and Long-legged Buzzard are found throughout the island. Goshawk and Sparrowhawk occur mostly in wooded areas, Long-legged Buzzard is mostly seen in the west and north, where it also breeds (11, 13, 14, 17 and sites Q, R, T, V). A handful of Short-toed Eagles also breed on the island (routes 11, 16, 17 and sites R and V). Hen Harrier winters in low numbers (6, 7), including some late returning migrants in spring.

Falcons Kestrel and Peregrine are uncommon breeding birds throughout the island. Lesser Kestrel breeds off-shore on islands near Sigri, and are often seen on 15, 16 and site V. Eleonora's Falcon is suspected to breed as well on the islands near Sigri and is most often seen in spring and autumn (8, 13, 15, 16, site V). Hobby passes through in small numbers, but Red-footed Falcon does so in large numbers. Both are most frequent in spring with Red-footed Falcon mostly seen at Kalloni (6, 7 and site P).

Rails and Coots The ever-elusive rails are among the highlights of bird migration on Lesbos as they can be seen here with relative ease. Water Rail breed in the reed-beds (2, 8) while Little Crake is fairly common and Spotted and Baillon's Crake rare in this habitat (5, best 8). Spring is the best season to see them. Coot and Moorhen occur with small numbers, the first most frequently in the winter.

Waders The Kalloni saltpans, Mesa and Polichnitos (6, 7, site O) are the best sites for waders. Apart from the occasional vagrant, you may expect to find here Oystercatcher (fairly common, best winter) Black-winged Stilt (common, also breeds), Avocet (fairly common, occasionally winters), Lapwing (a scarce, winter), Spur-winged Lapwing (rare but possibly increasing spring migrant), Golden, Grey and Ringed Plovers (scarce on passage), Kentish Plover (fairly common, also breeds), Jack Snipe (scarce in winter), Snipe (fairly common in winter and passage, but easily overlooked), Black-tailed Godwit (scarce migrant, mostly in spring), Whimbrel (rare on passage), Curlew (scarce in winter and autumn passage), Spotted Redshank, Marsh Sandpiper and Greenshank (all scarce on passage), Redshank (common in winter up to spring), Green Sandpiper (scarce in winter), Wood Sandpiper (common migrant), Common Sandpiper (scarce migrant), Turnstone (scarce in spring), Sanderling (scarce migrant), Little and Temminck's Stint (both common migrants, most in spring), Curlew Sandpiper (fairly common migrant, most in spring), Broad-billed Sandpiper (rare migrant, most in autumn), and Ruff (fairly common passage migrant).

Collared Pratincole is fairly common on passage at Kalloni and Almeropotamos (5, 7 and site P). Stone Curlew breeds at Kalloni (6, 7 and site P) and is most easily seen in autumn. Little Ringed Plover, Wood, Green and Common Sandpipers are also found in freshwater sites inland.

Gulls Slender-billed, Black-headed, Mediterranean and Little Gulls are frequent to scarce visitors, mainly of the Kalloni saltpans (7). All occur in winter and on passage. Audouin's Gull is a rare breeding bird of off-shore islands in the north. It is best seen on routes 11, 13, sometimes also at Kalloni (7). Yellow-legged Gull also breeds on off-shore islands but can be seen all over Lesbos, especially at the coast. Lesser Black-backed Gull is uncommon in winter off-shore.

Terns Little Tern is a common breeding bird of the coastal lowlands (breeds at 7, also seen at 5, 6, 13, 15 and 16 and site O and P). Common Tern is a scarce breeding bird and common migrant to the same sites. Whiskered and White-winged Tern pass through in large numbers and Black Tern and Gull-billed Tern in small numbers at the same sites, both in spring and autumn. Sandwich Tern is common in winter off-shore.

Pigeons Rock Dove breeds in low numbers at the coast (e.g. 14 and 15). Wood Pigeon is a scarce breeding bird and common winter visitor. Turtle Dove is a common breeding bird and migrant which can be seen all over the island. Collared Dove is common in town and villages.

Cuckoos Great Spotted Cuckoo is a rare migrant in spring, which frequently turns up at Dexameni Lake (10). Common Cuckoo is a frequent migrant and seen all over the island.

Owls Barn and Long-eared Owl are widespread but scarce. Little Owl is most common in the rocky western part of the island (16, 17). Scops Owl is common all around the island. It is particularly common around the Gulf of Gera and can be seen with relative ease at night in the large Plane Trees on the main square at Andissa and the monastery of Perivolis (13).

Nightjar Common spring migrant but rare breeding bird. A good site is at Achladeri forest (6). Also found around Mt Lepetimnos.

Swifts Swift is a common breeding bird. The Pallid Swift is surprisingly absent as a breeding bird, although it passes through in small numbers. Alpine Swift passes through commonly (best 17), but does not breed. Birds seen in summer are thought to come from off-shore islands and nearby Turkey.

Hoopoe, Kingfisher, Roller and Bee-eater Hoopoe is common throughout the island. Bee-eater is a common migrant, but breeds only very locally. Routes 5, 10, 11, 13, 14, 15 and 16 and sites O and P are good for finding Bee-eaters on passage. Roller is a scarce passage migrant, infrequently seen at 5, 6, 10, 13, 15 and 16, and site O. Kingfisher is most common at the coast in autumn and winter. It breeds at the bridge of the Vouvaris (6) and is often seen in the harbour of Skala Sikaminia (11).

Woodpeckers Only Middle-spotted Woodpecker breeds on Lesbos. It is fairly common in old olive groves and chestnut and oak woodlands (2, 3, 4, 5, 8, 12 and 14 and site C). Wryneck is seen only occasionally on passage.

Larks Crested Lark is common, especially along roads in open areas. Woodlark is a scarce breeding bird of open woodland (6). Greater short-toed Lark breeds in low numbers in coastal saline wetlands and grasslands (6, 7). Skylark is a winter visitor of the coastal lowlands (6, 7).

Swallows and martins Sand Martin breeds at Voulgaris (13). Swallow and House Martin are common and widespread, as is Red-rumped Swallow (e.g. 10, 11, 15, 16 and site J). Crag Martin is restricted to cliffs (2, 10, 13, 16 and site J).

Wagtails and pipits Various types of 'yellow' Wagtails are common in the coastal lowlands (2, 6, 7). Black-headed is the most common and also breeds. Other forms (or species) that pass through include Blue-headed (common), Grey-headed (common) and Ashy-headed (rare). White Wagtail is surprisingly rare on Lesbos. Grey Wagtail breeds along stony rivers (2, 3, 16). Their numbers increase in winter. Citrine Wagtail is an uncommon passage migrant (7, 13, 15, 16). Tawny Pipit passes through and perhaps breeds at 6, 7, 16 and site O. Meadow Pipit is a common winter visitor at the same sites. Tree Pipit and Red-throated Pipit are scarce passage migrants (7, 15 and site O).

Robin, nightingales and rufous bush-chat Robin is fairly common in the eastern mountains (2, 4). Nightingale is a common breeding bird of riverside woodlands and wooded marshes. Thrush Nightingale is a scarce passage migrant. Rufous Bush Robin is a localised bird of dry, rocky and scrubby terrain (7, 9, 15, 16 and site V).

Redstarts Black Redstart is common in winter and Common Redstart is scarce on passage.

Wheatears and chats Whinchat is a common passage migrant. Stonechat breeds and winters in small numbers. Isabelline Wheatear is fairly rare and a localized breeding bird (16, 17 and site T and V). Northern Wheatear also breed in small numbers in the western part of the island (e.g. 16, 17 and site Q). Black-eared Wheatear is a common breeding bird, especially in the western part of the island (e.g 2, 5, 9, 10, 11, 15, 16, 17). Pied Wheatear is a very rare passage migrant – some sightings are disputed. On passage, Kalloni (7) attracts many wheatears.

Thrushes Blackbird is a common bird and winter visitor. Song Thrush is a common winter visitor and localised breeding bird of the eastern mountains (4). Fieldfare and Redwing are both scarce winter visitors. Mistle Thrush is a rare breeding bird of open pinewoods (2, 4, 6 and site M). Blue Rock Thrush is a widespread breeding bird of rocky areas (6, 10, 13, 16, 17).

Warblers Subalpine Warbler is the most common of the warblers of the *Sylvia*-genus. Blackcap is also common in wooded areas. Sardinian Warbler is surprisingly rare and restricted to coastal areas (1, 9, 10, 11, 12, 13 and 16). Orphean Warbler breeds across the island (5, 6, 9, 10, 11). Rüppell's Warbler is a rare bird, best known from route 10. Whitethroat, Garden and Barred Warbler occur in small numbers on passage (e.g. 6, 11, 15, 16).

Cetti's Warbler is a common breeding bird of freshwater marshes and riversides. Bonelli's Warbler is frequent in woodlands around Olympos (2, 3, 4) and infrequent elsewere.

Great Reed Warbler is common and Reed Warbler is scarce in reedbeds (1, 2, 8, also 5, 13 and 15), Moustached Warbler is listed at 2 and 5 as winter visitor (to February). Olivaceous Warbler is a common breeding bird of dry scrubland. Olive-tree Warbler is a widespread but scarce breeding bird of open woodland with some scrub (5, 8 and 14, and sites Q and R).

On passage, Willow Warbler, Chiffchaff, Wood Warbler and Sedge Warbler are common. Marsh Warbler is scarce and Icterine and River Warblers are rare passage birds. Chiffchaff also occurs commonly in winter. Zitting Cisticola breeds in grasslands in the coastal lowlands (2, 6, 7 and site O). Goldcrest is restricted to coniferous woods (e.g. 2, 4)

Wren and flycatchers Wren is a widespread but fairly scarce breeding bird. Spotted and Pied Flycatchers are common passage migrants, especially at 15 and 16. Spotted also breeds in pinewoods. Collared and Semi-collared are rare and very rare respectively on spring passage, again at 15 and 16.

Tits Great and Blue Tits are common throughout. Coal and Long-tailed Tits are local birds of pine forests (2, 4, 6 and site T). Sombre Tit is a widespread and fairly common bird of open deciduous woodland and scrub (5, 8, 10, 14, 16, 17).

Nuthatches and Treecreeper Nuthatch is an uncommon breeding bird of old oak stands (e.g. 4, 10, 14 and site Q). Krüper's Nuthatch is restricted to pinewoods in the east, as is Short-toed Treecreeper (2, 4, 6 and site M). Rock Nuthatch is a widespread but scarce bird of rocky terrain (6, 8, 10, 11, 13 16, 17 and sites R, T, U and V).

Shrikes Red-backed and Woodchat Shrike are common on passage (5, 6, 10, 12, 13, 15 and 16) Lesser Grey Shrike is a scarce passage migrant and breeding bird at roughly the same sites (best 6, 10 and 16). Woodchat Shrike is a common breeding bird all over the island. Masked Shrike is a local but not uncommon breeding bird of olive groves and open (pine) woods (1, 2, 5, 6, 8, 9, 10, 11, 13, 15, 16 and sites C and O).

Starlings and Golden Oriole Starling is a widespread winter visitor. Rosy Starling is mostly a rare but annual migrant (most frequent at site P). However, in invasion years it can be common, particularly in the lowlands. Golden Oriole is a common passage migrant and frequent breeding bird of riparian forest (2, 3, 5, 10, 13, 15, 16).

Crows and allies Hooded Crow is the most common member of the crow family. The Asian atricapilus form of Jay is common in wooded areas.
Colonies of Jackdaw are present in most towns. Raven breeds in the Olymbos area and western mountains (2 and site T).

Sparrows House Sparrow is common throughout. Spanish Sparrow breeds colonially in agricultural land (e.g. 7, 11, 15) and can occur in large numbers during migration. Rock Sparrow is a localised breeding bird of the dry rocky west (13, 16 and 17).

Finches Chaffinch is a common breeding bird and winter visitor in well-wooded areas. Greenfinch and Goldfinch are common and widespread. Linnet is an uncommon breeding bird of dry terrain (e.g. 16, 17 and site U). Brambling, Siskin and Hawfinch are scarce winter visitors in varying numbers. Hawfinch also breeds near Agiasos (3, 4). Serin breeds in pinewoods (e.g. 6, site M and N).

Buntings Cirl Bunting is a common breeding bird of open oak woodland (e.g. 2, 6, 10, 14, 17). Cretschzmar's Bunting is a fairly common breeding bird of the dry western part of the island (9, 10, 12, 14, 16, 17 and site R, T, U and V). Corn and Black-headed Bunting are widespread and particularly common in agricultural land (2, 5, 7, 11, 13, 16, O, V). Cinereous Bunting is an uncommon and localised breeding bird of the rocky west (16, 17 and site U). Ortolan Bunting is a very scarce passage migrant.

ACKNOWLEDGEMENTS

This guidebook is not simply the product of a single author, but a synthesis of the combined efforts of a number of people.
First of all, I would like to thank Dirk Hilbers, director and founder of Crossbill Guides, who wrote important sections of the text and made a number of vital suggestions. He has been a constant source of knowledge, support and encouragement throughout the writing process.
A number of experts have also contributed to make this book live up to the high standards of the Crossbill Guides. For information on wildflowers and other natural treasures of the island I would like to thank Makis Axiotis, Panayiotis Dimitrakopoulos (University of the Aegean) and Ioannis Bazos (Hellenic Botanical Society and University of Athens). With regard to the orchids, I received enthusiastic support from local resident Jan van Lent to whom I am grateful for sharing his information and sites.
I would like to thank Steven Wytema for his valuable information on birds, and for checking the bird sections in this book.
Regarding geology I received enthusiastic support from Gino Smeulders and Nikos Zouros (Director of the Petrified Forest).
Local knowledge on the wildlife, history and daily life of the island was vital in the creation of this guidebook. Accordingly, I'm grateful to Spyros Psomas, Panayiotis Karavatakis, Costas Artakianos, Stavritsa and Stavros Vlotidelis, Nikos and Myrta Kalabokas, Myrsini Vaxevani (Archaeological Museum of Skala Eresou), Maria Kourli (Mesotopos Women's Cooperation), Panayiotis Krinelos, Apostolis Makaratzis and Aggeliki Politaki for their help in these areas.
Many thanks to all the photographers who made their splendid images, which reflect their enthusiasm for Lesbos, available for this book. They are named in the picture credits on the facing page.
Within the ranks of the Crossbill Guides team I thank Kim Lotterman, Cees Hilbers, Riet Hilbers and Oscar Lourens for their efficient and excellent work on this book. Particular gratitude goes to John Cantelo, for his suggestions and polite, but always accurate and swift, editorial savaging of text.
Finally I want to thank my partner Christiana Bairaktari for information on food, translations and great support. And of course my dear parents for passing on the love and fascination for nature, setting the path and the drive for making this book.
I hope my readers will enjoy Lesbos as much as I do and that they will find my enthusiasm for the island infectious. Have a great trip!

Alex Tabak, Crossbill Guides Foundation, Januari 2016

PICTURE CREDITS

Crossbill Guides / Hilbers, Dirk: cover, 4 (3rd from top), 34, 36, 51 (t), 71, 106, 109, 124, 125, 142 (t), 143, 155 (b), 156 (b), 164 (t), 170 (b), 171, 174
Crossbill Guides / Tabak, Alex: cover, 4 (2nd and 4th from top), 5 (2nd and 3rd from top), 10, 16, 17 (t+b), 18, 19 (b), 25, 26, 27 (t), 28, 31 (l+r), 35 (t+b), 39 (t+b), 40, 41 (b), 45, 51 (b), 52, 56, 59 (1st, 2nd and 3rd from top), 60 (b), 61 (t+b), 63, 64 (l+r), 66, 67 (l+r), 68 (t), 69, 70 (t+b), 73, 75 (1st, 2nd, 3rd and 4th from top), 76, 84 (t), 90, 94 (b), 98 (b), 99 (t), 104, 105 (t+b), 110, 111 (b), 114, 116, 118, 121 (t), 126 (t), 129, 132 (t), 134 (t), 142 (b), 146 (t+b), 150 (c+b), 155 (t), 156 (t), 157, 159 (t+b), 160, 165, 166 (b), 168 (t), 173 (t+c+b), 182, 184, 186
Crossbill Guides / Hoogenstein, Luc: 77, 80 (c), 83 (b), 130
Crossbill Guides / Verstrael, Theo: 37, 99 (b)
Crossbill Guides / Vliegenthart, Albert: 27 (b), 98 (t), 100, 113, 150 (t), 153 (b)
Dansen, Koos: 4 (1st from top), 5 (1st from top), 24 (t+b), 30, 79, 80 (t+b), 85, 86, 120, 132 (b), 134 (b), 136 (t+b), 137, 139 (t+b), 144, 153 (t), 162 (t), 170 (t)
Fikkert, Cor (www.corfikkert.blogspot.nl): 81, 89 (b)
Goula, Katerina: 183
Greef, Jan van der (www.janvandergreef.com): 42, 89 (t), 94 (t)
Heijne, Bart: 46, 102 (b), 140
Herder, Jelger (www.digitalnature.org): 32, 47, 92, 95, 102 (t), 121 (b)
Hoogenboom, Dick (www.dickenmirahoogenboom.nl): 41 (t), 84 (b), 111 (t)
Leijgraaf, Jos van de (www.pbase.com/jleijgraaf): 54, 83 (t), 128, 162 (b), 168 (b)
Lent, Jan van (www.janvanlent.com): 68 (b), 123, 126 (c+b)
Mager, Jörg: cover
Makaratzis, Apostolos: 5 (4th from top), 60 (t)
Oostveen, Martine van: 19, 164 (b), 175, 179, 180
Saxifraga / Vastenhouw, Bart: 151
Saxifraga / Uchelen, Edo van: cover, 185
Smeenk, Harm: 133
Winkel, Edwin: 166 (t)

All illustrations by Crossbill Guides / Alex Tabak

SPECIES LIST & TRANSLATION

The following list comprises all species mentioned in this guidebook and gives their scientific, German and Dutch names. It is not a complete checklist of the species of Lesbos. Some names have an asterisk (*) behind them, indicating an unofficial name. See page 7 for more details.

Plants

English	Scientific	German	Dutch
Alexanders, Perfoliate	Smyrnium perfoliatum	Stängelumfassende Gelbdolde	Doorwaskervel
Alison, Golden	Aurinia saxatilis	Felsen-Steinkraut	Rotsschildzaad
Alison, Lesbos*	Alyssum lesbiacum	Lesbos-Steinkraut*	Lesbos-schildzaad*
Alison, Sweet	Lobularia maritima	Strand-Silberkraut	Zilverschildzaad
Anemone, Crown	Anemone coronaria	Kronen-Anemone	Kroonanemoon
Anemone, Peacock	Anemone pavonina	Pfauen-Anemone	Pauwanemoon
Arum, Dragon	Dracunculus vulgaris	Gemeine Drachenwurz	Drakenwortel
Arum, Elongated*	Arum elongatum	Verlängerter Aronstab	Stinkende aronskelk*
Asparagus, Spiny*	Asparagus acutifolius	Stechender Spargel	Stekelige asperge*
Asphodel, Summer	Asphodelus aestivus	Kleinfrüchtiger Affodill	Gewone affodil
Aster, Sea	Aster tripolium	Strand-Aster	Zulte
Aubretia	Aubrieta deltoidea	Griechisches Blaukissen	Aubrietia
Azalea, Pontic	Rhododendron luteum	Pontische Azalee	Pontische azalea
Bartsia, Southern Red	Parentucellia latifolia	Breitblättriges Teerkraut	Kleinbloemige ogentroost*
Bartsia, Yellow	Parentucellia viscosa	Gelbes Teerkraut	Kleverige ogentroost
Bastard-toadflax, Berger's*	Thesium bergeri	Berger's Leinblatt*	Berger's bergvlas*
Bean, Prickly Caterpillar	Scorpiurus muricatus	Stacheliger Skorpionsschwanz	Schorpioenstaart
Bellflower, Rock	Campanula lyrata	Leier-Glockenblume	Rotsklokje*
Bindweed, Sea	Calystegia soldanella	Strandwinde	Zeewinde
Bird's-foot-trefoil, Grey	Lotus cytisoides	Geisskleeartiger Hornklee	Bremrolklaver*
Bird's-nest, Violet	Limodorum abortivum	Violetter Dingel	Paarse aspergeorchis
Birthwort, Hairy	Aristolochia hirta	Haarige Osterluzei	Behaarde pijpbloem*
Blackberry, Woolly	Rubus canescens	Filz-Brombeere	Sterviltbraam*
Blackthorn	Prunus spinosa	Schlehe	Sleedoorn
Broom, Spanish	Spartium junceum	Pfriemenginster	Bezemstruik
Broom, Spiny	Calicotome villosa	Behaarter Dornginster	Stekende brem*
Bryony, Black	Tamus communis	Schmerwurz	Spekwortel
Buckler-mustard, Annual	Biscutella didyma	Einjähriges Brillenschötchen	Eenjarig brilkruid
Buckthorn, Mediterranean	Rhamnus alaternus	Immergrüner Kreuzdorn	Altijdgroene wegedoorn*
Bugle, Eastern	Ajuga orientalis	Orientalischer Günsel	Oostelijk zenegroen
Burnet, Thorny	Sarcopoterium spinosum	Dornige Bibernelle	Stekelige pimpernel
Bush, Caper	Capparis spinosa	Echter Kapernstrauch	Kappertjesplant
Buttonweed	Cotula coronopifolia	Krähenfuss-Laugenblume	Goudknopje
Caraway, Horse	Laser trilobum	Rosskümmel	Siler
Carrot, Dune	Pseudorlaya pumila	Dünen-Möhre	Duinpeen*

Catchfly, Cretan	*Silene cretica*	Kreta-Leimkraut	Kretenzische silene*
Cattail, Southern	*Typha domingensis*	Südlicher Rohrkolben	Zuidelijike lisdodde*
Centaury, Yellow	*Cicendia filiformis*	Fadenenzian	Draadgentiaan
Chamomile, Corn	*Anthemis arvensis*	Acker-Hundskamille	Valse kamille
Chamomile, Rayless	*Anthemis rigida*	Kretische Kamille	Knopkamille*
Cherry, Mountain	*Prunus prostrata*	Niederliegende Kirsche	Liggende kers*
Chestnut, Sweet	*Castanea sativa*	Ess-Kastanie	Tamme kastanje
Cistus, Cretan	*Cistus creticus*	Kretische Zistrose	Kreta cistusroos*
Cistus, Sage-leaved	*Cistus salviifolius*	Salbeiblättriges Zistrose	Salieblandige cistusroos*
Clary, Wild	*Salvia verbenaca*	Eisenkraut-Salbei	Kleinbloemige salie
Clover, One-flowered	*Trifolium uniflorum*	Einblütiger Klee	Eenbloemige klaver
Clover, Persian	*Trifolium resupinatum*	Persischer Klee	Perzische klaver
Clover, Woolly	*Trifolium tomentosum*	Filziger Klee	Viltige klaver
Club-rush, Sea	*Bolboschoenus maritimus*	Strandsimse	Heen; Zeebies
Coral-necklace	*Illecebrum verticillatum*	Knorpelkraut	Grondster
Cornflower	*Centaurea cyanus*	Kornblume	Korenbloem
Corydalis, Eastern Aegean*	*Corydalis integra*	Balkan Lerchensporn*	Balkan-helmbloem
Cottonweed	*Otanthus maritimus*	Strand-Filzblume	Katoenkruid*
Crane's-bill, Shining	*Geranium lucidum*	Glänzender Storchschnabel	Glanzige ooievaarsbek
Crocus, Two-flowered*	*Crocus biflorus*	Zweiblütiger Krokus	Tweebloemige crocus
Crowfoot, Threadleaf	*Ranunculus trichophyllus*	Haarblättriger Wasserhahnenfuss	Kleine waterranonkel
Cucumber, Squirting	*Ecballium elaterium*	Spritzgurke	Springkomkommer
Cyclamen, Greek	*Cyclamen graecum*	Griechisches Alpenveilchen	Griekse cyclaam
Cyclamen, Ivy-leaved	*Cyclamen hederifolium*	Herbst-Alpenveilchen	Napolitaanse cyclaam
Cyclamen, Persian	*Cyclamen persicum*	Persisches Alpenveilchen	Perzische cyclaam
Daffodil, Sea	*Pancratium maritimum*	Strandlilie	Zeenarcis
Daffodil, Winter	*Sternbergia lutea*	Herbst-Goldbecher	Gewone goudkrokus*
Daisy, Crown	*Glebionis coronarium*	Kronen- Wucherblume	Gekroonde ganzenbloem
Fennel, Giant	*Ferula communis*	Riesenfenchel	Reuzenvenkel
Fern, Maidenhair	*Adiantum capillus-veneris*	Venushaarfarn	Venushaar
Fern, Royal	*Osmunda regalis*	Königsfarn	Koningsvaren
Fritillary, Lesbos*	*Fritillaria theophrasti*	Lesbos-Schachblume*	Lesbos kievitsbloem*
Galingale, Dune	*Cyperus capitatus*	Dünen-Zypergras	Duincypergras*
Garlic, Hairy	*Allium subhirsutum*	Wimperblättriger Lauch	Harig look
Garlic, Neapolitan	*Allium neapolitanum*	Neapolitanischer Lauch	Napolitaanse look
Germander, Felty	*Teucrium polium*	Polei-Gamander	Viltgamander*
Gladiolus, Italian	*Gladiolus italicus*	Acker-Gladiole	Italiaanse gladiool
Glasswort, Button	*Halocnemum strobilaceum*	Knopf-Queller*	Knopzeekraal*
Glasswort, Common	*Salicornia europaea*	Europäischer Queller	Kortarige zeekraal
Glasswort, Glaucous	*Arthrocnemum macrostachyum*	Graue Gliedermelde	Grijze zeekraal*
Grape-hyacinth, (Common)	*Muscari neglectum*	Weinbergs-Traubenhyazinthe	Troshyacint
Grass-poly	*Lythrum hyssopifolia*	Ysopblättriger Weiderich	Kleine kattenstaart
Gratiole	*Gratiola officinalis*	Gottes-Gnadenkraut	Genadekruid
Ground-pine	*Ajuga chamaepitys*	Gelber Günsel	Akkerzenegroen
Harebell, Balkan*	*Asyneuma limonifolium*	Balkan Stern-Glöckchen*	Balkan sterklokje*
Hawk's-beard, Pink	*Crepis rubra*	Roter Pippau	Roze streepzaad
Hawthorn, Common	*Crataegus monogyna*	Eingriffeliger Weissdorn	Eenstijlige meidoorn
Heath, Tree	*Erica arborea*	Baum-Heide	Boomhei
Helleborine, Broad-leaved	*Epipactis helleborine*	Breitblättrige Stendelwürz	Brede wespenorchis

English	Scientific	German	Dutch
Helleborine, Dense-leaved	Epipactis densifolia	Dichtblättrige Ständelwurz	Dichtbladige wespenorchis*
Helleborine, Narrow-leaved	Cephalanthera longifolia	Schwertblättriges Waldvögelein	Wit bosvogeltje
Helleborine, Small-leaved	Epipactis microphylla	Kleinblättrige Stendelwurz	Kleinbladige wespenorchis
Helleborine, Spurred	Cephalanthera epipactoides	Gesporntes Waldvögelein	Stijf bosvogeltje
Helleborine, Turkish	Epipactis turcica	Türkische Ständelwurz	Turkse wespenorchis*
Helloborine, White	Cephalanthera damasonium	Weisses Waldvögelein	Bleek bosvogeltje
Hemp, False	Datisca cannabina	Scheinhanf	Valse hennep
Horned-poppy, Yellow	Glaucium flavum	Gelber Hornmohn	Gele hoornpapaver
Hottentot-fig	Carpobrotus edulis	Hottentottenfeige	Hottentotvijg
Hyacinth, Tassle	Muscari comosum	Schopfige Traubenhyazinthe	Kuifhyacint
Hypecoum	Hypecoum procumbens	Gelbäugelchen	Hypecoum
Hypocist, Pink	Cytinus ruber	Rote Zistrosenwürger	Rode hypocist
Hypocist, Yellow	Cytinus hypocistis	Gelbe Zistrosenwürger	Gele hypocist
Iris, Oriental	Iris orientalis	Orientalische Schwertlilie	Oosterse lis*
Ironwort, Woolly	Sideritis lanata	Wolliges Gliedkraut	Wollig ijzerkruid
Ivy	Hedera helix	Efeu	Klimop
Juniper, Prickly	Juniperus oxycedrus	Stechwacholder	Spaanse jeneverbes
Knapweed, Spiny	Centaurea spinosa	Stachel-Flockenblume*	Stekelcentaurie*
Lady's-tresses, Autumn	Spiranthes spiralis	Herbst-Drehwurz	Herfstschroeforchis
Laurel, (Bay)	Laurus nobilis	Echter Lorbeer	Echte laurier
Lavender, French	Lavandula stoechas	Schopf-Lavendel	Kuiflavendel
Leadwort, Common	Plumbago europaea	Europäische Bleiwurz	Europees loodkruid
Leek, Yellow	Allium flavum	Gelber Lauch	Gele look
Lineseed, Mediterranean	Bartsia trixago	Bunte Bellardie	Bellardia
Loosestrife, Purple	Lythrum salicaria	Blut-Weiderich	Grote kattenstaart
Lupin, Narrow-leaved	Lupinus angustifolius	Schmallblättrige Lupine	Blauwe lupine
Maple, Cretan	Acer sempervirens	Kreta-Ahorn	Kretenzische esdoorn
Marigold, Common	Calendula officinalis	Garten-Ringelblume	Tuingoudsbloem
Marigold, Corn	Glebionis segetum	Saat-Wucherblume	Gele ganzenbloem
Marigold, Field	Calendula arvensis	Acker-Ringelblume	Akkergoudsbloem
Medick, Button	Medicago orbicularis	Scheiben-Schneckenklee	Bolrupsklaver*
Medick, Sea	Medicago marina	Strand-Schneckenklee	Zeerupsklaver
Medick, Shore	Medicago littoralis	Meer-Schneckenklee	Strandrupsklaver*
Medick, Tree	Medicago arborea	Strauch-Schneckenklee	Struikrupsklaver
Milk-vetch, Shrubby*	Astragalus angustifolius	Schmalblättriger Tragant	Struiktragant*
Mistletoe	Viscum album	Mistel	Maretak
Myrtle	Myrtus communis	Myrte	Mirte
Navelwort	Umbilicus rupestris	Echter Venusnabel	Muurnavel
Navelwort, Horizontal	Umbilicus horizontalis	Waagrechter Venusnabel	Platte muurnavel*
Nut, Barbary	Gynandriris sisyrinchium	Mittagsschwertlilie	Barbarijse iris*
Oak, Downy	Quercus pubescens	Flaum-Eiche	Donzige eik
Oak, Gall	Quercus infectoria	Gall-Eiche	Galeik*
Oak, Holm	Quercus ilex	Stein-Eiche	Steeneik
Oak, Kermes	Quercus coccifera	Kermes-Eiche	Hulsteik
Oak, Turkey	Quercus cerris	Zerr-Eiche	Moseik
Oak, Valonia	Quercus macrolepis	Wallonen-Eiche	Valonia-eik
Oleander	Nerium oleander	Oleander	Oleander
Olive, Broad-leaved False	Phillyrea latifolia	Breitblättrige Steinlinde	Breedbladige steenlinde

Orchid, Anatolian	Orchis anatolica	Anatolisches Knabenkraut	Anatolische orchis
Orchid, Balkan Lizard	Himantoglossum caprinum	Ziegen-Riemenzunge	Geitenorchis
Orchid, Bee	Ophrys apifera	Bienen-Ragwurz	Bijenorchis
Orchid, Bergoni's Tongue*	Serapias bergonii	Schlankwüchsiger Zungenstendel	Slanke tongorchis
Orchid, Bridled	Ophrys argolica	Argolische Ragwurz	Brilorchis*
Orchid, Bug	Anacamptis coriophora	Wanzen-Knabenkraut	Wantsenorchis
Orchid, Bull-headed	Ophrys bucephala	Stier-Ragwurz*	Stierorchis*
Orchid, Dense-flowered	Neotinea maculata	Gefleckte Waldwurz	Nonnetjesorchis
Orchid, Dull Bee	Ophrys fusca	Braune Ragwurz	Bruine orchis
Orchid, Eastern Lizard	Himantoglossum affine	Orientalische Riemenzunge	Oosterse bokkenorchis*
Orchid, Eastern Tongue	Serapias orientalis	Orientalischer Zungenstendel	Oosterse tongorchis
Orchid, Eastern Yellow Bee	Ophrys phryganae	Phrygana-Ragwurz	Oostelijke gele orchis*
Orchid, Elegant Marsh	Anacamptis elegans	Elegantes Sumpf-Knabenkraut	Sierlijke moerasorchis*
Orchid, Fan-lipped	Anacamptis collina	Hügel-Knabenkraut	Heuvelorchis
Orchid, Four-spotted	Orchis quadripunctata	Vierpunkt-Knabenkraut	Vierpuntjesorchis
Orchid, Green-winged	Anacamptis morio	Kleines Knabenkraut	Harlekijn
Orchid, Heart-flowered Tongue	Serapias cordigera	Herzförmiger Zungenstendel	Brede tongorchis
Orchid, Holmboe's Butterfly	Platanthera holmboei	Holmboes Waldhyazinthe	Holmboe's nachtorchis*
Orchid, Holy	Orchis sancta	Heiliges Knabenkraut	Heilige orchis
Orchid, Homer's	Ophrys homeri	Homers Ragwurz*	Homer's orchis*
Orchid, Horned	Ophrys (scopolax ssp.) cornuta	Gehörnte Ragwurz	Gehoornde orchis
Orchid, Horseshoe	Ophrys ferrum-equinum	Hufeisen-Ragwurz	Hoefijzerorchis
Orchid, Komper's	Himantoglossum comperianum	Bartorchis	Kompers orchis
Orchid, Lady	Orchis purpurea	Purpur-Knabenkraut	Purperorchis
Orchid, Lesbos*	Ophrys lesbis	Lesbos Ragwurz	Lesbosorchis*
Orchid, Long-lipped Tongue	Serapias vomeracea	Pflugschar Zungenstendel	Lange tongorchis
Orchid, Loose-flowered	Anacamptis laxiflora	Lockerblütiges Knabenkraut	IJle moerasorchis
Orchid, Mammose	Ophrys mammosa	Busen-Ragwurz	Vrouwtjesorchis
Orchid, Man	Orchis anthropophora	Ohnhorn	Poppenorchis
Orchid, Marsh	Anacamptis palustris	Sumpf-Knabenkraut	Moerasorchis
Orchid, Milky	Orchis lactea	Milchweisses Knabenkraut	Maskerorchis
Orchid, Mirror	Ophrys speculum	Spiegel-Ragwurz	Spiegelorchis
Orchid, Monkey	Orchis simia	Affen-Knabenkraut	Aapjesorchis
Orchid, Naked Man	Orchis italica	Italienisches Knabenkraut	Italiaanse orchis
Orchid, Pink Butterfly	Anacamptis papilionacea	Schmetterlings-Knabenkraut	Vlinderorchis
Orchid, Provence	Orchis provincialis	Provence-Knabenkraut	Stippelorchis
Orchid, Pyramidal	Anacamptis pyramidalis	Hundswurz	Hondskruid
Orchid, Rainbow	Ophrys iricolor	Regenbogen-Ragwurz	Regenboogorchis
Orchid, Reinhold's	Ophrys reinholdii	Reinholds Ragwurz	Reinhold's orchis*
Orchid, Roman	Dactylorhiza romana	Römisches Knabenkraut	Romeinse orchis
Orchid, Sawfly	Ophrys tenthredinifera	Wespen-Ragwurz	Wolzweverorchis
Orchid, Sicilian	Ophrys sicula	Kleinblütige Gelbe Ragwurz	Siciliaanse orchis*
Orchid, Small Horned	Ophrys minutula	Kleinblütige Schnepfen-Ragwurz*	Kleinbloemige gehoornde orchis*
Orchid, Small-flowered Tongue	Serapias parviflora	Kleinblütiger Zungenstendel	Kleine tongorchis

English	Scientific	German	Dutch
Orchid, Three-toothed	*Neotinea tridentata*	Dreizähniges Knabenkraut	Drietandorchis
Orchid, Umbilical	*Ophrys umbilicata*	Nabel-Ragwurz	Navelorchis
Orchid, Violet Bird's-nest	See: Bird's-nest, Violet		
Pea, Red	*Lathyrus cicera*	Rote Platterbse	Kekerlathyrus
Pear, Almond-leaved	*Pyrus amygdaliformis*	Mandelblättrige Birne	Amandelbladpeer
Pearlwort, Sea	*Sagina maritima*	Strand-Mastkraut	Zeevetmuur
Peony, Balkan	*Paeonia mascula*	Korallen-Pfingstrose	Koraalpioenroos*
Pillwort, Small	*Pilularia minuta*	Zwerg-Pillenfarn	Kleine pilvaren*
Pimpernel, Scarlet	*Anagallis arvensis*	Acker-Gauchheil	Rood guichelheil
Pine, Black	*Pinus nigra*	Schwarzkiefer	Zwarte den
Pine, Turkish	*Pinus brutia*	Kalabrische Kiefer	Turkse den
Plane, Oriental	*Platanus orientalis*	Orientalische Platane	Oosterse plataan
Plant, Curry	*Helichrysum stoechas*	Mittelmeer-Strohblume	Mediterrane strobloem
Poplar, Black	*Populus nigra*	Schwarz-Pappel	Zwarte populier
Poplar, White	*Populus alba*	Silber-Pappel	Witte abeel
Poppy, Common	*Papaver rhoeas*	Klatsch-Mohn	Grote klaproos
Purslane, Sea	*Atriplex portulacoides*	Portulak-Salzmelde	Gewone zoutmelde
Rocket, Sea	*Cakile maritima*	Europäischer Meersenf	Zeeraket
Rockrose, Spotted	*Tuberaria guttata*	Geflecktes Sonnenröschen	Gevlekt zonneroosje
Rockrose, Thyme-leaved	*Fumana thymifolia*	Thymianblättriges Nadelröschen	Tijmbladig zonneroosje*
Rosemary	*Rosmarinus officinalis*	Rosmarin	Rozemarijn
Rue, Fringed	*Ruta chalepensis*	Gefranste Raute	Winterwijnruit
Rue, White-flowered*	*Haplophyllum megalanthum*	Weisse Raute*	Witte ruit*
Rush, Sharp	*Juncus acutus*	Stechende Binse	Stekende rus
Sage, Sclary	*Salvia sclarea*	Muskateller-Salbei	Scharlei
Sage, Silver	*Salvia argentea*	Silber-Salbei	Zilversalie
Sage, Three-lobed	*Salvia triloba*	Dreilappen-Salbei	Drielobbige salie
Sainfoin, Small	*Onobrychis arenaria*	Sand-Esparsette	Zandesparcette
Salsify	*Tragopogon porrifolius*	Haferwurz	Paarse morgenster
Saltwort, Prickly	*Salsola kali*	Kali-Salzkraut	Stekend loogkruid
Samphire, Rock	*Crithmum maritimum*	Meerfenchel	Zeevenkel
Samphire, Silver-leaved*	*Inula heterolepis*	Silber-Alant*	Zilveralant*
Saxifrage, Greek	*Saxifraga graeca*	Griechischer Steinbrech*	Griekse steenbreek*
Saxifrage, Meadow	*Saxifraga granulata*	Knöllchen-Steinbrech	Knolsteenbreek
Sea-blite, Annual	*Suaeda maritima*	Strand-Sode	Klein schorrenkruid
Sea-heath, Hairy	*Frankenia hirsuta*	Behaarte Frankenie	Behaarde zeehei*
Sea-holly	*Eryngium maritimum*	Strand-Mannstreu	Blauwe zeedistel
Sea-lavender, Narbonne*	*Limonium narbonense*	Narbonne-Strandflieder	Narbonne lamsoor*
Sea-lavender, Winged	*Limonium sinuatum*	Geflügelter Strandflieder	Bochtig lamsoor
Sedge, Pendulous	*Carex pendula*	Hänge-Segge	Hangende zegge
Silk-vine	*Periploca graeca*	Griechische Baumschlinge	Melkwingerd
Smilax, Common	*Smilax aspera*	Stechwinde	Steekwinde
Snowdrop, Greater	*Galanthus elwesii*	Elwes-Schneeglöckchen	Groot sneeuwklokje
Spearwort, Adder`s-tongue	*Ranunculus ophioglossifolius*	Zungenblättriger Hahnenfuss	Addertongboterbloem*
Spurge, Sea	*Euphorbia paralias*	Strand-Wolfsmilch	Zeewolfsmelk
Squill, Alpine	*Scilla bifolia*	Zweiblättriger Blaustern	Vroege sterhyacint
Squill, Autumn	*Scilla autumnalis*	Herbst-Blaustern	Herfststerhyacint
Squill, Sea	*Drimia maritima*	Meerzwiebel	Zeeui

English	Scientific	German	Dutch
St. John's-wort, Turkish	Hypericum aviculariifolium	Türkisches Johanniskraut*	Turks hertshooi*
Star-of-Bethlehem, Drooping	Ornithogalum nutans	Nickender Milchstern	Knikkende vogelmelk
Star-of-Bethlehem, Grecian	Gagea graeca	Griechische Faltenlilie	Witte geelster*
Star-of-Bethlehem, Stalked	Gagea peduncularis	Langstieliger Gelbstern	Gesteelde geelster*
Star-thistle, Yellow	Centaurea solstitialis	Sonnenwend-Flockenblume	Zomercentaurie
Stock, Eastern Sand*	Malcolmia flexuosa	Geschlängelte Meerviole	Bochtige violier*
Stock, Sea	Matthiola sinuata	Strand-Levkoje	Strandviolier
Stock, Three-horned	Matthiola tricuspidata	Dreihörnige Levkoje	Driehoornige violier*
Stonecrop, Pale	Sedum sediforme	Felsen-Fetthenne	Rotsvetkruid*
Tamarisk, Greek*	Tamarix hampeana	Griechischer Tamariske*	Griekse tamarisk*
Thistle, Milk	Silybum marianum	Mariendistel	Mariadistel
Thistle, Syrian	Notobasis syriaca	Syrische Kratzdistel	Syrische distel
Toadflax, Jersey	Linaria pelisseriana	Pellicier-Leinkraut	Hoorntjesleeuwenbek*
Tree, Carob	Ceratonia siliqua	Johannisbrotbaum	Johannesbroodboom
Tree, Eastern Strawberry	Arbutus andrachne	Östlicher Erdbeerbaum	Oostelijke aardbeiboom
Tree, Judas	Cercis siliquastrum	Gemeiner Judasbaum	Europese judasboom
Tree, Locust	See: Tree, Carob		
Tree, Mastic	Pistacia lentiscus	Mastixstrauch	Mastiekstruik
Tree, Turpentine	Pistacia terebinthus	Terpentin-Pistazie	Terpentijnboom
Tulip, Wrinkle-leaved*	Tulipa undulatifolia	Gewelltblättrige Tulpe	Golfbladige tulp*
Twayblade, Common	Neottia ovata	Grosses Zweiblatt	Grote keverorchis
Venus's-looking-glass	Legousia speculum-veneris	Echter Frauenspiegel	Groot spiegelklokje
Venus's-looking-glass, Larger	Legousia pentagonia	Fünfkantiger Frauenspiegel	Balkanspiegelklokje*
Viper's-bugloss, Italian	Echium italicum	Italienischer Natternkopf	Italiaans slangekruid
Viper's-bugloss, Purple	Echium plantagineum	Wegerichblättriger Natterkopf	Weegbreeslangenkruid
Vitex	Vitex agnus-castus	Mönchspfeffer	Monnikspeper
Water-plantain, Lesser	Baldellia ranunculoides	Igelschlauch	Stijve moerasweegbree
Willow, White	Salix alba	Silber-Weide	Schietwilg
Yellow-wort	Blackstonia perfoliata	Durchwachsener Bitterling	Zomerbitterling

Mammals

English	Scientific	German	Dutch
Bat, Blasius's Horseshoe	Rhinolophus blasii	Blasius-Hufeisennase	Blasius' hoefijzerneus
Bat, Greater Horseshoe	Rhinolophus ferrumequinum	Grosse Hufeisennase	Grote hoefijzerneus
Boar, Wild	Sus scrofa	Wildschwein	Wild zwijn
Deer, Fallow	Damus damus	Dammhirsch	Damhert
Dolphin, Bottlenose	Tursiops truncatus	Grosser Tümmler	Tuimelaar
Dolphin, Common	Delphinus delphis	Gemeiner Delfin	Gewone dolfijn
Dolphin, Striped	Stenella coeruleoalba	Blau-Weisser Delfin	Gestreepte dolfijn
Fox, Red	Vulpes vulpes	Rotfuchs	Vos
Hare	Lepus europaeus	Feldhase	Haas
Hedgehog, Northern White-breasted	Erinaceus roumanicus	Nördlicher Weissbrustigel	Oostelijke egel
Marten, Beech	Martes foina	Steinmarder	Steenmarter
Otter	Lutra lutra	Fischotter	Otter
Rabbit	Oryctolagus cuniculus	Wildkaninchen	Konijn
Rat, Lesser Mole	Spalax leucodon	Westblindmaus	Westelijke blindmol

English	Scientific	German	Dutch
Seal, (Mediterranean) Monk	Monachus monachus	Mittelmeer-Mönchsrobbe	Mediterrane monniksrob
Shrew, Bicolored	Crocidura leucodon	Feldspitzmaus	Veldspitsmuis
Shrew, Lesser White-toothed	Crocidura suaveolens	Gartenspitzmaus	Tuinspitsmuis
Squirrel, Persian	Sciurus anomalus	Kaukasisches Eichhörnchen	Kaukasuseekhoorn
Vole, Günther's	Microtus guentheri	Mittelmeer-Feldmaus	Mediterrane woelmuis

Birds

English	Scientific	German	Dutch
Avocet	Recurvirostra avosetta	Säbelschnäbler	Kluut
Bee-eater	Merops apiaster	Bienenfresser	Bijeneter
Bittern, Little	Ixobrychus minutus	Zwergdommel	Woudaapje
Blackbird	Turdus merula	Amsel	Merel
Blackcap	Sylvia atricapilla	Mönchsgrasmücke	Zwartkop
Brambling	Fringilla montifringilla	Bergfink	Keep
Bunting, Black-headed	Emberiza melanocephala	Kappenammer	Zwartkopgors
Bunting, Cinereous	Emberiza cineracea	Türkenammer	Smyrnagors
Bunting, Cirl	Emberiza cirlus	Zaunammer	Cirlgors
Bunting, Corn	Miliaria calandra	Grauammer	Grauwe gors
Bunting, Cretzschmar's	Emberiza caesia	Grauortolan	Bruinkeelortolaan
Bunting, Ortolan	Emberiza hortulana	Ortolan	Ortolaan
Buzzard	Buteo buteo	Mäusebussard	Buizerd
Buzzard, Honey	Pernis apivorus	Wespenbussard	Wespendief
Buzzard, Long-legged	Buteo rufinus	Adlerbussard	Arendbuizerd
Chaffinch	Fringilla coelebs	Buchfink	Vink
Chiffchaff	Phylloscopus collybita	Zilpzalp	Tjiftjaf
Chukar	Alectoris chukar	Chukarhuhn	Aziatische steenpatrijs
Cisticola, Zitting	Cisticola juncidis	Cistensänger	Graszanger
Coot	Fulica atra	Blässhuhn	Meerkoet
Cormorant, Great	Phalacrocorax carbo	Kormoran	Aalscholver
Crake, Baillon's	Porzana pusilla	Zwergsumpfhuhn	Kleinst waterhoen
Crake, Little	Porzana parva	Kleines Sumpfhuhn	Klein waterhoen
Crake, Spotted	Porzana porzana	Tüpfelsumpfhuhn	Porseleinhoen
Crow, Hooded	Corvus corone cornix	Nebelkrähe	Bonte kraai
Cuckoo, Common	Cuculus canorus	Kuckuck	Koekoek
Cuckoo, Great Spotted	Clamator glandarius	Häherkuckuck	Kuifkoekoek
Curlew	Numenius arquata	Grosser Brachvogel	Wulp
Curlew, Stone	Burhinus oedicnemus	Triel	Griel
Diver, Black-throated	Gavia arctica	Prachttaucher	Parelduiker
Dove, Collared	Streptopelia decaocto	Türkentaube	Turkse tortel
Dove, Rock	Columba livia	Felsentaube	Rotsduif
Dove, Turtle	Streptopelia turtur	Turteltaube	Tortelduif
Eagle, Bonelli's	Hieraaetus fasciatus	Habichtsadler	Havikarend
Eagle, Booted	Hieraaetus pennatus	Zwergadler	Dwergarend
Eagle, Short-toed	Circaetus gallicus	Schlangenadler	Slangenarend
Egret, Great White	Ardea alba	Silberreiher	Grote zilverreiger
Egret, Little	Egretta garzetta	Seidenreiher	Kleine zilverreiger
Falcon, Eleonora's	Falco eleonorae	Eleonorenfalke	Eleonora's valk
Falcon, Red-footed	Falco vespertinus	Rotfussfalke	Roodpootvalk
Fieldfare	Turdus pilaris	Wacholderdrossel	Kramsvogel
Flamingo, Greater	Phoenicopterus roseus	Flamingo	Europese flamingo

English	Scientific	German	Dutch
Flycatcher, Collared	*Ficedula albicollis*	Halsbandschnäpper	Withalsvliegenvanger
Flycatcher, Pied	*Ficedula hypoleuca*	Trauerschnäpper	Bonte vliegenvanger
Flycatcher, Semi-collared	*Ficedula semitorquata*	Halbringschnäpper	Balkanvliegenvanger
Flycatcher, Spotted	*Muscicapa striata*	Grauschnäpper	Grauwe vliegenvanger
Garganey	*Anas querquedula*	Knäkente	Zomertaling
Godwit, Black-tailed	*Limosa limosa*	Uferschnepfe	Grutto
Goldcrest	*Regulus regulus*	Wintergoldhähnchen	Goudhaan
Goldfinch	*Carduelis carduelis*	Distelfink	Putter
Goshawk	*Accipiter gentilis*	Habicht	Havik
Grebe, Black-necked	*Podiceps nigricollis*	Schwarzhalstaucher	Geoorde fuut
Grebe, Great Crested	*Podiceps cristatus*	Haubentaucher	Fuut
Grebe, Little	*Tachybaptus ruficollis*	Zwergtaucher	Dodaars
Greenfinch	*Carduelis chloris*	Grünling	Groenling
Greenshank	*Tringa nebularia*	Grünschenkel	Groenpootruiter
Gull, Audouin's	*Ichthyaetus audouinii*	Korallenmöwe	Adouins meeuw
Gull, Black-headed	*Chroicocephalus ridibundus*	Lachmöwe	Kokmeeuw
Gull, Lesser Black-backed	*Larus fuscus*	Heringsmöwe	Kleine mantelmeeuw
Gull, Little	*Hydrocoloeus minutus*	Zwergmöwe	Dwergmeeuw
Gull, Mediterranean	*Ichthyaetus melanocephalus*	Schwarzkopfmöwe	Zwartkopmeeuw
Gull, Slender-billed	*Chroicocephalus genei*	Dünnschnabelmöwe	Dunbekmeeuw
Gull, Yellow-legged	*Larus michahellis*	Weisskopfmöve	Geelpootmeeuw
Harrier, Hen	*Circus cyaneus*	Kornweihe	Blauwe kiekendief
Harrier, Marsh	*Circus aeruginosus*	Rohrweihe	Bruine kiekendief
Harrier, Montagu's	*Circus pygargus*	Wiesenweihe	Grauwe kiekendief
Harrier, Pallid	*Circus macrourus*	Steppenweihe	Steppekiekendief
Hawfinch	*Coccothraustes coccothraustes*	Kernbeisser	Appelvink
Heron, Grey	*Ardea cinerea*	Graureiher	Blauwe reiger
Heron, Night	*Nycticorax nycticorax*	Nachtreiher	Kwak
Heron, Purple	*Ardea purpurea*	Purpurreiher	Purperreiger
Heron, Squacco	*Ardeola ralloides*	Rallenreiher	Ralreiger
Hobby	*Falco subbuteo*	Baumfalke	Boomvalk
Hoopoe	*Upupa epops*	Wiedehopf	Hop
Ibis, Glossy	*Plegadis falcinellus*	Braunsichler	Zwarte ibis
Jackdaw	*Corvus monedula*	Dohle	Kauw
Jay	*Garrulus glandarius*	Eichelhäher	Gaai
Kestrel	*Falco tinnunculus*	Turmfalke	Torenvalk
Kestrel, Lesser	*Falco naumanni*	Rötelfalke	Kleine torenvalk
Kingfisher	*Alcedo atthis*	Eisvogel	IJsvogel
Lapwing	*Vanellus vanellus*	Kiebitz	Kievit
Lapwing, Spur-winged	*Vanellus spinosus*	Spornkiebitz	Sporenkievit
Lark, Crested	*Galerida cristata*	Haubenlerche	Kuifleeuwerik
Lark, Greater Short-toed	*Calandrella brachydactyla*	Kurzzehenlerche	Kortteenleeuwerik
Linnet	*Carduelis cannabina*	Bluthänfling	Kneu
Mallard	*Anas platyrhynchos*	Stockente	Wilde eend
Martin, Crag	*Ptyonoprogne rupestris*	Felsenschwalbe	Rotszwaluw
Martin, House	*Delichon urbicum*	Mehlschwalbe	Huiszwaluw
Martin, Sand	*Riparia riparia*	Uferschwalbe	Oeverzwaluw
Merganser, Red-breasted	*Mergus serrator*	Mittelsäger	Middelste zaagbek
Moorhen	*Gallinula chloropus*	Teichhuhn	Waterhoen
Nightingale	*Luscinia megarhynchos*	Nachtigall	Nachtegaal

SPECIES LIST & TRANSLATION

English	Scientific	German	Dutch
Nightingale, Thrush	Luscinia luscinia	Sprosser	Noordse nachtegaal
Nightjar	Caprimulgus europaeus	Ziegenmelker	Nachtzwaluw
Nuthatch, (Common)	Sitta europaea	Kleiber	Boomklever
Nuthatch, (Western) Rock	Sitta neumayer	Felsenkleiber	Rotsklever
Nuthatch, Krüper's	Sitta krueperi	Türkenkleiber	Turkse boomklever
Oriole, Golden	Oriolus oriolus	Pirol	Wielewaal
Osprey	Pandion haliaetus	Fischadler	Visarend
Owl, Barn	Tyto alba	Schleiereule	Kerkuil
Owl, Little	Athene noctua	Steinkauz	Steenuil
Owl, Long-eared	Asio otus	Waldohreule	Ransuil
Owl, Scops	Otus scops	Zwergohreule	Dwergooruil
Oystercatcher	Haematopus ostralegus	Austernfischer	Scholekster
Pelican, Dalmatian	Pelecanus crispus	Krauskopfpelikan	Kroeskoppelikaan
Pelican, Great White	Pelecanus onocrotalus	Rosapelikan	Roze pelikaan
Peregrine	Falco peregrinus	Wanderfalke	Slechtvalk
Pigeon, Wood	Columba palumbus	Ringeltaube	Houtduif
Pintail	Anas acuta	Spiessente	Pijlstaart
Pipit, Meadow	Anthus pratensis	Wiesenpieper	Graspieper
Pipit, Red-throated	Anthus cervinus	Rotkehlpieper	Roodkeelpieper
Pipit, Tawny	Anthus campestris	Brachpieper	Duinpieper
Pipit, Tree	Anthus trivialis	Baumpieper	Boompieper
Plover, Golden	Pluvialis apricaria	Goldregenpfeifer	Goudplevier
Plover, Grey	Pluvialis squatarola	Kiebitzregenpfeifer	Zilverplevier
Plover, Kentish	Charadrius alexandrinus	Seeregenpfeifer	Strandplevier
Plover, Little Ringed	Charadrius dubius	Flussregenpfeifer	Kleine plevier
Plover, Ringed	Charadrius hiaticula	Sandregenpfeifer	Bontbekplevier
Pratincole, Collared	Glareola pratincola	Rotflügel-Brachschwalbe	Vorkstaartplevier
Quail	Coturnix coturnix	Wachtel	Kwartel
Rail, Water	Rallus aquaticus	Wasserralle	Waterral
Raven	Corvus corax	Kolkrabe	Raaf
Redshank	Tringa totanus	Rotschenkel	Tureluur
Redshank, Spotted	Tringa erythropus	Dunkler Wasserläufer	Zwarte ruiter
Redstart, Black	Phoenicurus ochruros	Hausrotschwanz	Zwarte roodstaart
Redstart, Common	Phoenicurus phoenicurus	Gartenrotschwanz	Gekraagde roodstaart
Redwing	Turdus iliacus	Rotdrossel	Koperwiek
Robin	Erithacus rubecula	Rotkehlchen	Roodborst
Robin, Rufous Bush	Cercotrichas galactotes	Heckensänger	Rosse waaierstaart
Robin, White-throated	Irania gutturalis	Weisskehlsänger	Perzische roodborst
Roller	Coracias garrulus	Blauracke	Scharrelaar
Ruff	Philomachus pugnax	Kampfläufer	Kemphaan
Sanderling	Calidris alba	Sanderling	Drieteenstrandloper
Sandpiper, Broad-billed	Limicola falcinellus	Sumpfläufer	Breedbekstrandloper
Sandpiper, Common	Actitis hypoleucos	Flussuferläufer	Oeverloper
Sandpiper, Curlew	Calidris ferruginea	Sichelstrandläufer	Krombekstrandloper
Sandpiper, Green	Tringa ochropus	Waldwasserläufer	Witgat
Sandpiper, Marsh	Tringa stagnatilis	Teichwasserläufer	Poelruiter
Sandpiper, Wood	Tringa glareola	Bruchwasserläufer	Bosruiter
Serin	Serinus serinus	Girlitz	Sijs
Shag	Phalacrocorax aristotelis	Krähenscharbe	Kuifaalscholver
Shearwater, Cory's	Calonectris borealis	Gelbschnabelsturmtaucher	Kuhls pijlstormvogel
Shearwater, Scopoli's	Calonectris diomedea	Gelbschnabelsturmtaucher	Scopoli's pijlstormvogel
Shearwater, Yelkouan	Puffinus yelkouan	Mittelmeer-Sturmtaucher	Vale pijlstormvogel

Shelduck	Tadorna tadorna	Brandgans	Bergeend
Shelduck, Ruddy	Tadorna ferruginea	Rostgans	Casarca
Shoveler	Anas clypeata	Löffelente	Slobeend
Shrike, Lesser Grey	Lanius minor	Schwarzstirnwürger	Kleine klapekster
Shrike, Masked	Lanius nubicus	Maskenwüger	Maskerklauwier
Shrike, Red-backed	Lanius collurio	Neuntöter	Grauwe klauwier
Shrike, Woodchat	Lanius senator	Rotkopfwürger	Roodkopklauwier
Siskin	Carduelis spinus	Erlenzeisig	Sijs
Skylark	Alauda arvensis	Feldlerche	Veldleeuwerik
Snipe	Gallinago gallinago	Bekassine	Watersnip
Snipe, Jack	Lymnocryptes minimus	Zwergschnepfe	Bokje
Sparrow, House	Passer domesticus	Haussperling	Huismus
Sparrow, Rock	Petronia petronia	Steinsperling	Rotsmus
Sparrow, Spanish	Passer hispaniolensis	Weidensperling	Spaanse mus
Sparrowhawk	Accipiter nisus	Sperber	Sperwer
Sparrowhawk, Levant's	Accipiter brevipes	Kurzfangsperber	Balkansperwer
Spoonbill	Platalea leucorodia	Löffler	Lepelaar
Starling	Sturnus vulgaris	Star	Spreeuw
Starling, Rosy	Pastor roseus	Rosenstar	Roze spreeuw
Stilt, Black-winged	Himantopus himantopus	Stelzenläufer	Steltkluut
Stint, Little	Calidris minuta	Zwergstrandläufer	Kleine strandloper
Stint, Temminck's	Calidris temminckii	Temminckstrandläufer	Temmincks strandloper
Stonechat	Saxicola torquata	Schwarzkehlchen	Roodborsttapuit
Stork, Black	Ciconia nigra	Schwarzstorch	Zwarte ooievaar
Stork, White	Ciconia ciconia	Weissstorch	Ooievaar
Swallow	Hirundo rustica	Rauchschwalbe	Boerenzwaluw
Swallow, Red-rumped	Cecropsis daurica	Rötelschwalbe	Roodstuitzwaluw
Swift, (Common)	Apus apus	Mauersegler	Gierzwaluw
Swift, Alpine	Apus melba	Alpensegler	Alpengierzwaluw
Swift, Pallid	Apus pallidus	Fahlsegler	Vale gierzwaluw
Teal	Anas crecca	Krickente	Wintertaling
Tern, Black	Chlidonias niger	Trauerseeschwalbe	Zwarte stern
Tern, Common	Sterna hirundo	Flussseeschwalbe	Visdief
Tern, Gull-billed	Gelochelidon nilotica	Lachseeschwalbe	Lachstern
Tern, Little	Sternula albifrons	Zwergseeschwalbe	Dwergstern
Tern, Sandwich	Thalasseus sandvicensis	Brandseeschwalbe	Grote stern
Tern, Whiskered	Chlidonias hybrida	Weissbart-Seeschwalbe	Witwangstern
Tern, White-winged	Chlidonias leucopterus	Weissflügel-Seeschwalbe	Witvleugelstern
Thrush, Blue Rock	Monticola solitarius	Blaumerle	Blauwe rotslijster
Thrush, Mistle	Turdus viscivorus	Misteldrossel	Grote lijster
Thrush, Song	Turdus philomelos	Singdrossel	Zanglijster
Tit, Blue	Cyanistes caeruleus	Blaumeise	Pimpelmees
Tit, Coal	Periparus ater	Tannenmeise	Zwarte mees
Tit, Great	Parus major	Kohlmeise	Koolmees
Tit, Long-tailed	Aegithalos caudatus	Schwanzmeise	Staartmees
Tit, Sombre	Poecile lugubris	Trauermeise	Rouwmees
Treecreeper, Short-toed	Certhia brachydactyla	Gartenbaumläufer	Boomkruiper
Turnstone	Arenaria interpres	Steinwälzer	Steenloper
Wagtail, Ashy-headed	Motacilla (flava) cinereocapilla	Aschkopf-Schafstelze	Italiaanse kwikstaart
Wagtail, Black-headed	Motacilla (flava) feldegg	Maskenschafstelze	Balkankwikstaart

SPECIES LIST & TRANSLATION

Wagtail, Blue-headed (Yellow)	*Motacilla (flava) flava*	Wiesenschafstelze	Gele kwikstaart
Wagtail, Citrine	*Motacilla citreola*	Zitronenstelze	Citroenkwikstaart
Wagtail, Grey	*Motacilla cinerea*	Gebirgsstelze	Grote gele kwikstaart
Wagtail, Grey-headed	*Motacilla (flava) thunbergii*	Thunberg-Schafstelze	Noordse kwikstaart
Wagtail, White	*Motacilla alba*	Bachstelze	Witte kwikstaart
Warbler, Barred	*Sylvia nisoria*	Sperbergrasmücke	Sperwergrasmus
Warbler, Cetti's	*Cettia cetti*	Seidensänger	Cetti's zanger
Warbler, (Eastern) Bonelli's	*Phylloscopus orientalis*	Balkanlaubsänger	Balkanbergfluiter
Warbler, (Eastern) Olivaceous	*Iduna pallida*	Blassspötter	Oostelijke vale spotvogel
Warbler, Fan-tailed	See: Cisticola, Zitting		
Warbler, Garden	*Sylvia borin*	Gartengrasmücke	Tuinfluiter
Warbler, Great Reed	*Acrocephalus arundinaceus*	Drosselrohrsänger	Grote karekiet
Warbler, Icterine	*Hippolais icterina*	Gelbspötter	Spotvogel
Warbler, Marsh	*Acrocephalus palustris*	Sumpfrohrsänger	Bosrietzanger
Warbler, Moustached	*Acrocephalus melanopogon*	Mariskensänger	Zwartkoprietzanger
Warbler, Olive-tree	*Hippolais olivetorum*	Olivenspötter	Griekse spotvogel
Warbler, Reed	*Acrocephalus scirpaceus*	Teichrohrsänger	Kleine karekiet
Warbler, River	*Locustella fluviatilis*	Schlagschwirl	Krekelzanger
Warbler, Rüppell's	*Sylvia rueppelli*	Maskengrasmücke	Rüppells grasmus
Warbler, Sardinian	*Sylvia melanocephala*	Samtkopf-Grasmücke	Kleine zwartkop
Warbler, Sedge	*Acrocephalus schoenobaenus*	Schilfrohrsänger	Rietzanger
Warbler, Subalpine	*Sylvia cantillans*	Weissbart-Grasmücke	Baardgrasmus
Warbler, Willow	*Phylloscopus trochilus*	Fitis	Fitis
Warbler, Wood	*Phylloscopus sibilatrix*	Waldlaubsänger	Fluiter
Wheatear, (Eastern) Black-eared	*Oenanthe melonoleuca*	Balkansteinschmätzer	Oostelijke blonde tapuit
Wheatear, Isabelline	*Oenanthe isabellina*	Isabellsteinschmätzer	Izabeltapuit
Wheatear, Northern	*Oenanthe oenanthe*	Steinschmätzer	Tapuit
Wheatear, Pied	*Oenanthe pleschanka*	Nonnensteinschmätzer	Bonte tapuit
Whimbrel	*Numenius phaeopus*	Regenbrachvogel	Regenwulp
Whinchat	*Saxicola rubetra*	Braunkehlchen	Paapje
Whitethroat, (Common)	*Sylvia communis*	Dorngrasmücke	Grasmus
Whitethroat, Lesser	*Sylvia curruca*	Klappergrasmücke	Braamsluiper
Wigeon	*Anas penelope*	Pfeifente	Smient
Woodlark	*Lullula arborea*	Heidelerche	Boomleeuwerik
Woodpecker, Middle-spotted	*Dendrocopos medius*	Mittelspecht	Middelste bonte specht
Wren	*Troglodytes troglodytes*	Zaunkönig	Winterkoning
Wryneck	*Jynx torquilla*	Wendehals	Draaihals

Reptiles and Amphibians

English	Scientific	German	Dutch
Agama, Starred	*Stellagama stellio*	Hardun	Hardoen
Boa, Sand	*Eryx jaculus*	Sandboa	Zandboa
Frog, Levant Water	*Pelophylax bedriagae*	Bedriagas Wasserfrosch	Levantijnse meerkikker
Frog, Marsh	*Pelophylax ridibundus*	Seefrosch	Meerkikker
Frog, Tree	*Hyla arborea*	Europäischer Laubfrosch	Boomkikker

Gecko, Kotschy's	Cyrtopodion kotschyi	Ägäische Nacktfinger	Europese naaktvingergekko
Gecko, Mediterranean House	Hemidactylus turcicus	Europäischer Halbfinger	Europese tjiktjak
Lizard, European Glass	Pseudopus apodus	Scheltopusik	Scheltopusik
Lizard, Snake-eyed	Ophisops elegans	Europäisches Schlangenauge	Slangenooghagedis
Lizard, Three-lined	Lacerta trilineata	Riesen-Smaragdeidechse	Reuzensmaragdhagedis
Skink, Snake-eyed	Ablepharus kitaibelii	Johannisechse	Slangenoogskink
Worm, Slow	Anguis fragilis	Blindschleiche	Hazelworm
Snake, Caspian Whip	Dolichophis caspius	Balkan-Springnatter	Kaspische toornslang
Snake, Cat	Telescopus fallax	Europäische Katzennatter	Katslang
Snake, Coin	Hemorrhois nummifer	Münzennatter	Muntslang
Snake, Dahl's Whip	Platyceps najadum	Schlanknatter	Slanke toornslang
Snake, Dice	Natrix tessellata	Würfelnatter	Dobbelsteenslang
Snake, Dwarf	Eirenis modestus	Kopfbinden-Zwergnatter	Maskerdwergslang
Snake, Grass	Natrix natrix	Ringelnatter	Ringslang
Snake, Leopard	Zamenis situlus	Leopardnatter	Luipaardslang
Snake, Montpellier	Malpolon monspessulanus	Eidechsennatter	Hagedisslang
Snake, Worm	Typhlops vermicularis	Blödauge	Slanke wormslang
Spadefoot, Eastern	Pelobates syriacus	Syrische Schaufelkröte	Syrische knoflookpad
Terrapin, Balkan	Mauremys rivulata	Balkan-Bachschildkröte	Balkanbeekschildpad
Terrapin, European Pond	Emys orbicularis	Europäische Sumpfschildkröte	Europese moerasschildpad
Toad, Common	Bufo bufo	Erdkröte	Gewone pad
Toad, Green	Pseudepidalea viridis	Wechselkröte	Groene pad
Tortoise, Marginated	Testudo marginata	Breitrandschildkröte	Klokschildpad
Tortoise, Spur-thighed	Testudo graeca	Maurische Landschildkröte	Moorse landschildpad
Viper, Ottoman	Vipera xanthina	Bergotter	Kleinaziatische adder

Invertebrates

English	Scientific	German	Dutch
Admiral, Southern White	Limenitis reducta	Blauschwarzer Eisvogel	Blauwe ijsvogelvlinder
Apollo, False	Archon apollinus	Osterluzei Apollo	Pijpbloemapollo
Beetle, European Oil	Meloe proscarabeus	Schwarzblauer Ölkäfer	Gewone oliekever
Blue, Amanda's	Polyommatus amandus	Vogelwicken-Bläuling	Wikkeblauwtje
Blue, Eastern Baton	Pseudophilotes vicrama	Östlicher Quendelbläuling	Oostelijk tijmblauwtje
Blue, Green-underside	Glaucopsyche alexis	Himmelblauer Steinkleebläuling	Bloemenblauwtje
Blue, Lang's Short-tailed	Leptotes pirithous	Kleiner Wander-Bläuling	Klein tijgerblauwtje
Blue-eye	Erythromma lindenii	Pokaljungfer	Kanaaljuffer
Bluet, Dainty	Coenagrion scitulum	Gabel-Azurjungfer	Gaffelwaterjuffer
Bluetail, Common	Ischnura elegans	Grosse Pechlibelle	Lantaarntje
Bluetail, Small	Ischnura pumilio	Kleine Pechlibelle	Tengere grasjuffer
Brown, Large Wall	Lasiommata maera	Braunauge	Rotsvlinder
Brown, Lattice	Kirinia roxelana	Gelbbrauner Ringaugenfalter	Grote schaduwzandoog
Brown, Meadow	Maniola jurtina	Grosses Ochsenauge	Bruin zandoogje
Brown, Oriental Meadow	Hyponephele lupinus	Orientalisches Ochsenauge*	Zuidelijk grauw zandoogje
Brown, Persian Meadow	Maniola telmessia	Türkisches Ochsenauge	Levant bruin zandoogje
Brown, Turkish Meadow	Maniola megala	Lesbos-Ochsenauge	Turks bruin zandoogje
Burnet, Blood Droplet	Zygaena minos	Bibernell-Widderchen	Bevernel-sint-jansvlinder*

English	Scientific	German	Dutch
Burnet, White-collar	Zygaena carniolica	Esparsetten-Widderchen	Oogvlek-sint-jansvlinder
Butterfly, Nettle-tree	Libythea celtis	Zürgelbaum-Schnauzenfalter	Snuitvlinder
Cardinal	Argynnis pandora	Kardinal	Kardinaalsmantel
Centipede, Megarian Banded	Scolopendra cingulata	Riesenläufer/Gürtelskolopender	Scolopendra*
Chaser, Blue	Libellula fulva	Spitzenfleck	Bruine korenbout
Chaser, Broad-bodied	Libellula depressa	Plattbauch	Platbuik
Cleopatra	Gonepteryx cleopatra	Mittelmeer-Zitronenfalter	Cleopatra
Clubtail, Turkish	Gomphus schneiderii	Türkische Keiljungfer	Turkse rombout
Comma	Polygonia c-album	C-Falter	Gehakkelde aurelia
Comma, Southern	Polygonia egea	Südlicher C-Falter	Zuidelijke aurelia
Copper, Purple-shot	Lycaena alciphron	Violetter Feuerfalter	Violette vuurvlinder
Damsel, Common Winter	Sympecma fusca	Gemeine Winterlibelle	Bruine winterjuffer
Darter, Red-veined	Sympetrum fonscolombii	Frühe Heidelibelle	Zwervende heidelibel
Darter, Southern	Sympetrum meridionale	Südliche Heidelibelle	Zuidelijke heidelibel
Demoiselle, Banded	Calopteryx splendens	Gebänderte Prachtlibelle	Weidebeekjuffer
Demoiselle, Beautiful	Calopteryx virgo	Blauflügel-Prachtlibelle	Bosbeekjuffer
Dropwing, Violet	Trithemis annulata	Violetter Sonnenzeiger	Purperlibel
Emerald, Yellow-spotted	Somatochlora flavomaculata	Gefleckte Smaragdlibelle	Gevlekte glanslibel
Emperor, Blue	Anax imperator	Grosse Königslibelle	Grote keizerlibel
Emperor, Lesser	Anax parthenope	Kleine Königslibelle	Zuidelijke keizerlibel
Emperor, Vagrant	Anax ephippiger	Schabrackenlibelle	Zadellibel
Featherleg, Blue	Platycnemis pennipes	Blaue Federlibelle	Blauwe breedscheenjuffer
Festoon, Eastern	Zerynthia cerisy	Östlicher Osterluzeifalter	Oostelijke pijpbloemvlinder
Fritillary, Aegean	Melitaea telona	Östlicher Flockenblumen-Scheckenfalter	Oostelijke knoopkruid-parelmoervlinder
Fritillary, Knapweed	Melitaea phoebe	Flockenblumen-Scheckenfalter	Knoopkruid parelmoervlinder
Fritillary, Lesser Spotted	Melitaea trivia	Bräunlicher Scheckenfalter	Toortsparelmoervlinder
Fritillary, Marbled	Brenthis daphne	Brombeer-Perlmuttfalter	Braamparelmoervlinder
Fritillary, Spotted	Melitaea didyma	Roter Scheckenfalter	Tweekleurige parelmoervlinder
Goldenring, Blue-eyed	Cordulegaster insignis	Türkische Quelljungfer	Blauwoogbronlibel
Goldenring, Turkish	Cordulegaster picta	Gezeichnete Quelljungfer	Turkse bronlibel
Grasshopper, Long-nosed	Acrida ungarica	Gewöhnliche Nasenschrecke	Gewone langneus-sprinkhaan*
Grayling, Aegean	Hipparchia mersina	Mersin-Waldportier	Egeïsche heivlinder
Grayling, Balkan	Hipparchia senthes	Griechischer Samtfalter*	Verborgen heivlinder
Grayling, Eastern	Hipparchia pellucida	Türkischer Samtfalter*	Turkse heivlinder
Grayling, Eastern Rock	Hipparchia syriaca	Balkan-Waldportier	Balkanboswachter
Grayling, Freyer's	Hipparchia fatua	Freyers Samtfalter*	Donkere heivlinder
Grayling, Great Banded	Brintesia circe	Weisser Waldportier	Witbandzandoog
Grayling, White Banded	Pseudochazara anthelea	Weissband-Samtfalter	Witbandheremiet
Hairstreak, Green	Callophrys rubi	Grüner Zipfelfalter	Groentje
Hairstreak, Ilex	Satyrium ilicis	Brauner Eichen-Zipfelfalter	Bruine eikenpage
Hawker, Blue-eyed	Aeshna affinis	Südliche Mosaikjungfer	Zuidelijke glazenmaker
Hawker, Green-eyed	Aeshna isosceles	Keilflecklibelle	Vroege glazenmaker
Hawker, Hairy	Brachytron pratense	Frühe Schilfjäger	Glassnijder

Hawk-moth, Hummingbird	*Macroglossum stellatarum*	Taubenschwänzchen	Kolibrievlinder
Hawk-moth, Striped	*Hyles livornica*	Linienschwärmer	Gestreepte pijlstaart
Mantis, Conehead	*Empusa pennata*	Hauben-Fangschrecke	Kegelbidsprinkhaan*
Mantis, European	*Mantis religiosa*	Gottesanbeterin	Bidsprinkhaan
Odalisque	*Epallage fatime*	Blaue Orientjungfer	Oriëntjuffer
Owlfly, Eastern*	*Libelloides macaronius*	Östlicher Schmetterlingshaft	Oostelijke vlinderhaft*
Owlfly, Yellow-veined*	*Libelloides longicornis*	Langfühleriger Schmetterlingshaft	Langsprietvlinderhaft*
Pennant, Black	*Selysiothemis nigra*	Teufelchen	Zwarte korenbout
Pincertail, Small	*Onychogomphus forcipatus*	Kleine Zangenlibelle	Kleine tanglibel
Scarlet, Broad	*Crocothemis erythraea*	Feuerlibelle	Vuurlibel
Scorpion, Mediterranean Checkered	*Mesobuthus gibbosus*	Östliche Skorpion*	Oostelijke schorpioen*
Shrimp, Brine	*Artemia salina*	Salinenkrebs	Pekelkreeftje
Skimmer, Black-tailed	*Orthetrum cancellatum*	Grosser Blaupfeil	Gewone oeverlibel
Skimmer, Epaulet	*Orthetrum chrysostigma*	Rahmstreif-Blaupfeil	Epauletoeverlibel
Skimmer, Keeled	*Orthetrum coerelescens*	Kleiner Blaupfeil	Beekoeverlibel
Skimmer, Small	*Orthetrum taeniolatum*	Zierlicher Blaupfeil	Kleine oeverlibel
Skimmer, Southern	*Orthetrum brunneum*	Südlicher Blaupfeil	Zuidelijke oeverlibel
Skipper, Hungarian	*Spialia orbifer*	Südöstlicher Roter Würfel-Dickkopffalter	Oostelijke kalkgrasland-dikkopje
Skipper, Inky	*Erynnis marloyi*	Schwarzlicher Dickkopffalter*	Zwartbruin dikkopje
Skipper, Levantine	*Thymelicus hyrax*	Levant-Dickkopffalter*	Turks geelsprietdikkopje
Skipper, Mediterranean	*Gegenes nostrodamus*	Grosser Mittelmeer Dickkopffalter	Groot kustdikkopje
Skipper, Millet	*Pelopidas thrax*	Wander-Dickkopffalter*	Gierstdikkopje
Skipper, Oriental Marbled	*Carcharodus orientalis*	Östlicher Dickkopffalter*	Oostelijk andoorndikkopje
Skipper, Small	*Thymelicus sylvestris*	Braunkolbiger Braun-Dickkopffalter	Geelsprietdikkopje
Spectre, Eastern	*Caliaeschna microstigma*	Schattenlibelle	Schaduwlibel
Spider, Giant Ladybird*	*Eresus walckenaeri*	Griechische Röhrenspinne	Griekse vuurspin
Spreadwing, Dark	*Lestes macrostigma*	Dunkle Binsenjungfer	Grote pantserjuffer
Spreadwing, Eastern Willow	*Chalcolestes parvidens*	Östliche Weidenjungfer	Oostelijke houtpantserjuffer
Spreadwing, Robust	*Lestes dryas*	Glänzende Binsenjungfer	Tangpantserjuffer
Spreadwing, Small	*Lestes virens*	Kleine Binsenjungfer	Tengere pantserjuffer
Streamertail, Grecian	*Nemoptera coa*	Griechischer Fadenhaft	Griekse wimpelstaart
Swallowtail, Scarce	*Iphiclides podalirius*	Segelfalter	Koningspage
Swallowtail, Southern	*Papilio alexanor*	Südlicher Schwalbenschwanz	Zuidelijke koninginnenpage
Tiger, Cream-spot	*Arctia villica*	Schwarzer Bär	Roomvlek
Tortoiseshell, Large	*Nymphalis polychloros*	Grosser Fuchs	Grote vos
White, Balkan Marbled	*Melanargia larissa*	Balkan Schachbrett	Oostelijk dambordje
White, Black-veined	*Aporia crataegi*	Baumweissling	Groot geaderd witje
White, Eastern Dappled	*Euchloe ausonia*	Östlicher Gesprenkelter Weissling	Oostelijk marmerwitje
White, Krueper's Small	*Pieris krueperi*	Krüpers Weissling	Schildzaadwitje
Yellow, Clouded	*Colias crocea*	Postillion	Oranje luzernevlinder

TOURIST INFORMATION & OBSERVATION TIPS

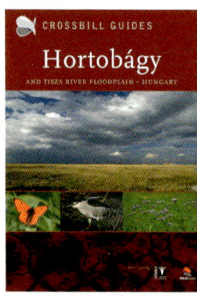 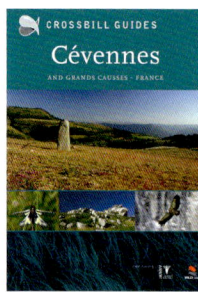 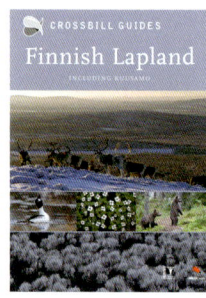 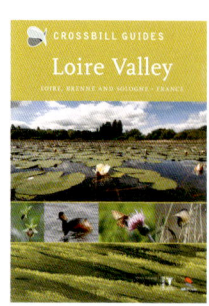

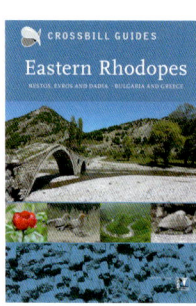 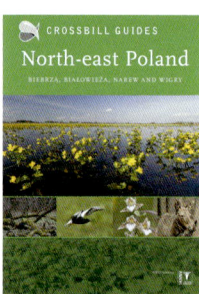  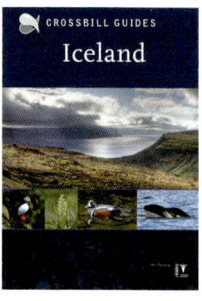

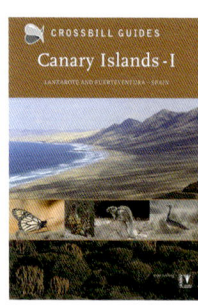 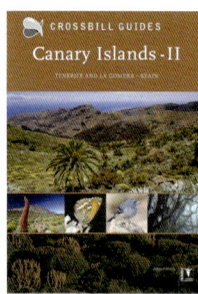 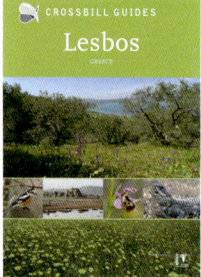 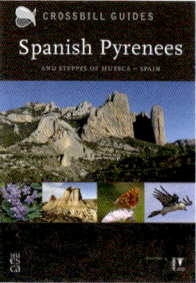

More titles are in preparation. Check our website for further details and updates.

WWW.CROSSBILLGUIDES.ORG